The End of the Rope

Volume I: The remnants of war, 1945

Andrew Warmington

Copyright 2023 Andrew Warmington

The people, places and events described in this book are real and every attempt has been taken to ensure the facts are correct. Any errors or omissions are unintended.

All rights reserved. No part of this publication may be reproduced, stored in a retrieval system, or transmitted, in any form or by any means, electronic, mechanical, photocopying, recording or otherwise, without the prior permission of the publishers.

Foreword

This is the first in a planned series of 12 books reviewing the 201 cases that ended with one or more executions in Britain between the end of World War II in 1945 and the last hangings in 1964. The cases are covered in chronological order, interspersed with a prologue in this issue, two interludes in years when the future of hanging was in doubt and a final word about when it really did end. Each individual story, where possible, is told chronologically and the cases are listed consecutively throughout the volumes and cross-referenced using their number in square brackets. The key sources are listed for each chapter. These are not meant to be complete and reference only those that were used in writing the story.

Some of these cases are very famous, indeed: those where there was or may have been a miscarriage of justice; those where the sheer horror of the murder(s) led to massive press coverage; and those where, for one reason or another, there was something to elevate the case above the ordinary. A few cases have become veritable cottage industries. At the time of publishing, I Googled 'Ruth Ellis' and got nearly 300,000 hits, while other famous cases yielded 20,000 to 50,000; 'Frank Freiyer', at the opposite extreme, yielded seven, none of them remotely informative. Both Ellis and Freiyer were individuals who killed their partner and were hanged for it. They and their victims were people of equal importance. These books will try, as far as is practicable, to consider them equally. I have therefore sought to write at least 2,500 words and no more than 6,000 on each case.

I would like to thank Ray Sullivan for his invaluable help in formatting this book and proof-reading, Charlotte Niemiec for proof-reading and Joyce Mason for the cover design. I suppose I could thank Rishi Sunak for creating the COVID-19 furlough scheme, which created a vast amount of paid free time in which I could substantially complete the work. But he's a Tory, so I won't.

Andrew Warmington

Ledbury

September 2023

CONTENTS

Prologue: The end of the rope - The hanged of post-war Britain - 1

1. "My name should be 'Trouble', not 'Smith'": George Smith - 59

2. "Oh dear, master, whatever do you want?": Aniceto Martinez - 79

3. "Two men attacked us. I missed them and shot my wife": Howard Grossley - 93

4. "I could see Laura's face in front of me": Thomas Richardson – 113

5. "The righteous death of a traitor": Erich König & four others - 134

6. "There are six more I have got to kill, then I will kill myself": Ronald Mauri - 160

7. "I am a German soldier and as such have had no interest in politics": Emil Schmittendorf & Armin Kühne - 180

8. "That little guttersnipe": John Amery - 194

9. "It was me and I want to get it off my chest": John Young - 215

10. "This is the first mistake he ever made in his life": James McNicol - 237

11. "The other one hit him when I was holding him": Robert Blaine - 256

12. "In death as in life, I defy the Jews, who caused this last war": William Joyce - 276

13. "A poor, uneducated fool who was caught young": Theodore Schurch - 295

14. "I am nobody": William Batty - 314

15. "Now you can meet the boyfriend": Michał Nieścior - 329

Prologue: The end of the rope – The hanged of post-war Britain

The past, as the saying goes, is another country.

In 1972, when I was nine, I was given the Guinness Book of Records for Christmas. It was a dense, fact-filled publication in those days, far more substantial than the heavily illustrated modern version. The 'Judicial' section enthralled me. I learned young, and have never forgotten, that the last two men to be hanged in Britain went to the gallows on 13 August 1964 in Liverpool and Manchester respectively. That might as well have been the Bronze Age to me in 1972, even though I could work out that at the time I had been a baby of 17 months and my mother was heavily pregnant with my sister. But I could not remember it and could not really relate to it. The earliest memories to which I can put a date are in 1970. I do not remember the abolition of capital punishment becoming permanent in 1969, or Woodstock, or the first Moon landings, which all took place that year.

From the perspective of decades later, it seems hard to reconcile the age of the Beatles with the one where a few hapless murderers had their necks broken on behalf of us all every year. This era seems so strange from the vantage point of today. It was a time when a man could raise suspicion because he was not wearing a collar and tie in a cinema; where a female juror's oath was technically invalid because she had failed to take her gloves off while making it; where childless couples wanting to adopt a baby would steer clear of one whose father was unknown because his supposed bad character might somehow impact that of the child; where the date of a death could be worked out from the number of uncollected milk bottles on the doorstep; where magistrates could call an adult defendant 'boy' and tell him to take his hands out of his pockets – and he would obey them.

And yet, it was not so very long ago. Everyone from the generation above me had grown up with hanging. Only a few people got worked up about it either way. Among the many who experienced reflex, retributive and often rough justice in their own lives, like a clip around the ear for being cheeky as a child or a kicking by the police as a young tearaway, being killed by the state for killing someone else may have seemed reasonable enough.

As a wealth of literature has shown, Britain has a long, broadly comfortable relationship with capital punishment: from the ritual of beheadings for treason at the Tower of London, to the 'Bloody Code' of the eighteenth century when even petty theft could lead to you dangling on a rope at Tyburn, right through to the twentieth century when sanitised executions took place behind closed doors and the curious public could only see a notice being put up to say that it had taken place.

Which is not to say that Britain was a particularly crime-ridden country. In the twentieth century, the homicide rate was low and rarely varied very much.

In the first decade, 1900-9, there were 4.4 homicides per million of the population, falling in successive decades to a low of 130 per year (3.2 per million) in 1930-9. The figures for the 1940s were 152 per year. This is harder to put into a 'per million' figure because so many potential perpetrators and victims were away on wartime service during the first half of the decade, though they suggest a sharp rise, as would be expected during wartime.

Arthur Koestler, a prominent voice against the rope, calculated that there were 1,666 murders known to the police in England and Wales in the following decade, leading to 127 executions. In 1951-55, the average number of murders was 137 per year (3.1 per million). From 1957, when the Homicide Act came into force, murder was split out from manslaughter in the statistics. In each of the years to 1962, there were between 125 and 151 murders, between 14 and 36 manslaughters and thus between 147 and 179 in total or 3.3-4.0 per million. It is hard to extrapolate any trends from this, other than that there was a slight but uneven upward trend in the homicide rate, which was still lower than it had been six decades before.

The availability – or not – of the rope seemed to make no appreciable difference to the number of people being killed. Between 1922 and 1944, there were 3,241 homicides known to the police in Britain, an average of 141 per year. Of these, 1,341 (41%) led to a charge of murder, 58 per year. A high proportion of the perpetrators killed themselves too at the time or later. The rest of the homicides were either never cleared up or ended in lesser charges or acquittals. Of those who were charged with murder, 517 were convicted. Subtracting the 17 who were found 'guilty but insane' or insane on arraignment, that leaves exactly 500, or a little under 22 per year. Thus, 37% of those who were charged were sentenced to death, of whom 325 (about 14 per year, or 65% of those sentenced) were executed.

A different set of statistics tells us that, of the 3,130 people (2,176 men and 654 women) committed for trial on a charge of murder in England and Wales between 1900 and 1949, 1,210 (1,080 men and 130 women) were sentenced to death. Of these, 34 were ultimately 'detained during His [or Her] Majesty's Pleasure' and 47 were certified insane after sentencing and committed to Broadmoor, while 632 (621 men and 11 women) were hanged. Thus, the reprieve rate was 47.8%: 40.3% for men and 90.8% for women.

That discrepancy masks the fact that the vast majority of the women had been condemned for killing their own infant children, usually when they were in a terrible emotional state. This crime was no longer punished by death in practice, whatever the law said – and it was not capital murder at all if the child was less than a year old. For other female murderers, criminologist Annette Ballinger has worked out, the reprieve rate was slightly lower than it was for men.

With a few spikes here and there, these figures changed little from one year to another. Added all together, they say that almost exactly one in every ten homicides led to the perpetrator paying for it with his or her life. The trend in the post-war era was much the same, with an average of 11 executions per year, or somewhere between 12 and 13 when one factors in the two periods in 1948 and 1955-7, during which hanging was informally suspended.

On the eve of World War II, it had seemed to many that capital punishment was on the way out. Not only was the murder rate declining, but fewer death sentences were being imposed and the average number of executions had fallen to just over eight per year. The Parliamentary Labour Party was almost unanimously abolitionist and there were plenty of the same mind in other parties, although most Conservative MPs were retentionists. The general public's view had shifted in the same direction, though not nearly so far. A Gallup poll in 1938 found that 55% of those who expressed an opinion were in favour of keeping the death penalty in some form and 45% were for abolition; 11% had no opinion, so at 49% in favour, it was the lowest level of support for hanging ever recorded.

The war slammed the brakes shut on any move towards abolition. This was partly because the reality of millions of people being massacred for an insane political end made the public less worried about killing everyday murderers, partly because

Nazi war atrocities made the public aware of the depths of depravity people can sink to but, more probably, because of the very real violent crime wave that followed the war. That violent crime in general and murder have very little, if anything, to do with each other went largely unnoticed. People, the press and politicians fixed their attention largely on the cases where young hoodlums killed during the course of a robbery, even though these remained a small minority of the capital cases.

In carrying on hanging, Britain was out of step with most of Europe, which, the Soviet Bloc excepted, was turning its back on putting murderers to death, even as war criminals were being executed in large numbers. Civilian executions had not happened in some West European countries, such as Denmark, Norway, the Netherlands and Portugal, since the nineteenth century; Sweden carried out its last in 1910; Switzerland in 1940; Italy in 1947; West Germany in 1949; Belgium and Austria in 1950; the Republic of Ireland in 1954.

A few countries carried on after Britain – Greece carried out its last execution by firing squad in 1972, Spain its last five by firing squad and garrotting in 1975 and France its last by guillotine in 1977 – but Britain was the most dedicated killer of civilian murderers, executing more of them between 1945 and 1977 than any other West European country and possibly more than all the rest combined. There were 58 post-war civilian executions in France, spread over 32 years, compared to the 19 when Britain was still using the rope; Spain, which was still a quasi-fascist dictatorship where military and civil justice shaded into each other, had 96; Greece was also under dictatorships for much of the time.

It would take a different kind of book to address why Britain was so disproportionately keen to do away with civilian murderers. It was certainly not because Britain was a more violent country than any other, despite periodic moral panics about rising crime and violence. The parliamentary system may have had something to do with it, because neither of the main parties that formed governments was inclined to defy public opinion and abolish capital punishment outright until public opinion shifted sufficiently that way. And 'sufficiently' is the word. When hanging was finally abolished, it was still against the wishes of the British public and the MPs who voted it through knew as much. Even in the 2010s, the British remained keener on the idea than any other nation in Western Europe, with one poll suggesting that 50% favoured capital punishment. This makes it the only country without a majority opposed.

Who were the condemned?

Between the end of World War II and the abolition of capital punishment just over 20 years later, 215 people were hanged in Britain. Of these, one was condemned for rape and another for murder under US military law; two were hanged for treason under an eighteenth-century statute; and one more for treachery under a wartime regulation and under military jurisdiction. All the rest were convicted of what was, in peacetime, the only capital crime on the statute book. Of the 211 murderers, only four were women, reflecting both women's far lower tendency to violence and general squeamishness about putting women to death. Taking out the German POWs sentenced by military courts and the American servicemen condemned under US military law, that leaves 199 men and four women.

The post-war hanged were in many ways the epitome of ordinariness in Britain. The commonest first name among them was John the commonest surname was Smith. Mostly at the start of the period, when large numbers of men were still in arms, a fair number were recorded as soldiers. In all, 14 were still either serving, former or demobilised soldiers, as were six victims. Later, their jobs were more likely to be those of working-class men of the day. Miners (11, including unemployed miners) and vehicle drivers of all kinds (13) were well represented, though the stereotypical figure of the serial killer lorry driver was not yet current and the man's work as a driver was rarely integral to the opportunity he got to kill, though his mobility in an era when having access to any kind of motor vehicle was unusual made it easier for him to do so.

The commonest description by far was the catch-all term of 'labourer', denoting the unskilled jacks-of-all-trades, mostly young men who moved around between low-paid, unskilled jobs, and sometimes in and out of petty crime. Of the 215, 54 were identified as labourers, including eight with more specific titles, like builder's labourer or farm labourer. Most of the rest happened to be doing something more specific at the time of their arrest but would have been classified as labourers at other points in their lives.

They were also mainly young. Throughout this period, the lowest age eligible for the death penalty was 18 and efforts to raise it to 21 were repeatedly argued down on the (correct) basis that 18- to 21-year-olds were disproportionately liable to commit violent crime. Post-war Britain hanged two 18-year-olds and four 19-year-olds. Of the rest, 125 (58%) were in their twenties, 75 (35%) in their thirties and 29 (13%) in their forties. Only five were over 50; the oldest, [153] William Hepper, was 62. The Homicide Act 1957 lowered the age profile somewhat, because the murders it classed as capital murder tended to be those of younger men.

The vast majority of the condemned were white and British, as one would expect, but there were many other nationalities among them in a society that was becoming more diversified and was drawing in growing numbers of refugees and migrants from across the world: the aforementioned American and German soldiers, another German-born civilian, two Canadians, two Jamaicans, a Spaniard, a Maltese, a Yugoslav, a Hungarian, a Ukrainian, two South Africans (one black, one Asian), one West African, two British-born mixed-race men, one Pakistani from West and one from East Pakistan (as Bangladesh was then), a Somali, a Cypriot and 12 Poles. This latter number reflected the large number of Poles absorbed into the population in the aftermath of war.

The inter-war years had seen a smattering of high profile, high society murder trials; there were almost none after 1945 and none at all that ended on the rope. Where any sniff of poshness hung around a case by association, it was likely to attract heavy press coverage. That extends to the raffish air affected by the likes of [30] Neville Heath and [65] John Haigh, whose origins were actually quite humble; the part played by the exiled King of Greece's house in Belgravia in the case of [31] Arthur Boyce; or the fact that [131] Miles Giffard had gone to public school and played Minor Counties cricket. In an age where only 5% of men and even fewer women went to university, few of the condemned had more than a basic education and some did not even have that. Only the wartime traitor [12] William 'Lord Haw Haw' Joyce and [181] Bernard Walden had degrees, and the latter's working life was blighted by lost opportunity because of his disability.

The means by which the victims were killed were generally mundane too. Most commonly (in 61 cases), they were battered with an implement, ranging from work hammers to a casually picked-up brick or lump of concrete, with a few 'exotic' implements, including a marlin spike and a knobkerrie. Surprisingly, until one realises how many more guns were available then than now, 53 of the victims were shot. Stabbing and throat-cutting accounted for 35, while 23 were strangled with a ligature and a further 23 were strangled manually. In 21 cases, usually where the killer was in a state of frenzy or finishing the task incompetently, multiple means were used.

Seven more victims were beaten and/or kicked to death. Asphyxiation – usually of children and other relatively incapacitated or helpless victims, or where murder was not specifically intended – accounted for five more. Three babies or young children were drowned. One woman was deliberately and repeatedly run over by a car. Her killer, also uniquely, was a serving policeman. For all the crime fiction where poison is used, it was very rare after World War II and the single case confirmed the stereotype of this being a woman's way of killing.

The serial killer, though not unknown, was still far from being a common concept in this age. Of the 197 murder cases leading to the gallows, 176 involved a single individual killing once. Put another way, of the 211 people hanged for murder, only about 17 killed, alone or jointly, more than one person and only five killed on more than one occasion. The exact number is uncertain because they include some cases of possible miscarriages of justice, while two men who were convicted together for one murder – [20] Marian Grondkowksi and

Henryk Malinowski – may have committed another for which they were never tried.

Only Haigh, [133] Reginald Christie and [173] Peter Manuel were true serial killers: the first murdered cynically for gain; the second for his own weird form of sexual gratification; the last for a form of nihilistic gratification that was essentially about power. Haigh had six known victims and claimed three more, almost certainly untruthfully; Christie also had six known victims, but probably two more; Manuel was convicted for seven murders, but probably killed nine and any number of other unsolved murders have been linked to him. Two more, Heath and [166] Norman Green, were serial killers in the making but were caught before they had accumulated the three known victims usually seen as the threshold, although Green may well actually have killed a third victim.

With two – and in one case five – men going to the gallows for a single murder on 14 occasions, the number of victims is only slightly greater than the number of hanged. It was not until the death penalty was limping towards the exit door that the modern serial killer became better known in the UK. The Moors Murderers began their reign of terror while the noose was still available and were charged a mere 11 days after the bill that would suspend capital punishment was passed; then came the still unsolved 'nudes' murders in West London, the Cannock Chase killings of Raymond Morris, and many, many more in the decades after.

The rest of the hanged were – leaving aside the potentially innocent – a collection of the 'bad, mad and sad', as prominent abolitionists dubbed them. They lived ordinary, often difficult lives. Where there are photographs of murder scenes, they often show scenes of squalor that are hard to imagine now. It has been said that murder may be the worst of crimes, but murderers are rarely the worst of criminals. Indeed, it was a truism even then: many years before, Sir John Macdonell had concluded based on examination of the records from 1885 to 1905 that murder "is not generally the crime of the so-called criminal classes and is rather in most cases an incident in miserable lives".

Post-war Britain suggests that there is some truth in this observation. Those who were hanged for murder were somewhat more likely than the population at large to have a criminal record and/or a propensity to violence, but most had neither. A fair few came from very large families, where poverty and casual neglect at the least were pretty much inevitable, but this does not necessarily lead us very far, given that they did not always have a criminal record and their siblings generally led respectable lives. A few were apparently very gentle characters before an explosion of rage led them to kill, even allowing for the fact that this often came from relatives pleading for their lives. Very few of these men woke up on the morning they committed their murders with the specific intention of doing so. Most snapped into uncontrolled anger against their partner, lost their temper in an argument and/or under the influence of alcohol, or panicked and lashed out during a bungled robbery, precisely because they were not cool, calculating villains.

That is not to excuse them; it is simply to note that their crimes were as mundane and sometimes as random as they were horrible. Very few killed calmly and cynically, and few had planned what to do next even if they had planned the killing before. Many could not explain afterwards, even to themselves, why they had done what they did. Many were clearly dissociated mentally from their actions or remained in denial. A large number, while sane by the legal standards of the day, had suffered head injuries and were prone to odd behaviour as a result. Several confessed out of guilt or attention-seeking when they would probably have escaped by keeping their mouths shut, notably [67] William Jones, [105] Alfred Bradley and [103] Herbert Mills.

Quite a few of those who went to the gallows seem to have been palpably mad, even allowing for the fact that insanity was almost the only option for the obviously guilty to plead, outside Scotland, until the Homicide Act brought the concept of diminished responsibility into the equation. An alarmingly high number of men 'killed the thing they loved' and had a morbid desire to die as well or claimed to have killed as part of a suicide pact. Then there is the extraordinary case of [165] Frederick Cross, whose life was in ruins and who killed a total stranger to get himself hanged, because he did not have the courage to kill himself. It also turned out, in the end, that he did not have the courage to face the gallows either. Most would-be romantic killers did not. Their death wishes usually evaporated when the reality of their situation came home to them.

Who were the victims?

Their victims of these killings were by and large as ordinary as the perpetrators. Only two of the 233 victims were eminent figures: the retired diplomat and author [1] Sir Eric Teichman and the war heroine [120] Countess Krystyna Skarbek, also known as Christine Granville. Often, in the nature of things, it is much harder to know anything about the victims, though a few – notably [34] Mona Vanderstay and [59] Harry Michaelson – had fascinating lives too and some others, like [36] Dr Neil McLeod, were eminent in their field.

They ranged through all ages, from a newborn baby without even a name in the case of [92] William Watkins' son to [52] Minnie Freeman Lee, who was in her mid-nineties. Generally, though, victims were more likely than not to be young: 57 (25% of them) were in their twenties when they were killed, 31 (14%) were in their thirties and 45 (20%) in their forties. Ten (4.5%) were aged below ten and 29 (12.5%) aged 10-20; 21 (9%) were in their fifties, 17 (7%) in their sixties and 23 (1%) were over 70. They were also disproportionately female. Women and girls accounted for 144 of the 233 (62%), men and boys for the remaining 89, leaving aside four more male victims whose attribution to a particular killer is uncertain.

The victims were also less diverse in their ethnic origin than the killers and more likely to be white and British. Two were German POWs who were lynched by other German POWs. There were two more Germans, two Belgians and seven other nationalities or ethnicities among them, who usually died at the hands of people of the same or similar origin. Only Skarbek and [102] Eugenie Le Maire were foreign-born people who were killed by white British men. There was thus something in the figures that, anecdotally at least, could reinforce any xenophobes in their view that serious and violent crime was probably the work of foreigners.

Certain professions were more vulnerable than most, because their occupations were relatively likely to put them in the way of harm. The victims included 13 prostitutes or other sex workers, though half of these were killed by a boyfriend or a man who thought he was her boyfriend. There were 11 shopkeepers and shop assistants who were killed by strangers in robberies and five more shop workers whose profession was incidental to how they died. Near the start of the period, there were eight soldiers among the victims, including POWs and demobilised troops, who were often killed by other soldiers. Later there were six policemen. Most victims, however, were none of these things and had the same sort of backgrounds as the people who killed them.

Predictably, the most dangerous 'occupation' to have in these years was to be the partner, ex-partner or casual squeeze of a jealous, unstable man with an anger problem. Definitions of relationships are hard to categorise, but 57 of the victims, about one quarter, were women who were or had been in a relationship with the man who killed her. A handful more killings were inspired by jealous rage on the part of a man who desired a woman but could not have her. Ten more victims were the male love rivals of these men, some of them killed alongside the woman who had taken up with them after spurning their killer. The second most vulnerable group comprised retired elderly people. They accounted for 20 more of the victims, usually because they were killed in robberies gone wrong, or were landlords or landladies killed by their tenants.

Another truism, that a serious crime is generally solved straight away or not at all, is largely borne out from these cases. Of the 198 capital cases of murder and rape studied here, the perpetrator was arrested at the scene or gave himself up soon after in 22 (11%) of them. Another 75 (38%) were arrested the day after the crime, a further 63 (32%) within a week, 17 (9%) more within a month and 21 (11%) more within the year. Only William Jones is an outlier, confessing four years on to a crime he had indubitably got away with, although Haigh, Christie and Manuel had all been killing for years before they were finally caught soon after their last murder.

From crime to trial

The responsibility for investigating a murder fell to the local constabulary, of course, but where resources were stretched, the case seemed complex or heavy publicity was making their job difficult, help could be sought from London in the form of Department Central or CI, which was usually referred to as the Murder Squad; the CID called them the 'Glory Boys'. It was entirely at their chief constable's discretion: many local forces did not much want some 'fancy Dan' from London wading in and taking over. A superintendent and his sergeant, usually chosen on the cab rank principle, would be sent to the scene complete with a 34 lb 'murder bag', comprising scalpels, forceps and other surgical instruments, a magnifying glass, strong plastics bags to hold a body and a mass of stationery to take down statements in this pre-computer age.

The Murder Squad had doubled in size from only four chief inspectors to eight in the 1930s and the wartime crime wave led to regional forces calling on it more often than before. The members were typically in their forties. All had begun life on the beat and were brought in after showing particular promise. Between them, these men took on some of the most infamous murder cases of their day.

Although lionised by many, including *The People*'s famous crime reporter Duncan Webb, who called them "the world's finest instrument for hunting down killers", the Murder Squad was not particularly well paid, even compared to others of their rank, and the temptation of better paid, easier work in private security was never far away. In addition, the top job was rotated regularly, some being promoted out or retiring after only a year. No fewer than ten men headed it between 1945 and 1967: Thomas Thompson, George Hatherill, Harold Hawkyard, William Rudkin, William Chapman, Alexander Finlay, Albert Griffin, Joseph Kennedy, John Du Rose and Jack Mannings.

After arrest, under the 'Judges Rules', the suspect would be cautioned, questioned, taken to the nearest police station, cautioned again and invited to make a statement. Almost invariably, he would appear before the nearest magistrates' court that same day or the next. This would be a formality, lasting just long enough for evidence of arrest and the crime to be given, and would be followed by a remand in custody, usually for a week, while evidence was gathered.

In addition to a post mortem by a regular doctor, the body would need to be examined by a forensic pathologist to determine cause of death. This was usually a senior figure attached to a regional Home Office forensic laboratory and/or a university. Those who appeared most frequently in cases in the post-war period were Professor James Matthewson Webster, covering most of the Midlands (17 known cases); Professor Keith Simpson and Dr Donald Teare in London and the south (16 and 13 respectively), along with the no less eminent Dr

Francis Camps (seven); and Dr David Price in Yorkshire (ten).

A succession of remands would follow, until the police had enough evidence to present to the Director of Public Prosecutions, who would then decide whether to proceed to a committal hearing. When this was all ready, solicitors on both sides would be allowed to present evidence before the same magistrates, though the defence counsel usually did not call witnesses and exercised the right to reserve the defence. If the magistrates felt that a *prima facie* case had been made against the defendant, the case would be sent for trial.

In parallel, he would be kept under close observation in the hospital wing of the prison and interviewed regularly by the chief medical officer and psychiatrists. They would decide if he was mentally capable of standing trial and they sometimes disagreed with each other: the former were often old school types, suspicious of the new-fangled science of the mind, as were most judges. A plea of guilty or not guilty was made at this point but it could be changed before or at the trial. This normally took place at the assizes nearest to the location of the crime, unless there were compelling reasons for it not to be – usually widespread knowledge of the case and possible prejudice against the defendant among jurors.

How much time elapsed between committal and trial was the single main determinant of how long the entire process took. In theory, especially if the case was a relatively simple one, there was space in the calendar and the assizes were coming up immediately, it could go straight there. In practice, with the need to instruct barristers, one to three months was the norm. In some instances, there was no trial at all because the defendant pleaded guilty, but this was rare. Even when he had made a full confession to the crime and there was no chance of an acquittal, they usually pleaded not guilty.

Of the 215 who were hanged after World War II, only nine had pleaded guilty. Two more wanted to: one had his plea overruled by the judge at his counsel's request so that evidence could be heard and the other was not permitted to do so under Scottish law. One more tried to change his plea mid-trial but was persuaded not to by his counsel. They were the exception, though. To plead guilty was to admit not just the facts but also that there were no extenuating circumstances; only those who actively wanted to hang did it. Except in very rare cases, none of which occurred after 1945, no appeal was possible if there had been no trial. The judge might advise the defendant to plead not guilty, and had to check that he was of sound mind and knew the consequences of what he was doing. Sentence of death could then be passed immediately, with a few cases done and dusted in under ten minutes.

Presiding over all this and ultimately passing sentence was the judge, who had no discretion in the matter because death was the only sentence that could be imposed on one who was convicted of murder and was not insane. The judge was invariably male and rarely younger than 55, following a long career in the law that began with finding chambers, then 'taking silk' as King's Counsel (KC) or, from the reign of Elizabeth II, Queen's Counsel (QC). Many had experience of presiding as town Recorders.

There were normally 17 judges in King's (later Queen's) Bench, though more could be added to deal with a backlog of cases, as happened in 1939 when Mr Justice Cassels and Mr Justice Hallett were elevated. The vast majority of the judges had been educated at Oxbridge and the Inns of Court and were of fully 'establishment' backgrounds, although there were exceptions. A large number had doubled up as MPs in their time as KCs or QCs. Most of them, though, again, not all, were Conservatives. An exception was Mr Justice Donovan, a Labour MP who always voted for abolition yet applied the law as it then stood in passing death sentences.

In all, 54 judges passed the 205 death sentences that were carried out between 1945 and 1964 from civilian courts. However, 16 of them accounted for more than half of these. Mr Justice Stable – Sir Wintringham Norton Stable, to give him his full name – was the most prolific, with 13, followed by Mr Justice Oliver with 11 and Mr Justice Cassels with ten. Others who donned the square black cloth frequently were Justices Hallett (nine), Croom-Johnson and Lynskey (eight), Byrne and Finnemore (seven), Gorman, Jones, Parker and Streatfield (six apiece), Donovan, Hilbery, Morris and Sellers (five). Many instances will be discussed in individual cases, but the post-war judicial bench was clearly not a particularly distinguished group and some can rightly be described as old fools who were out of touch with the world they lived in.

Because of the gravity of the crime, a KC or QC would lead for both prosecution and defence at a capital trial. The defence counsel was paid for by legal aid in almost every murder case: only Giffard had a wealthy and sympathetic relative to pay for his costs. These were the most eminent barristers of their day. All bar two were male, the exceptions being Rose Heilbron and Elizabeth Lane, who took silk at the same time. They were generally from privileged backgrounds. Many of them were the sons of eminent QCs and judges, and some went on to become judges themselves.

KCs and QCs were, at least in theory, assigned to cases on the 'cab rank' principle and could either prosecute or defend. This led to some confirmed abolitionists, such as Labour MP and QC Reginald Paget, conscientiously prosecuting murderers to the gallows. Particularly in London, however, there were some eminent KCs and QCs who only ever prosecuted in murder trials, such as Anthony Hawke and – with one exception towards the end of his career, where he defended in a prominent case – Christmas Humphreys.

The trials themselves, compared to today, were remarkably short. Many were over in a day or two, if the facts were not in serious dispute and few witnesses were called. [196] James Hanratty's took 21 and was the longest in British criminal history at the time. That record has been beaten many times over since then. Sentence almost always followed the prescribed mantra, which was shortened after the Homicide Act of 1957 from one of "being hanged by the neck until you are dead" to having to "suffer death by hanging". In Scotland, there was even more convoluted form of words in which the condemned man was addressed as 'panel'. (There was an exceptional occasion in March 1963 when Mr Justice Avory told George Frederick Thatcher, who killed a lorry driver during an armed robbery at a dairy depot in Mitcham: "You shot this man brutally and without pity and that the law prescribes but one sentence, that you too shall die!" In fact, Thatcher's sentence was reduced to non-capital murder on appeal.) Having done this, the judge would write a short formal letter to the Home Secretary to notify him of the sentence.

Post-war juries were pretty much always a reflection of respectable society. To be selected for jury service required being a property owner, someone who was unlikely to have much insight into crime and the motivations behind it. The balance was typically ten men and two wome. There was never a single case with a majority of women jurors in England and Wales; Scotland, where a jury of 15 was usually chosen for a serious crime like murder, was likelier to have a more even balance. More invidious still, for a group of ordinary citizens who were meant to be making a decision based on facts alone, the 'facts' they were deciding on were often about the state of the defendant's mind when he killed rather than whether or not he killed.

The law on this was based on the M'naghten rules, which dated back to 1843, when a jury acquitted Daniel M'naghten of the murder of Sir Robert Peel's private secretary and he was instead committed to an asylum on the grounds of insanity. The disquiet this case provoked led to a debate in the House of Lords and the end result was the formulation that: "To establish a defence on the ground of insanity, it must clearly be proved that, at the time of the committing of the act, the party accused was labouring under such a defect of reason, from disease of the mind, as not to know the nature and quality of the act he was doing; or if he did know it, that he did not know what he was doing was wrong".

Since the 1880s, juries had also been permitted to reach a verdict of 'guilty but insane' and the Home Secretary was required to order a medical examination of any prisoner under sentence of death by at least two qualified medical practitioners, where there was reason to believe that he was insane. If there was evidence that he was, he would automatically be reprieved and sent to Broadmoor. There was only a little more tinkering around the edges of the rules after that.

By 1947, the sanity of a person charged with murder could be analysed before, during or after trial, and this was not uncommon. Nearly 14% of the 3,130 people committed for trial for murder in the first half of the twentieth century were found to be insane. Of the 1,210 convicted of murder, medical inquiries were held in 192 cases (16%). This led to 48 being certified insane, 38 being reprieved on the grounds of their mental state and 106 being executed. In some instances where insanity was not alleged at the trial, it was found afterwards: this happened in 15 of the 33 cases between 1923 and 1950 where there was a reprieve after the statutory enquiry.

As Home Secretary in the Labour government of 1945-51, Sir James Chuter Ede set up a panel of psychiatrists who could be called on to advise on the mental state of a condemned prisoner, instead of always using the same few. Ironically, it was Chuter Ede's Permanent Under-Secretary of State, Sir Frank Newsam, who was reviled by abolitionists as a heartless and ill-tempered man bent on sending killers to the gallows, who directed that wherever there were grounds for suspecting any mental abnormality, there should be an informal inquiry outside the provisions of the Act. This enabled medical professionals, rather than simply decide whether or not to certify the condemned as a lunatic, to advise on whether there were medical reasons for recommending the Home Secretary to grant a reprieve. Where they did so, he always followed their advice and as a result spared a great many who were mentally abnormal but not strictly insane.

Outside Scotland, where even a majority of one was acceptable, juries had to reach a unanimous verdict. Whilst the private nature of their deliberations was sacrosanct, this meant that any dissenting voices would come under pressure to fall into line so that it could be over with as swiftly as possible. In [74] George Kelly's case, it has been claimed that the jury at his first trial were 11 to one for acquittal, but the one juror holding out for a conviction meant that he could be, and was, tried again. His was one of only two cases in this period to be tried twice and to lead to the gallows.

Sometimes juries came back without a verdict and asked for further direction on a point of law. In many cases, they were out and back in a matter of minutes because the guilty verdict was obvious. Defence counsels' rule of thumb was that the longer the jury was out, the better the chance of acquittal. Even then, deliberations did not take long: the jury that convicted Hanratty and was the exception that proved the rule, was out for ten hours. This is another record that has been broken many times over since abolition.

According to Gerald Gardiner QC, an abolitionist, juries would almost always reach verdicts of insanity, manslaughter or acquittal "if given almost any opportunity". This may be stretching it a bit, but juries certainly could recommend mercy and did not have to give a reason for it. They did so in 468 cases between 1900 and 1949. Of these, 68% ended in a reprieve. Usually, this recommendation was because there were extenuating circumstances but sometimes it happened because a single juror was holding out against conviction because he disliked the death penalty and was persuaded or browbeaten into line with the promise that if they recommended mercy, there would be no hanging. This was not always the case, even where a strong recommendation was made, as some jurors found out to their lasting regret.

From trial to gallows

Once he had been convicted and sentenced, the condemned would be sent to the prison where his execution was to be carried out, if he was not there already. The governor would write to the local Under-Sheriff notifying him that the prisoner was in his custody under sentence of death. It was for the Under-Sheriff, a local solicitor, to begin the process by choosing a day for the execution and contract with the hangman and his assistant(s).

The prisoner would be lodged in the condemned cell. This was more spacious than a conventional cell, furnished with a bed, table, chairs, and a private toilet and washroom. He wore prison clothes, including soft slippers and tapes instead of buttons on his jacket, until the morning of the execution when he was allowed to dress in his own clothes. The governor would see him every day, the prison doctor twice daily and the chaplain as often as he wished. His solicitor could also come to see him as often as necessary, though always in the presence of warders.

Everything was organised to ensure the condemned could not harm himself until the state did. A rotating team of two warders on eight-hour shifts would guard him night and day. Their task was to keep him calm, distract him with games and encourage him to go quietly when the time came. If he went to chapel or was taken out for exercise, he was kept out of sight of the other prisoners. Female warders kept watch on the female condemned until the last couple of hours, when a male team took over; it was thought that being there during the execution was too much to ask of a woman.

In Scotland, warders were required to record any notable things that the prisoner said or make comments on his demeanour in an 'Occurrences Book' as they went off shift. This would be available to the Secretary of State for Scotland and might inform his thinking about granting a reprieve. Some prisons in England compiled the warders' and other officials' remarks into something which was essentially the same thing, but this was not a formal requirement and was often not done. As retired warders later admitted, they would not in practice record everything and when they did it would usually be something that could help the man they had built a friendship of sorts with. However, some have claimed that prisoners hanged themselves by making remarks to the effect that they had spun the doctors a line about their mental state.

The time between trial and execution was, by modern standards, very swift. The only stipulation was that 'three clear Sundays' must pass and executions did not usually take place on a Monday. Thus, in theory, a man could be sentenced on a Saturday and hanged 17 days later. This is exactly what happened in the case of [84] Patrick Turnage. Three weeks were thought to be about right in terms of enabling the prisoner to settle his affairs and prepare himself for the end. Any longer, some thought, would have been too much of a strain all round, as it was universally agreed that the waiting period was the worst for all involved. An appeal automatically led to the postponement of the originally scheduled execution date, typically by about a month.

From 1945 to the hiatus in the summer of 1955, 61 (39%) of the 162 who were ultimately hanged and had been eligible to appeal – or strictly speaking, apply for leave to appeal – chose not to do so, mostly because their counsel thought it pointless. That said, some palpably pointless appeals did happen and the right to appeal was enshrined in law. Nine more condemned men could not appeal because they had pleaded guilty or because of wartime regulations.

One side effect of the Homicide Act 1957 – and perhaps also of the retirement of Lord Chief Justice Goddard, who made his views on hopeless appeals known – was that more verdicts were appealed. The introduction of degrees of murder and the complexity of the issues meant that it at least seemed more likely that judges might misdirect juries. There is thus a striking contrast in the periods before and after the Act. After it, 35 men were hanged: of these, only [199] Henry Burnett chose not to appeal; [182] Francis Huchet could not do so under Jersey law; the other 33 all did.

Appeals, for England and Wales, were held at the Court of Criminal Appeal in London. If available, the Lord Chief Justice of the day would preside with two other senior judges. If he did not (usually because he had been the judge at the original trial or was engaged on another case at the time), any three senior Appeal Court judges would sit together. If they could not agree or if a major point of law was at stake, this could be increased to five in very rare instances. It was basically similar in Scotland, where the legal hierarchy was headed by the Lord Justice-General and the Lord Justice-Clerk, who might both sit among three or five judges at the Court of Criminal Appeal in Edinburgh.

The first post-war Lord Chief Justice in England and Wales was Thomas Inskip, First Baron Caldecote, a Conservative MP who had previously been both Solicitor-General then Attorney-General. However, he suffered a stroke in 1945, which meant that he was not involved in any post-war capital cases. The new Labour Prime Minister, Clement Attlee, appointed as his successor Rayner Goddard, Baron Goddard. Attlee had never met Goddard, who was a strong Conservative. It was a political appointment and every previous appointee to the role had hitherto been the Attorney-General. However, the incumbent, Hartley Shawcross, who was the lead British prosecutor at the Nuremberg trials and was also a Labour MP, did not want the job. He had only just been appointed to the role in August 1945.

Goddard was the first Lord Chief Justice to have a degree in law and he was full of paradoxes: irascible and domineering on the bench, he could be generous and humble in private. He undoubtedly had a fine legal mind and was as hard on errors by himself and his peers as he was on defendants, but he was also brutal, heartless and legalistic to the last degree. His support for both capital and corporal punishment was so obsessive that it might well have been a fetish. Ludovic Kennedy described him as "a bully and a sexual deviant" and a senior QC, John Parris, relayed a story from Goddard's own clerk that he put out fresh trousers for Goddard after he had to pass sentenced, because he was liable to ejaculate when he did. As Kennedy remarked, this act was probably not entirely spontaneous. It must be said, however, that the clerk in question published a book that was entirely favourable in his memories.

Goddard lasted until 1958, presiding over more appeals in capital cases than any other judge, and finally retired at the age of 81 because of his failing eyesight and hearing. His successor was Hubert Lister Parker, Baron Parker of Waddington. Once again, Parker was not the first choice. Lord Kilmuir, the former Home Secretary Sir David Maxwell-Fyfe, was Prime Minister Harold Macmillan's preference, but he preferred to stay in the government, and the then Attorney-General, Sir Reginald Manningham-Buller, was so similar in temperament to Goddard that his colleagues nicknamed him 'Bullying Manner'. Parker was a conservative figure too but was widely seen as a breath of fresh air after Goddard. His Oxford DNB biographer says that his advocacy was characterised by "fairness, clarity and good temper – passionate rhetoric was not for him". By 1965, he also leaned towards abolition as preferable to the Homicide Act.

Although some appeals were made on the basis that the jury verdict was 'against the evidence', the Appeal Court was a court of law, not fact. Evidence that was known at the time of the trial but had not been used for whatever reason could not be introduced now; only evidence which had genuinely emerged since the trial could be admitted, and that at the court's discretion. For instance, at [37] Walter Rowland's appeal, David Ware, who had confessed to the crime after Rowland was convicted, was present in the cells underneath and ready to give evidence but the court refused to call him on technical legal grounds.

The proceedings at appeal were in some respects a reversal of the trial, with the defence giving evidence first. There was no specific requirement for the prosecution to reply and the judges often decided not to call them to testify if the defence had not made a sufficiently strong case, even if counsel had spoken for hours on end to find some tiny flaw in the case. The court was not there to re-run the question of whether the accused was guilty, because the verdict of a jury was sacrosanct. The only real hope was of finding an error in law made by the judge in his charge to the jury or summing-up – 'misdirection', to give it its correct term – that might, in the opinion of the Appeal Court judges, have led the jury to come to a different opinion.

The cases examined here, by definition, did not result in such a finding and the Appeal Court judges were being asked to find fault in their colleagues, but if there was a scintilla of doubt, the justices would overturn the verdict or, if appropriate, substitute a manslaughter verdict. In one case, in 1961, they quashed George Anthony Porritt's non-capital murder conviction and substituted a verdict of manslaughter on the grounds of provocation, despite this never having mentioned at the trial. This was a very rare exception, however. Post-1957, the option of substituting a capital murder verdict for a non-capital one was also there. After reaching their verdict, the senior judge would read it out. This could take many hours, though the outcome would be obvious within a few paragraphs.

One of the oddities of the system was that, at least in the later years, the Home Office tacitly wanted appeals to be made, however hopeless, on the basis that the condemned should not decline to do so in the hope of mercy being granted. At least lawyers thought this was the case and they made appeals even where they could not advance any reason for them. This created tensions with the Court of Appeal, where the justices were forthright if they did not think the appeal had any substance. In 1955, Mr Justice Hilbery, one of the least distinguished of the post-war judges, said, in the course of dismissing Michael Xinaris's appeal: "Too often grounds are framed in order to give an appeal the appearance of substance, which, on examination, are found to be worthless." Xinaris was, however, ultimately reprieved.

Once the appeal process was over and those on the ground – the doctors and the governor - had made their final reports, it went to the Home Office. The Permanent Under-Secretary and his deputy would prepare a memorandum on the case for the man – it always was a man – who had the final power of life and death. This was the Home Secretary of the day in England, Wales and the Crown dependencies, and the Secretary of State for Scotland in Scotland. In this respect too, the UK was unique: nowhere else in the world did life or death decisions fall so squarely on a single pair of shoulders. (In Northern Ireland, the matter was decided by the entire cabinet.) He would take advice from senior civil servants, who had inevitably more experience of the process than him and look at the judge's recommendation as well as those from inside the prison. The final decision, however, was his alone. It was often communicated by writing the words 'The law must take its course' on the case file if he declined a reprieve.

A jury's recommendation to mercy would be taken into account but would not necessarily be listened to. Of the 468 (360 men and 108 women) recommended to mercy between 1900 and 1949, 348 (245 men and 103 women, 74% of the total) were reprieved. That left a not inconsiderable 120 who were not. From 1940 to 1949, again according to Gardiner, 75 were recommended to mercy, of whom 24 were hanged, and from 1949 to 1960, recommendations to mercy of varying strength were ignored in 13 cases.

Chuter Ede recalled in 1955 that on two or three occasions a juror wrote to him saying that he had let them down by not granting a reprieve despite a recommendation to mercy. "I did not grant a reprieve when, after consulting with the trial judge, and asking him the grounds for making a strong recommendation for mercy, the judge said, 'I really have not the remotest idea'," he wrote. By contrast, if the judge joined the recommendation, a reprieve would almost certainly follow. There were only six occasions in the first half of the twentieth century where the Home Secretary ignored a judge's recommendation to mercy.

In all, ten men made life or death decisions over convicted murderers between 1945 and 1964: five in England and Wales, five in Scotland. The most prolific were those who spent a long time as Home Secretary and the most prolific of all was Chuter Ede, an abolitionist by inclination who said that he never overrode a departmental recommendation to mercy and sometimes overrode ones against, nonetheless declined to reprieve no fewer than 93 condemned people. In fact, measured by the number of executions per month of holding the position, he had more (1.5) than any twentieth century Home Seretary bar his successor, the utterly grim Sir David Maxwell Fyfe (1.6).

Other than chief hangman Albert Pierrepoint, Sir Frank Newsam, and perhaps Lord Goddard, no one was involved in more capital cases in this period than Chuter Ede. His three immediate successors in the Conservative government of 1964 accounted for most of the rest: Sir David Maxwell-Fyfe (49 reprieves declined between October 1951 and October 1954); Major Gwilym Lloyd-George, a member of the Liberal National Party that backed the Conservative government and another abolitionist by inclination (12 between October 1954 and January 1957), who also sometimes reprieved condemned men against official advice; and Richard Austen 'Rab' Butler (25 between January 1957 and July 1963). Henry Brooke made the last four decisions against a reprieve in England and Wales. He also turned against the death penalty in his later years.

How Home Secretaries reached their decisions is often described as being shrouded in mystery because it was confidential, as even the most ardent abolitionists believed it should be. Even when motions in the Commons reflected deep disquiet over a particular case, the Home Secretary did not have to answer questions. There were no formal rules governing how decisions were made, although it was widely believed that there were.

Inevitably, as politicians, Home Secretaries made decisions in the context of the times and more than once came down on the side of severity when there was a widespread public perception that young criminals were getting out of control. The decision was a political matter for the public too, in any case: Home Secretaries were assailed from both sides of the debate for being too lenient and too harsh, in general and/or in particular cases. Many decisions they made seem strange or wrong in retrospect.

Unless defence counsel then managed to convince the Attorney-General to issue his fiat for the appeal to be taken to the House of Lords, which was only possible on a point of law deemed to be of exceptional public importance, the Home Secretary's refusal to grant a reprieve was the last hurdle to clear. Petitions were often got up, but these had no standing in law, though it was not unknown for discreet enquiries to be made about what public opinion was in the place where the crime was committed. The Home Office would receive any reputable person who wanted to make representations, though officials would not make any comment about the likely outcome. Never were relatives allowed to meet the Home Secretary.

Direct appeals by families and solicitors to the monarch were not uncommon, but they would only be referred back to the Home Secretary as the

Crown had no powers in the matter, despite justice being nominally administered by them, and monarchs had not signed death warrants since the young Queen Victoria had been spared the task. Earlier kings had raised cases and George VI discussed some with Chuter Ede but he never tried to influence his decision. Elizabeth II was never brought into it at all. "She was never consulted in advance. If no reprieve was decided on, the papers did not even go to her," an insider said.

Once the decision was made that the law must take its course, the Permanent Under-Secretary would formally write to the Sheriff and the prison governor so that they could prepare for the execution, as well as to the judge who passed sentence and the judges who had dismissed the appeal. There was no formal requirement, awful though it sounds, to inform the prisoner's family. The governor would have to inform the prisoner, whether by reading out the letter or simply telling him its contents. It was actually not impossible for the Home Secretary to change his mind after that, but this was extremely rare in practice.

Where it happened

Everything now passed into the hands of the prison governor. In all, 25 prisons carried out executions in the post-war period but nine of them were only used once or twice. The bulk, not surprisingly, were carried out in big city prisons, which generally served a defined area around them. The most used were in London (Pentonville, with 37 executed, and

Wandsworth with 33), Leeds (Armley, 21), Manchester (Strangeways, 17), Liverpool (Walton, 15), Durham (12), Birmingham (Winson Green, 11) and Glasgow (Barlinnie, 10). Others in regular use were at Lincoln (nine), Bristol (Horfield, seven) and Winchester (six). Cardiff, Norwich, Shrewsbury and Swansea each accounted for five more. These were the prisons that accounted for the vast majority of executions throughout the twentieth century; only Maidstone had accounted for more than ten before World War II and was not used after.

In most cases, the condemned suites had been built in the 1920s, though they continued to be remodelled right up to abolition. Typically, they occupied three floors. At the top accessible by a permanent wall ladder from the gallows room were the twin beams, with brackets for the chains. On the second floor were one or two condemned cells. These were normally adjacent to the 'hanging shed' where the execution took place, leaving only a few seconds' walk for the condemned to make. Two exceptions to the rule were HMP Oxford, where the execution suite was a short walk up a corridor and only had a single flap on the trap, and HMP Bedford, where it stood in a separate building about 50 yards from the condemned cell.

On the ground floor of every execution chamber was the 'drop room' into which the trap doors opened, also accessible by stairs and with sand on the ground to absorb any body materials that might be excreted, which was actually a very rare occurrence. Some prisons had an autopsy room next to this room. In Scotland, only Barlinnie and HMP Saughton in Edinburgh had permanent suites. The one used for [48] Stanisław Myszka's execution at Perth in 1948 was a temporary structure and was soon after replaced by a permanent one that was never actually used. Another was built at HMP Craiginches in Aberdeen and was to be used only once, for Henry Burnett in 1963.

At any one time, there were two 'number one' executioners available to the authorities, who were in charge and actually pulled the lever, plus usually six more who might act as assistants. By 1945, Thomas Pierrepoint had been in the role for 24 years and he officiated ten more times after the war. However, his advancing years were increasingly impacting his performance and he ceased to be called on after July 1946.

Thomas's nephew Albert was already a prolific hangman by 1945, having begun as an assistant in the 1930s and then become a 'number one' during the war after Stanley Cross retired. He assisted his uncle for the last time that year at [2] Aniceto Martinez's execution at Shepton Mallet, and he hanged 129 more people in Britain between September 1945 and July 1955. Albert also travelled regularly to Germany to hang convicted war criminals, and to Egypt and other places where the Army was stationed. The total number of his executions has been estimated at anything between 400 and 600. The most exhaustive recent analysis by Traugott Vitz and Matthew Spicer has yielded the number of 433: 48 as assistant and 385 as principal. These included exactly 200 war criminals at Hameln prison in Germany. This work helped to make him a public figure, arguably the first hangman since Victorian times who was.

Everything about hanging had been honed to an art form over many years. The Memorandum of Instruction produced in 1932 still applied at the start of the period. They specified that on the day before an execution, the apparatus should be tested, first without any weight and then with a bag of sand of the same weight as, or slightly more than, the condemned man attached to the rope. This would enable the executioners to ensure that the rope would be stretched with a force equating to the energy reached when the prisoner fell the correct length (1,100 ft. lbs., following the last amendments in 1939) to ensure that dislocation of the cervical vertebrae would take place, causing instant unconsciousness and rapid death.

On the day before the execution, the executioner and his assistant(s) would arrive, and go straight to the governor's office for a briefing on the prisoner's height and weight. They would take a discreet look at him, either at exercise in the yard (where he was taken so that he could not hear the crashing doors during testing) or through the 'Judas hole' in the condemned cell. This was done simply to look at his build and general physical condition, then consider whether any slight variation might be in order from the 'Table of Drops' that had been in use, though constantly updated, since Victorian times. It is a myth that the hangman would go into the condemned cell to shake hands with the condemned to calculate his weight. The process was far more scientific than that.

The equipment was stored off-site and couriered to the prison that same day: the box typically contained two 13-feet ropes, a block and tackle, two straps, a sandbag, chalk, a measuring rod, a piece of copper wire, a white linen cap and a pack of thread. After testing the gallows with the prison engineer, the apparatus was locked until the next morning, but the bag of sand remained suspended overnight, reducing the diameter of the rope by about five eighths of an inch and reducing the stretch to ensure that any extra slack in it did not cause the man to fall too far. A safety pin was also left in place to hold the lever, to be removed by the hangman next morning. He and his assistant were put up in vacant cells overnight. This requirement was a result of a Victorian reform to stop the often thoroughly disreputable hangmen of the day getting drunk.

As soon as possible after 6.00 a.m. on the day of execution, the bag of sand was raised out of the pit and dropped again to stretch the rope out completely. The executioner would measure off from a line previously painted thirteen inches from the end of the rope – equating roughly to the circumference of the neck – to the required drop length, which was marked with chalk. The copper wire fastened to the chain would now be stretched down the rope and cut off at the chalk mark; the sandbag would be removed and the chain adjusted at the bracket so that the lower end of the wire reached the same level from the floor as the prisoner's height. The cotter was securely fixed through the bracket and chain, and the executioner made a chalk mark on the floor, in a plumb line with the chain, where the prisoner should stand.

An officer could now be left in charge of the execution suite while the team had their breakfast. The prisoner would have the services of a chaplain and some rediscovered their faith as death loomed. Leslie Lloyd-Rees (1919-2013), who spent 38 years as a prison chaplain, recalled in a BBC documentary giving communion to a man who had been confirmed in his last days, who knelt alongside his warders to receive it. His experiences made him a firm abolitionist and he was far from alone in that. The team of warders for the last two hours would be new, unless the prisoner had made a specific request for any of them to be with him. It was natural for a relationship of sorts to develop in the close confines of the condemned cell and, if the presence of a friendly face was thought likely to help things proceed smoothly, this would be permitted.

The trapdoor opens

Shortly before the time of execution – which was not set by law but was almost always 8.00 or 9.00 a.m. – the official party would gather and move silently towards the condemned cell. Coconut matting would be put down to drown out the sounds of their approach and avoid panicking the prisoner. The door to the 'hanging shed' was opened only at the last second. There were no specific requirements in terms of who would be present, but they usually included the prison governor, the chief medical officer and the under-sheriff, plus the chaplain, if he was in the cell ministering to the condemned man.

On the stroke of the hour, the party would enter the condemned cell. Only in Scotland did the ritual of confirming his name and allowing him to speak any last words still prevail. The prisoner would know to stand and raise his arms behind his back to be pinioned by having them tied together at the wrists. Almost all cooperated. Often, the only words spoken were "Follow me" as the executioner led him through the door to where the noose waited. It was usually hidden behind a wardrobe, which the warders now rolled away to open the door into the execution suite.

There, the executioner positioned the prisoner under the part of the beam where the rope was attached, his feet by the chalk marks. He then put the cap over the prisoner's head and the rope round the neck with the knot to the left of the chin to ensure that the neck jerked backward. This, the memoranda said, should be done "quite tightly (with the cap between the rope and the neck), the metal eye being directed forwards, and placed in front of the angle of the lower jaw, so that with the constriction of the neck, it may come underneath the chin." By 1945, the rubber washer that held the eyelet of the noose in place had been replaced with an internal, star-shaped one, which gripped the rope better. The gutta-percha washer covering the rope over the attachment eye to the chain was still in use until 1952, when it was replaced with vulcanised rubber to prevent splintering.

As the executioner adjusted the rope, his assistant would strap the prisoner's legs tightly, step back behind the white safety line around the trap and signal that he was clear. The executioner would withdraw the safety pin and push the lever to open the trap doors. 'Cap [on prisoner's head], noose [around his neck], pin [i.e., put him in the correct place on the trap], push [the lever], drop' was the mantra.

The condemned man plunged through the floor to the length calculated the day before, then stopped abruptly. The knot would ensure that his neck was broken cleanly, by jerking it back. In theory, this would be between the second and third vertebrae, though in practice it was not always so. Either way, death was guaranteed and usually instantaneous, at least according to the authorities; there are some who still say that hanging actually only caused paralysis followed by strangulation. The whole process, from the team entering the condemned cell to the prisoner's death, normally took less than 15 seconds and it could be as few as seven or eight.

A telegram would be sent to the Home Secretary or Secretary of State for Scotland immediately after, certifying that the execution had taken place. At this point, the official party would disperse. The body was left to hang for an hour, then removed to a post mortem chamber where the hangman and his assistant would prepare it for the formal inquest by the coroner and a jury of 12. This would take place the same afternoon to certify the cause of death, as would have happened if he had died of natural causes. The prisoner would also have to be formally identified, sometimes by the police officer who had arrested him, or by a relative. He was then buried within the confines of the prison, the prison chaplain who had ministered to him hours before presiding over a lonely and macabre event.

The Homicide Act of 1957 brought some minor changes in procedure, notably that the findings of the inquest were published in the *London Gazette*. Double, side-by-side executions, at least six of which had taken place since the war, were abolished. Instead, where two prisoners were to be hanged for the same crime, they would take place simultaneously in different prisons. This happened on three occasions, including the last two hangings of all. In addition, the need to wait an hour after the execution for the removal of the body ended and it was normally taken down after the chief medical officer had pronounced the prisoner dead.

Normally, 20 minutes were enough but, after the execution in 1959 of [178] Joseph Chrimes, who had to be re-suspended when the medical officer found that his heartbeat had not stopped, a wait of

45 minutes was stipulated. A new Memorandum of Instructions was issued as a result, including this detail, but it made no other significant changes.

When a hangman resigned or retired, an experienced assistant would be promoted to replace him. The recommendations of the existing or previous 'number one' behind the scenes counted for a lot when such decisions were made. In 1946, the ageing Thomas Pierrepoint was replaced by Steve Wade, who hanged 29 men, mostly at Armley and Durham, and assisted 17 more times. Albert Pierrepoint had warmly commended Wade for his reliability and discretion. No mistakes were tolerated. Harry Kirk's career ended immediately after he botched his first and only execution as 'number one', that of [85] Norman Goldthorpe at Norwich in 1950.

Executioners and assistants did not have to be sacked as such, because they were not employees but contractors, called on by local officials from a Home Office list. Where their skills or conduct no longer came up to scratch or they otherwise blotted their copybooks, they were simply not called on again, as Syd Dernley found in 1954. (That said, it appears that Herbert Morris and Herbert Allen were notified of their removals.) After a last flurry of executions in the summer of 1955, hanging went into abeyance for nearly two years. During this time, Wade was removed from the list for the same reason as the man he had replaced, advancing age, while Albert Pierrepoint resigned for reasons that have been much discussed ever since.

When capital punishment resumed in 1957, two of the most senior and reliable men were promoted again, though Harry Allen was the main man. It is highly likely that Pierrepoint recommended them. As well as three trips to Cyprus to hang convicted EOKA 'terrorists' and civilian murderers, Allen executed 26 men in the UK in the following seven years, having previously assisted 41 times. Robert Leslie Stewart presided at the other six and also assisted Allen as often as not. In addition to these six men, 12 others assisted between 1945 and 1964 but never actually pulled the lever themselves: 18 times in Harry Smith's case, 15 in Dernley's, 13 in Henry Critchell's.

As already noted, the whole process was very swift. Every single person executed in Britain after the end of World War II was dead within a year of being arrested. The longest gaps were 313 days in the case of Northern Ireland's last condemned man, [195] Robert McGladdery, in 1961, and 311 for the last man tried and condemned under US military law, [2] Aniceto Martinez, in July 1945. At the opposite extreme, it could be as fast as 54 days, in the most obscure case of all, that of [32] Frank Freiyer in 1946, and 55 days for [25] Thomas Hendren in the same year. Three others were also hanged within two months of committing their crime.

On average, throughout the period, the time from arrest to execution was 126 days. If the outliers – those hanged under US or British military law, in Northern Ireland, or for treason or treachery, where the processes involved were longer – are removed, the average falls to 120 days, or almost exactly four months. In the pre-Homicide Act era, it was 122 days, 114 without the outliers. Once the Homicide Act came in, it went up to 146 days, 135 without the outliers. The much higher proportion of appeals after the Homicide Act became law almost entirely explains this.

The system was incredibly quick by comparison with the long-drawn-out processes that make capital punishment in modern America so degrading for all concerned – though in fact some American cases in the 1950s were equally quick. At the time, the speed of the process was one reason among the many why abolitionists found it barbaric. Compared to modern US processes, it all seems quite humane and at least it addressed what should be the whole point of the death penalty: that it judges someone guilty of so heinous a crime that he should not be allowed to grow into another person. Justice in post-war Britain was sometimes rough, but it was never delayed.

How guilty were they?

Miscarriages of justice were rare among 1945-64 capital cases, but they did happen. Already, four of those hanged since 1945 have been posthumously pardoned because their convictions have been ruled unsafe. Such rulings do not explicitly say that they were innocent, merely that the trials were not conducted properly, or new evidence came to light too late to save them.

[73] Timothy Evans was pardoned because Reginald Christie's murderous activities in the same house, unsuspected at the time of his trial, cast serious doubt on his conviction; 74] George Kelly because new evidence undermined the credibility of the police and a key prosecution witness against him; [118] Mahmood Mattan for basically similar reasons; [13] Derek Bentley largely because the judge at his trial was blatantly biased against him and the law, even if applied correctly, was clearly nonsensical in this case.

There are real doubts in several other cases, notably those of [106] Alfred Moore, [110] Edward Devlin and Alfred Burns, and [160] George Riley. In many more where the facts are clear, there appears to be at least a reasonable case for a verdict of manslaughter rather than murder, or at least circumstances that would have been seen as extenuating in later years. Conversely, three of the cohort had already been convicted of killing before: the indubitably guilty [21] Patrick Carraher and [128] James Alcott, as well as [3] Walter Rowland, whose guilt or innocence is one of the great imponderables of the period, though he was certainly a murderer earlier in his life. Modern science has also proved that one of the most famous victims of an apparent miscarriage of justice, [196] James Hanratty, was guilty after all.

Nonetheless, there are all too many instances of policemen blindly following one line of enquiry and ignoring other evidence, and of eccentric conduct by judges. Even though most of the condemned were guilty as charged, many were treated badly, even by the standards of the day. The law recognised this problem and tried, after much agonising and debate, to rectify that: hence the Homicide Act, which tried to please everyone but just created another layer of absurdity. It did at least greatly reduce the numbers going to gallows – from about 17 per year in 1945-55 to five in 1957-64 – and took most of the merely 'sad' and 'mad' out of the equation.

Far more common an issue than the wholly innocent being hanged in error was the number of mentally disturbed people who were executed. Neither the judiciary nor British society at the time as a whole had much grasp of psychology or psychiatry as they are understood today. Given that, before the Homicide Act, a defence of insanity was the only way to escape a mandatory death sentence when the basic facts were not in doubt, it was often pleaded in court and both sides would need to bring in experts to testify. However, they could only advise; it was for the jury to decide, based on their own life experience, whether or not the accused was fit to be sentenced, and it was far from certain that their advice would be taken.

All too often, psychiatrists had to endure the ill-concealed scorn of elderly judges or at best see their views given no more weight than those of prison medical officers. In one early case, that of [9] John Young, a psychiatric evaluation was carried out in the lunch break during his trial. This seems quite extraordinary when the life of a clearly very abnormal man depended on the outcome of this evaluation. Mr Justice Hilbery has been quoted as saying: "We're in the hands of the alienists or – as they're called nowadays – the psychiatrists ... If they say there's a medical reason for not hanging a murderer, he's not hanged." This was far from accurate but was certainly representative of attitudes on the bench.

'Temporary insanity' at the time of the crime was always very hard to assess during the trial, when the accused would be in a calmer state and would probably come across as perfectly sane. It is telling that Arthur Koestler and C.H. Rolph in *Hanged by the Neck*, published in 1961, argued along with the Royal Commission of the early 1950s that "there is no sharp dividing line between sanity and insanity; they shade into each other imperceptibly". This statement is so obviously correct that it scarcely needs saying now. Back then, it was quite a contentious view.

And so, in the years before, many men of dubious sanity went to the gallows. Koestler and Ralph listed 123 who were executed between 1949 and 1960, albeit in a list riddled with minor factual errors, including the names of two were not actually hanged. Of these, almost exactly half (61), they said, were either *crimes passionels* or crimes of the disordered mind. Only 30 were committed for gain, without any marked mental abnormality, and in most cases the psychiatric aspect of the case was never discussed. The vast majority were not truly premeditated but committed "in a fury or panic"; only one case was of cold-blooded murder for gain. That, incidentally, was the crime for which Kelly was wrongly hanged.

The most prevalent causes of murder, Koestler and Rolph found, were insanity and mental disorder, committed by the certifiably insane, epileptics, psychopaths and people with every shade of mental illness in between. "The result has been a tragic procession to the gallows of psychopaths, epileptic mental defectives, hysterics, sex maniacs, depressives and people on the border of paranoia and schizophrenia," they concluded. There is evidence to back this up from the comprehensive statistics from the years 1940-9, where of the 586 people tried for murder and not acquitted at trial or on appeal, 325 (55.5%) were insane, 164 being found guilty but insane under the M'Naghten rules, 144 more on arraignment and 17 in prison. As Gardiner put it, murder was essentially a result of disordered minds. There were also a few, though the ones he cited were pre-war, where men killed to achieve notoriety even though they knew what the result would be. Post-war, there were 15 cases where the defendant insisted on pleading guilty against legal advice or the judge's warning, or simply said that they were in a hurry to be hanged.

Insanity pleas became less common after Section 2 (1) of the Homicide Act of 1957 introduced the concept of diminished responsibility, leading to the alternatives of manslaughter and a life sentence, commitment to a mental hospital or even an absolute discharge. Koestler and Ralph calculated that in the 45 months from the passing of the Homicide Act to the end of 1960, 115 of those indicted for capital or non-capital murder pleaded diminished responsibility. Of these, 85 had their charge reduced to manslaughter. In 19, however, the prosecution sought to dispute the plea and succeeded 16 times.

Looking at the cases of the 203 people hanged for murder under UK law in 1945-64, I have attempted a ranking on the four criteria of guilt, mental state, premeditation and mitigating circumstances, where 5 is the highest score and 1 the lowest. This necessarily involves subjective judgements that can readily be disagreed with, but at least gives an indication of how guilty the post-war hanged were really in essentially legal rather than moral terms. The scores are as follows in each category:

Guilt:

1. Strong evidence of innocence
2. Serious doubt of guilt or strong case for manslaughter
3. Reasonable doubt/possible case for manslaughter or accident
4. Very small possibility of doubt, such as the evidence being purely circumstantial, but not enough to say there was a reasonable doubt

5. No doubt whatsoever, because of a valid confession, forensic evidence and/or excellent identification evidence

Premeditation:

1. Definitely no planning or intent to kill
2. Strong possibility of a lack of intent to kill
3. Violence/recklessness but not necessarily any intent to kill
4. Clear general readiness to kill
5. Clear and specific premeditation

Mental state:

1. Severe mental instability certified by doctors/unfit to plead
2. Very low intelligence/schizophrenia/mental problems from upbringing
3. Mixed evidence: not insane but in some way not right, such as chronic alcoholism, depression, damage from difficult upbringing or traumatic experiences, poor emotional state, etc.
4. Possible temporary insanity as defined by law or psychopathic state
5. Undoubtedly sane, legally and medically

Mitigating circumstances:

1. Clear evidence of mitigation, such as being an accomplice who did not kill and/or did not offer violence

2. Possible provocation/possibility that death caused by other conditions/suicide pact/plausible alternative killer/accused was an accomplice who did not kill but offered violence/clear evidence of police misconduct
3. Mixed, including youth/previous good character/uncertainty about who actually killed/element of self-defence/allegations of police misconduct/genuine grievance against victim
4. Suggestion of them but not of any standing in law, or no major previous criminal record
5. None at all, an utterly callous crime and/or the culmination of a long criminal record

None of the 203 score a 'perfect' 20 – but 32 of them score 19, 44 score 18, 36 score 17, 35 score 16 and 30 score 15. This, I would suggest, is the level at which, if one agrees with capital punishment at all, one can generally say that the condemned had little to complain about. However, that statement must be qualified. For instance, Kelly scores 15 because the crime for which he was hanged was clearly committed by someone who was sane, callous and ready to kill in the pursuit of a robbery, but there are serious doubts about his guilt.

Of the remainder, 13 scored 14, a figure where either the decision to hang them looks harsh and/or there are serious reasons to question whether the accused was guilty of murder. The remaining ten score less than 14 and fall into the category of possible miscarriages of justice. These include cases where, like Kelly, the guilt of the accused is in real doubt though the horror of the crime is not: those of Devlin and Burns (12), Mattan (12) and Riley (13).

There are more other cases where guilt in law is clear but there were mitigating factors that should have led to a reprieve. [90] Frank Griffin (12) did kill Jane Edge but did not intend to, was in an alcoholic fuddle at the time of the bungled act of theft he committed and was poorly served by the police and medical profession; William Watkins (13) very probably killed his baby son but was surely deserving of compassion for his wretched life circumstances; [145] Norman Harris (12) participated in a robbery where the victim died, but he did not intend to kill, offered no violence and was clearly repentant.

Right at the bottom, Timothy Evans (11) bears some blame for putting the noose around his neck because of his senseless lies, but was almost certainly innocent of the murders of his wife and daughter; while Bentley (8) was hanged for the murder committed by an accomplice when he was under arrest and no longer engaged in a common enterprise, had no intention to kill or even offer violence and was probably mentally unfit to be hanged, perhaps even to stand trial, in any case. It was perhaps the most appalling injustice ever perpetrated by the British state and the best answer that can be made to the 'Bring back the rope' brigade.

1. "My name should be 'Trouble', not 'Smith'": The murder of Sir Eric Teichman by Private George Edward Smith Junior in the grounds of Honingham Hall, Norfolk, on 3 December 1944 and his execution at HMP Shepton Mallet on 8 May 1945

Britain slept through the night of 7-8 May 1945, safe in the knowledge that there were no more bombing raids to come and the war in Europe was over. The next day had been declared to be Victory in Europe (VE) Day and it saw an explosion of celebrations across the land. Over in a quiet corner of Somerset, an American serviceman saw VE Day in too – but only just. Shortly after 1.00 a.m. on 8 May, at HMP Shepton Mallet, Private George Edward Smith Junior paid the ultimate price for the murder of Sir Eric Teichman in the grounds of his stately home on 3 December 1944.

Smith, 26, was one of ten children of a family who lived at 4418 Liberty Avenue in the Bloomington area of Pittsburgh. The only known picture of him, in the *Pittsburgh Press* on 13 January 1945, shows a handsome young man with thick hair draped across his right eyebrow, a prominent nose and heavy lips. According to his mother, he was always the black sheep of the family, the only one who got into trouble. He had spent time in mental hospitals and once served a year in a reformatory for stealing a car. She and his father had even tried to have him arrested or institutionalised at different times.

At his trial, it was stated that he had been court-martialled 18 times in 30 months and had gone absent without leave four times. "I wouldn't be surprised at anything I heard of him," Mrs Smith remarked when he was arrested. Later, she added: "I never did know why he was in the Army in the first place. He was a sick boy." Nevertheless, he had been allowed to join the military in August 1942. Nearly two and a half years later, he was with 784th Bombardment Squadron, 466th Bombardment Group, 96th Combat Bombardment Wing (Heavy), 2nd Air Division at RAF Attlebridge, adjacent to Honingham Hall. He was reportedly employed as a cook.

Smith was the last but one of 18 American servicemen to be executed at Shepton Mallet. He was condemned under US law, but the UK authorities had insisted that British hangmen perform the task. They disliked the amateurish way the US Army carried out hangings, often with poorly designed scaffolds, no standardised drop length and the wrong type of rope. This decision at least spared the condemned the slow, agonising death suffered by many of the Nazi war criminals hanged by American methods in continental Europe. Some American practices, however, continued. While rationing prevailed outside, hangman Albert Pierrepoint recalled that there was "the best running buffet and unlimited canned beer" for all involved prior to executions at Shepton Mallet.

Unlike British hangings, those conducted by the US military took place in the dead of night, rather than first thing in the morning. Smith was executed in uniform, but any badges or flashes marking him as a soldier were removed and his dishonourable discharge had been completed. Instead of the speedy process perfected at civilian executions in Britain, he had to stand strapped and hooded with the noose around his neck while the formalities were completed. "The part of the routine which I found it hardest to acclimatise myself to was the, to me, sickening interval between my introduction to the prisoner and his death," Pierrepoint wrote later.

"Under British custom I was working to the sort of timing where the drop fell between eight and 20 seconds after I had entered the condemned cell. Under the American system, after I had pinioned the prisoner, he had to stand on the drop for perhaps six minutes while his charge sheet was read out, sentence spelt out, and he was asked if he had anything to say, and after that I was instructed to get on with the job." Up to 20 people might have been crowding around the chamber. Smith had no last words. The 'number one' on this occasion was Albert's uncle Thomas Pierrepoint, who had been active as a hangman for just under 40 years and was now 74. Henry Critchell assisted. Thomas and/or Albert had officiated at 12 of the other executions of American troops and at every hanging in the UK for years before.

The murder Smith had committed was remarkable only for its pointlessness. His victim, however, was unquestionably one of the most eminent victims of people who were hanged between VE Day and abolition. Sir Eric – by birth, Erik - Teichman was born in 1884 and educated at Gonville & Caius College, Cambridge. He joined the British Embassy in China in 1907 as an interpreter in the consular service. He is said to have been a spy, as well as an explorer, a diplomat, an expert horseman and a linguist who understood a wide array of Chinese dialects. Teichman travelled widely through Central Asia as part of his work, publishing *Travels of a Consular Officer in North-West China* in 1921 and *Travels of a Consular Officer in Eastern Tibet* in 1922. Both are still widely read. He also left extensive notes about the Gansu and Xinjiang regions, then largely unknown in the West.

Undeterred by suffering a severe spinal injury he sustained while playing polo in 1932, Teichman was the first person in modern times to travel the full 2,500 miles of the 'Silk Road'; he did this in 1935 at the behest of the British Embassy to evaluate setting up a base in the remote city of Urumqi to alleviate Soviet pressure on British-controlled Kashgaria. He took a train from Beijing to Suiyuan on the eastern frontier of Inner Mongolia, then continued west with two Ford trucks and a staff of five, skirting the Gobi Desert on camel tracks for 1,500 miles to Urumqi. The next stage of the journey was to Kashgar, during which one of the trucks had to be abandoned, then on by yak and pony through the

Himalayas to Afghanistan and into British India. At Gilgit in the Karakoram, he was struck down by illness and later flew on to Delhi. The whole journey took four months.

Teichman wrote up the first part and published it as *Journey to Turkestan* in 1937. A review remarked that it was "a journey that should, one would think, have been redolent romance, of Marco Polo and Fletcher. We travel not for travelling alone: by hotter winds our fiery hearts are fanned ... But there is nothing of that here. True, of human obstacles there were few or none. The expedition's struggles were with nature – the sands from which they had to dig their wheels, the boulders which had to be thrown from mountain paths, the frozen rivers through which they had to break way for the ferry; yet Sir Eric writes such an unemotional style that even these seem little more than puncture in the Sperrins." Teichman said almost nothing of the fruits of the mission, the review observed. "One would not like to give a wrong impression of the book, solid and informative, and would be most useful to any future traveller over the route. But how one wishes that Defoe or Cobbett had had the opportunity to make the journey."

Another reviewer agreed, describing Teichman's writing style as "straightforward", while "his concentration on fact and exclusion of the inessential give austerity to the descriptive passages and authority to those in which he discusses the political conditions prevailing in Chinese

Turkistan". Very little of Teichman's character comes over in his writings. His travels were emphatically not the internal 'journeys' of modern psychobabble. As a *Spectator* review said, he seemed "quite uninterested in himself". A boy who encountered Sir Eric during the war years, when his house was given over to the charity Dr Barnardo's, remembered him as "a rather dour man", to whom he barely spoke in his years there, although another, Bill Cotton, recalled that Teichman played Father Christmas to the boys at special Christmas parties every year.

That house was Honingham Hall, which stood in a 3,000-acre estate eight miles west of Norwich. Honingham Hall was a Jacobean mansion that had originally been built for Sir Thomas Richardson, a justice of the King's Bench, in 1605 and since owned by the Townsend and Ailwyn families until Ronald Fellowes, Second Baron Ailwyn, sold it in 1935. Teichman retired from his post due to ill health in 1937 and bought the house that same year. He then worked on *Journey to Turkistan* and his last published work, *Affairs of China*, in 1938. In 1942, he was briefly in China again as an adviser to the British Embassy at Chongqing, returning to Britain for good in 1944.

Like most of Britain's stately homes, Honingham Hall had been turned over to other uses to support the war effort. It became a Barnardo's home, with the Teichmans staying in the main part and up to 50 boys at any time staying in the rest, some for up to seven years. Sir Eric was impressed enough that he left the house to Barnardo's in his will, provided that his widow could remain there.

By 1945, aged 60, he was in severe physical decline. Most obviously, he was hunchbacked. He had stood over six feet tall fully upright but his wife, Lady Ellen, a widow he had married late in life, commented that she was 5'2" and he barely came up to her shoulder. Indeed, at the time of his death, there was some speculation that he had been shot by accident by a poacher who had not seen him but heard rustling in the bracken that he assumed to be an animal. Some accounts say that Teichman had only been back at his home two weeks before his fatal encounter with Private Smith. His brusque manner may conceivably have played a part in what happened to him.

Their paths crossed because RAF Attlebridge, which both the RAF and the US Air Force used, adjoined the Honingham Hall estate. The base covered the northwest corner of Honingham parish, with the rest in East Tuddenham, Hockering and Weston Longville. At about 13.00 on Sunday 3 December, Smith and Private Leonard S. Wojtacha, 20, a boyish-looking man of Polish origin from Detroit who was attached to 61st Station Complement, 466th Bombardment Group, left the base and wandered into the grounds of the estate. Wojtacha's name is given as Wijpacha in some accounts, but this is clearly multiple repetitions of a transcription error; there is no such name.

They were armed with M1 0.38 carbines and ammunition. It has been said that they were poaching, but they probably had nothing quite so organised in mind and could have ended the day guilty only of trespass. According to the accounts later given by both men, they each fired several rounds at an oil drum in a field and at a cow. They then entered the woods on the estate, passed the house on an old, abandoned road and began firing at a squirrel, following it to an overgrown wooded area about 300 yards east of the house.

Hearing shots, at about 2.00 p.m., Teichman assumed it was poachers, left his drawing room to investigate and found the pair still looking up for the squirrel. It is possible that, because of his hunched posture, they did not see him until he was nearly on them. Smith told Wojtacha: "Look out. There is an old man behind you". Wojtacha, who had just become aware of Teichman's presence, walked towards him. Teichman called out: "Just a minute. What are your names?" Smith replied, "Get back, Pop" or "Old man, don't come any closer". When Teichman did not stop, Smith fired a single shot from his hip. Teichman slumped to the ground, face down, at a distance variously estimated as between eight and 42 feet. It was definitely more than six feet away, as no powder burns were found on him.

The two soldiers left in haste. Throughout, Wojtacha later testified, Smith was "happy, calm, gay and normal", probably detaching himself emotionally from what had happened. At one point on the way back, Wojtacha saw an old man walking with a dog and said: "There is the old man walking down the road". Smith answered, "I must have missed him. I should have shot him again", though anyone thinking rationally would surely have known that this was not the same man. Pausing only for Smith to push a twig into his gun barrel, either to clean it or jam it, they returned at about 2.50 p.m., hid the guns under a table in another soldier's room and parted. Smith remained calm and smiling; Wojtacha was badly frightened and remained so.

Searches began on the estate at about 5.00 when Sir Eric did not return. Nothing was found. Lady Ellen was unable to sleep for worry. She went out again at about midnight with a nurse, Victoria Childerhouse, and this time she found her husband's body. A copper, jagged-edged shell was found nearby, along with some chewing gum, which suggested that the bullet was fired from a US Army carbine. This was confirmed beyond doubt by the autopsy, which also revealed that the bullet had entered Teichman's right cheek, shattered the jaw completely, was deflected downward by two vertebrae in the neck, broke two ribs and passed out of the body under the left shoulder blade, lodging in his clothes. There was early speculation about organised skulduggery in the death of "a man who the Japs feared" but it soon evaporated in the face of the mundane truth.

By 5.00 p.m., rumours had started going about RAF Attlebridge. Smith, who woke up during a conversation about the shooting, reportedly said:

"Maybe it's a good thing the old bastard is dead". During the evening, he ate at the home of some civilian friends, played with their pets and went on to a pub, where he drank for about 90 minutes and "behaved normally", though he was ordered from the mess hall on his return because he was unkempt in appearance and slightly drunk.

The next morning, as the news was confirmed, the whole base was ordered to surrender their arms. Smith's gun, numbered 2036239 and bearing his name, still had a piece of weed stalk jammed in the barrel. On 5 December, Smith came up to Wojtacha's table at the mess hall and said: "Don't say anything. Let them find out for themselves". This took very little time. The Provost Marshal, Major Tyler Birch, learned that the two had "gone hunting" on the Sunday afternoon. Wojtacha was confronted with the evidence and casts of footsteps made at the scene of the crime, and was promised leniency if he disclosed what he knew. He promptly made a full statement.

Smith, when warned he would be charged as a result and read his rights, told Birch: "I shot him". He then made a written confession, which essentially agreed with Wojtacha's account, other than adding that he had drunk about 15 coffee cups of beer before leaving the base. The two then walked over the route and re-enacted the events with officials, who found evidence including bullet holes in the oil drum to corroborate it. Smith was still reportedly "calm, co-operative and friendly towards

Wojtacha", though he was excessively voluble at times. He was charged with murder, Wojtacha with being an accessory. Later a Home Office ballistics expert, Dr Henry Smith Holden, confirmed that the bullet had come from Smith's carbine and that five shots in total had been fired from it.

The case received press coverage both in the US and in the wider world, including Australia. The *Detroit Free Press* had tracked down Wojtacha's parents in their cottage in the suburb of Hamtramck less than a week after the shooting. His mother, Agnes, who had limited English, described him as "a good boy who never got into trouble". Another son, Edward, was also overseas with the Army; their father, Albert, was then a "war worker", it reported.

Smith's court martial began at RAF Attlebridge on 8 January 1945, in a hastily converted room that was used most of the week as a gymnasium and on Sundays as a chapel. About 400 people were reportedly present. The court consisted of 12 members, including the president, Colonel McInlay. The prosecution was led by trial judge advocate Major Frank Brockus; Major Peter Deisch and First Lieutenant Max Sokarl defended Smith. It lasted the unusually long space of five days due to the repeated hospitalisations of Smith, who had no doubt begun to contemplate his likely fate.

The main witness was Wojtacha, who told the story of their journey to the woods, Teichman challenging them and that the "next thing he knew a gun was fired". When Brockus asked "Whose gun?", he said that it was Smith's and that Smith fired it towards Teichman. Birch attested to Smith admitting "I shot him" and said he had recorded Smith's replies to questions "in language as near as his own [*sic*] as I could get". Detective Constable Sidell of the Norfolk Police showed the carbine he had taken from Smith during searches of the camp and said this was given to the defence to handle. Corporal Weaver of the US Army testified that Smith had handed it to him on 4 December and that a twig was stuck in the barrel.

Smith withdrew his confession and claimed it had been made under duress, but he did not testify, saying: "I prefer to remain silent". Brockus, on no clear basis, alleged that the motivation was simple and explicable: Smith had no intention of giving his name to Teichman and consequently being court-martialled. This was probably a long way removed from whatever went on in Smith's disordered mind.

The defence brought a total of 23 witnesses and 14 exhibits, taking three days to complete. Sokarl, the press reported, "put up a vigorous defence", portraying Smith as a split personality, and pleaded insanity on his behalf. Deisch likewise argued that his client was "subject to uncontrollable, irresistible and insane impulses over which he has no control". Going over Smith's troubled history of imprisonment and institutionalisation, Sokarl noted his 18 court-martials - something, one would think, that rather goes against the idea that the prospect of another would bother him enough to commit a killing to avoid another.

The idea that Smith had it in him to think out a motive on the spot was absurd, Sokarl averred; it was "a purposeless, motiveless and idiotic act" and Smith was "a person on whom fears of criminal law have no effect". Any reasonable man would have removed the twig from the carbine before handing it in, he said. Would a sane man have made a full confession, let alone re-enacted the crime for investigators? Smith could no more have refrained himself from carrying out the shooting than he could have refrained himself from admitting it.

Also brought in evidence were some essays Smith had written, apparently of his own volition, while under arrest. 'What I think about the man I shot' said that he did not know why he shot Teichman, who "had not done anything to me and I did not do anything to me. He did not know me and I did not know him. All I can say for myself is that I am very sorry for it … My name should be 'Trouble', not 'Smith'", he concluded. In 'Why I would like be a dog' [sic], Smith said he would have liked it, because house dogs were treated better than people. 'What I think about officers in the army' and, to laughter, 'What I think about my lawyer' were also read out.

At one point, during the trial, Sokarl had Smith disrobe and show the court the 17 tattoos he had "from neck to knee". These included the names 'Patsy', 'Dick', 'George' and 'Micky' on his chest, plus 'Ann' and a picture of a naked girl and a shamrock on his right leg, a "strange cross", an upside-down number 13 and a baby's face. Somehow, these were supposed to have a bearing on his mental state.

In his final address, Brockus asked the court to put insanity aside, arguing: "When Sir Eric came close to Smith and asked his name, Smith said to himself 'I will kill him. Nobody will ever know what happened to this old man. I can get rid of him'. Smith underestimated one man – Wojtacha, the soldier who was with him. Smith thought that Wojtacha would never tell. Wojtacha is very fortunate that he was not killed by Smith on that occasion". Perhaps he was, but it is absurd to project this train of thought onto Smith. "By his calm, deliberate act, he has become a cancerous growth on this world's face," Brockus concluded with a vitriol unimaginable in a British court, even then. "It is the duty of this court to remove that cancer."

As Sokarl made his final speech – during which he said, "Smith's life is no life. It is a living death. It is a great pity" – Smith "listened with his elbows resting on a table beside his chair. His eyes were fixed on his clashed hands". As the court reached its verdict, he was seen chatting happily to his guards but he "swayed noticeably" as the verdict of guilty and sentence of death were read out. He soon regained his composure, however, "walked smartly" to Sokarl's desk and thanked him. As he was led out in handcuffs, he "managed a smile". It has been stated that Wojtacha was later sentenced to a prison term of unrecorded length but there is no record of this and it may be that he was never tried.

Because the case was prosecuted under US law, the processes were much slower than in a British court. A mandatory review followed on 26 April, before the Board of Review to the Branch Office of the Judge Advocate General Within the European Theatre of Operations, before Judge Advocates Riter, Burrow and Stevens. They re-examined the evidence in great detail to decide whether to recommend upholding the sentence. One previous conviction by special court-martial for being disorderly in uniform in a public place had been brought up during the court but nothing emerged to suggest that drunkenness was anything to do with Smith's actions. Nor was there any discussion about his intentions. Given that he fired from his hip, he was probably not seeking to kill, if he was consciously seeking to do anything, and it was chance that the shot proved fatal. There was no question, however, that it was legally murder.

Most of the board's deliberations were to do with Smith's mental health. The defence cited his score of 67 on the Army's General Classification Test, putting him in the bottom 15-20% of personnel. Other stories about him suggested a rather disturbed, withdrawn personality, someone who was incapable of thinking through the consequences of his actions. Some suggest he may have been autistic, a condition that was little known or understood at the time.

In a chilling echo of the fatal shooting, Smith had once cut off the tails of two pet white mice "because he thought they would look cute with bob tails" and he once kicked his dog, despite being fond of animals generally. He was obsessively neat, a loner, not interested in meeting the local girls, and was generally calm and cheerful, but also prone to sudden, irrational acts and explosions of anger. In jail, he was reportedly happy and co-operative. The essays were looked at and said to "reveal incoherency, illiteracy and some viciousness".

Major Leo Alexander, chief of the Psychiatric Section at the 65th General Hospital, examined Smith three times in four days in early January and diagnosed his condition as "constitutional psychopathic state, with inadequate and immature personality, emotional instability, schizoid traits, and explosive (poorly repressed). Primitive-sadistic aggressiveness – severe. Mental deficiency, borderline, mental age nine years. In older psychiatric terminology: Mentally defective, homicidal degenerate."

Alexander (who also estimated the average mental age of the US Army as 14, probably revealing more about the state of psychological theory at the time than the soldiers themselves) went on to say that although Smith had a split personality, he was not insane. He "knew right from wrong but was not impressed with the seriousness of the difference" and lacked moral restraint. "His emotion was to kill the squirrel and the killing urge, which inhibitions did not restrain, was transferred suddenly but not automatically to the man who interfered with his wishes. The accused secured an emotional gain from the killing – from flaunting it before the investigating officer and from his predicament at the trial."

Smith, Alexander concluded, was "dangerous, might have killed men before and would probably do so again if left at large. Drinking liquor would reduce his conscious restraint against subconscious emotions. He bordered on insanity, but his criminal responsibility, though impaired, was not abolished." This view was substantially supported by Major Thomas March, chief of neuropsychiatry at the 231st Station Hospital, who diagnosed Smith as having a "constitutional psychopathic state; inadequate personality and schizoid tendencies or traits ... His will to adhere to the right was tainted not with insanity, but by abnormal emotional tendencies."

By contrast, Dr John V. Morris, medical superintendent of the Norfolk County Mental Deficiency Institutions, diagnosed schizophrenia. Smith's mental state, in his opinion, "was such that he might at times be able to distinguish right from wrong, but if he had an impulse to do something wrong, he would not have enough control or reasoning power to resist. He was subject to uncontrollable impulses" and needed "permanent restraint". Morris's view was that Smith shot

Teichman simply because Teichman "interfered with his pleasure". Smith had showed no signs of emotion or regret when questioned about the shooting, talking of it "as a man talked of killing a rabbit, with no sign that he had done anything wrong, and declared, 'I just lost my head. I didn't even aim at him. I fired a single shot.'"

The court went over the evidence, including photographs of the body, the re-enactment, ballistics and psychoanalysis, and concluded that it had all been properly admitted. Given that Smith "purposely shot the deceased without provocation and in no fear of his own safety", the only question was whether the court agreed with the US Army psychiatrists or the British civilian one. The test as to mental responsibility under military law at the time was whether the accused was "so far free from mental defect, disease, or derangement as to be able, concerning the particular acts charged, both to distinguish right from wrong and to adhere to the right". On this basis, it ruled, the original court had properly found him legally sane. The sentence was upheld.

Requests for clemency were made, notably by Lady Teichman, who, with extraordinary goodness of soul, made personal appeals first to Army headquarters, then to General Eisenhower and finally to the US ambassador in London, John Winant. To the latter, she wrote, on 4 May: "The law is hard, and it seems awful to me that a young man should be forced into eternity. If it is a death sentence, could anyone do anything to help him?". Winant passed this on to Brigadier-General E.C. McNeil, Assistant Judge Advocate General. It was to no avail and Smith kept his appointment with the hangmen four days later. With characteristic bureaucratic callousness, the US Army did not notify his mother and she found out from a reporter for the *Pittsburgh Press*, who arrived on her doorstep on 19 May. "It's happened? It's funny that the War Department wouldn't let me know about it," she said, before turning away, weeping.

Sir Eric Teichman is buried in St Andrew's Church in Honingham. Smith lies in Row 3, Grave 52 within Plot E of the Oisne-Aisne military cemetery in Northern France. This is also the burial place of 93 others executed by hanging or firing squad during World War II, including all bar one, possibly two, of those who died at Shepton Mallet. The plot is hidden from the rest of that cemetery, which has 6,012 graves in four other plots. There are flat stone markers instead of crosses and headstones, no flags and no names. Its very existence was kept quiet until a Freedom of Information request in 2009 forced the authorities to release the names and it still does not appear on the official guide pamphlet.

After his release, Wojtacha married Marilyn Sandstrom, by whom he had two daughters. At some point before 1981, they divorced and he remarried a woman called Lorene, giving him two stepdaughters. He lived in Ferndale, Michigan, while Marilyn moved to Chattanooga, Tennessee.

He died on 19 October 1992, aged 68, while his ex-wife lived to the age of 88. When she died on 10 November 2014, she had ten grandchildren, 15 great-grandchildren and seven great-great-grandchildren, who all owe something to her husband's sensible decision not to stand by Smith.

Lady Teichman remained at Honingham Hall with a much-reduced staff, though sometimes hosting the Queen's ladies-in-waiting while the Royal family was at Sandringham. Eventually, her advancing age forced her to retire to a nursing home. Barnardo's were not permitted by the terms of Sir Eric's will to sell it during her lifetime but soon the charity no longer wanted the cost of maintaining such vast houses. The Leonards, master and matron of the Barnado's home, remained there for a whileafter Lady Teichman's death. It then passed through three more owners until the last secured permission to demolish it in 1966, while keeping the stable building to convert into a house. Such was the fate of countless grand houses in post-war Britain.

A few traces of RAF Attlebridge survive, including air raid shelters, two fuel stores, two possible searchlight or gun positions, a sewage works and the remains of sentry boxes. The runway area is now occupied by sheds raising turkeys. Fragments of ammunition have also been found, suggesting that part of the area was used as a firing range. By an ironic chance, a Norwich auctioneer found a Churchill 12-bore boxlock ejector gun belonging to Sir Eric in 2006 and sold it at Kensington House.

2. "Oh dear, master, whatever do you want?": The rape of Agnes Cope by Private First-Class Aniceto Martinez at 15 Sandy Lane, Rugeley, Staffordshire, on 6 August 1944 and his execution at HMP Shepton Mallet on 15 June 1945

Terrible crime though it is, rape had not been punishable by death in Britain for over a century. The last civilian to be hanged for committing it had been Richard Smith at Nottingham back in 1836. However, rape was still punishable by death in most of the southern states of the US in the mid-twentieth century and continued apace until the same year that hanging ceased altogether in the UK, 1964. There were just over 300 rape executions (discounting those where the victim was also murdered) in the US between 1941 and 1964, the last being that of Ronald Wolfe in Missouri's gas chamber in May 1964. Under US military law too, specifically the 24th American Article of War, where a defendant was convicted of rape, there were only two possible sentences: death or life imprisonment. Thus, it became a potentially capital crime in the UK too when the British government passed the Visiting Forces Act of 1942.

In the eight months between August 1944 and June 1945, six GIs were to suffer death accordingly, as well as eight who were hanged for murder and four who committed both. Eliga Brinson and Willie Smith, both 22, were hanged in August 1944 for the rape of a 16-year-old girl in the fields outside a dance at Bishop's Cleeve in Gloucestershire that April; Madison Thomas raped and robbed a woman on her way home at Gunnislake in Cornwall on 26 July 1944 and was hanged on 12 October; Robert Pearson and Parson Jones swung side by side on 17 March 1945 for the rape of a heavily pregnant woman in an orchard at Chard, Somerset, on 3 December 1944.

And finally, on 15 June 1945, Private First-Class Aniceto Martinez of Vallecitos, New Mexico, 23, became the last man to be hanged for rape in Britain, as well the last of 18 US servicemen to suffer death at HMP Shepton Mallet in the 30 months since January 1943. He was also the last man ever to be hanged at this prison. Shepton Mallet had been the site of a civilian prison for centuries before the British military loaned it to the US Army as part of the Visiting Forces Act of 1942, which permitted American military justice to be carried out here. Built in 1910, it was already showing its age in 1942. The gallows had not been used since 1926 and a new two-storey red brick structure had to be added to one of the wings for a new set to be installed. Two cells were converted into the condemned cell. The prison also housed some priceless archives taken out of London for safety during the war, including the Domesday Book and a copy of the Magna Carta.

Although there is compelling evidence that all of the 18 of the men the US Army put to death at Shepton Mallet were guilty as charged, American military justice was not undiscriminating when it came to social class or colour. All, predictably, were from the ranks: one was a corporal, the rest were all privates or private first class. Their average age was 24. Ten were black, five were white and the other three, including Martinez, were Hispanics. They were a sub-set of the 96 American servicemen serving in the European and North African 'theatres of operations' during World War II to be executed for one or more of these crimes.

Two of the 18 were shot by firing squads at dawn and the rest hanged. It has been suggested that the authorities reverted to hanging because of complaints from locals about the noise, though this may be an urban legend. Their 18 victims were all white bar one and 14 of them were civilians. All five who preceded Martinez in being hanged for rape were black. One might speculate at length about whether the races were treated equally at a time when segregation was a simple fact of life in most of the US, especially in cases where a sexual crime perpetrated by a non-white man on a white woman would have been regarded with particular revulsion. There is not actually that much publicly available evidence in the US itself to show whether this is the case.

In 1993, J. Robert Lilly of North Kentucky University published figures showing that 70 GIs in total were executed following court-martials in all theatres in World War II, of whom 55 were black and 15 were not. Of the 28 executed for murder, 22 were black, while a further 25 blacks and four others, including Martinez, were executed for the rape of civilians.

Lilly has also established that the US military handed down 443 death sentences to its own soldiers: 198 to blacks, 245 to others. Blacks were disproportionately overrepresented among the condemned, considering that they were only about 10% of the troops. They were also far likelier than whites to be sentenced for rape, murder or both; only for desertion and similar crimes was this not the case. And when sentenced, they were disproportionately likelier to have their sentences carried out.

Almost all of the offenders had very speedy trials, typically lasting two working days, under procedures laid down in the 1928 American Forces Manual for Courts-Martial. [1] George Smith's trial was unusually long by contrast, taking five days for evidence to be heard; Martinez's was much more typical in its brevity. The defence, usually led by an officer of the rank of captain or above, had only two to three weeks to prepare their cases and the court rarely granted defence motions to delay the proceedings. More typically American was the longer gap between sentence and execution: three months as opposed to the 'three clear Sundays' conventional in the UK. Why Martinez waited six months from arrest to trial and another four to execution is unclear.

Martinez had joined the Army in Santa Fe in October 1942. At some point, he was a member of the 202nd Military Police Company, which was almost certainly a mainly white unit. By August 1944, he was working as a guard within Headquarters Detachment of Prisoner of War Enclosure No. 2. This stood at Flaxley Green Camp in Stilecop Field on the main road between Rugeley and Hednesford, near Cannock Chase, in Staffordshire. Built by the Royal Engineers in 1941-2, it housed Italian POWs in six main compounds. It has long since vanished from view.

On the night of 5 August 1944, Martinez left the camp to go into Rugeley, a town that had been made infamous by the murderous Victorian doctor, William Palmer, and vainly petitioned to change its name after his execution. By his own account, he visited two or three pubs from 6.00 p.m. onwards, ending up at the Crown Hotel, which is still in business. He had drunk enough beer to be "high" by the end of the evening but was not drunk – or so he claimed. After closing time at about 10.00 p.m., he left, walked around and finally came to a group of houses on the right-hand side where, he said, he had "talked to a lady in one of the houses on two prior occasions" and went to the house where I thought she lived, possibly confusing numbers 18 and 15 Sandy Lane. This was at about 10.30.

"I knocked, but no one answered, so I turned the knob and walked in. I went upstairs, and the lady asked me if I wanted money. I told her it was not money, and then pulled her down on the bed," he stated. There is a discrepancy in his timing and that of his victim, who said the rape began at 3.15 a.m. on 6 August. There is no doubt that Martinez was away from his base well before that: he was the only person missing during a bed check at about midnight and therefore became the prime suspect immediately. On the basis that the victim was almost certainly correct, nearly five hours of his movements remain unaccounted for.

Agnes Cope was a frail, 75-year-old widow, weighing eight stone and no match for a powerful young man. She lived alone in the small cottage at 15 Sandy Lane, where she had resided for 43 years – she had actually moved in on the day that Mafeking was relieved in the Boer War. Cope told investigators that she was awakened by the sound of someone moving on the stairs, then a man appeared in the doorway. Although she did not see his face, he sounded American, and was wearing khaki and a hat with a black peak.

"Oh dear, master, whatever do you want?" the terrified woman asked. "If it is money you want, I haven't got it." The man replied: "I don't want money. You know what I want. It be a woman I want", which was alternatively worded as "It is not money. I want woman". This happened at 3.15 a.m., a fact she said she knew because her assailant picked up the clock and said: "It's a quarter past three, missus". From the use of British colloquialisms like 'It be' and 'missus', it seems certain that these words are either those she ascribed to him or ones put down as an approximation by a policeman rather than literal quotes. This is totally unlike the speech pattern of a Texan.

The man placed his hat on the bed, moved her to one side, lifted her nightdress and forcibly raped her. Cope resisted as best she could and was struck every time she did so, receiving a black eye that lasted for a week. In court, she was later to say that "the more she squealed, the more the man hit her". After the assailant had gone, she sat on the side of the bed until she heard her daughter, who had come to visit, moving about downstairs. She told her daughter what had happened and, "as soon as she could pull herself together", which was some point between 7.30 and 8.30 a.m., they went to the police station, where she made a statement.

Police surgeon Dr L.D. Roberts, who examined her at 10.45, found small, recent bruises on her face and neck, bruising and swelling in her vagina, and traces of sperm, all of which fully bore out her story. She also had a sprained thumb. Inspector Horace J. Brooks of Staffordshire County Police looked at the house and found that the back doors had been forced, while outside there was an impression on the ground where someone had lain down and vomited. That afternoon at about 3.00 p.m., he went to the camp to report the crime.

Suspicion pointed to Martinez straight away because he had been absent at bed check. When questioned, he initially denied any knowledge of the offence. Brooks took possession of some clothes he had been wearing that evening and these were sent to the West Midlands Forensic Laboratory in Birmingham for examination by Professor James Matthewson Webster and Professor Long.

At the end, Brooks warned him that he would be handed over to the US authorities and cautioned him in the standard British format. Asked if he wanted to say anything in response to the charge, Martinez is recorded as replying: "I did go in the house. I did not break the door open. I had connections with a woman. She was not forced. It was at a little house at the bottom of the hill near the pub. It happened last night. I had had some drink. I was not drunk. I was sick near the house." This, again, is obviously a transcription of notes because it is totally unlike normal speech. At the end, however, Martinez refused to sign the statement, saying "then you can't use it at a court-martial against me".

The following day, Lieutenant Harold F. Ford, an agent of the 28th Military Police Criminal Investigations Department also interviewed Martinez. Ford reminded him of his right under Article of War 24 to remain silent and told him that anything he might say might be used in evidence against him. Martinez volunteered his story of going to the house he believed to be the same as the one he had been to before, knocking, then going in when there was no answer. In his version, the woman asked if he was looking for money. He said: "No, I've got plenty of money, you know what I want" and she replied: "Let's get it over so you can go back home".

He then described the intercourse in limited detail, saying it was over in a second and he did not recall hitting her. Then he grabbed his hat and went out the back door, jumped over the hedge onto the road and returned to camp. Martinez further stated that this house had been recommended to him by others: he believed it to be "a house of ill repute", had been there two weeks before but was told to come again another night. Furthermore, he had previously seen soldiers and "numerous women" inside the house and was once ordered away by military police, though he had not seen Agnes Cope before.

Whether any of this was true of the other house or not, it was not a credible defence to the charge. Martinez also denied wearing the hat, shirt and trousers produced in evidence that night. Even without the bed check and the doctor's evidence, a mountain of evidence pointed to him. Forensics had found the service cap he was said to have worn on the night contained a thorn similar to those on the six-foot hawthorn bush around the house and blue fibres similar to those in the quilt on Cope's bed (which she mistakenly said was red). Similarly, some white material found under the shirt, while around the bottom of two buttons of the trousers he admitted wearing on the night contained cotton fibres and threads consistent with her nightdress and the lower portion of the shirt contained a semen stain.

Martinez was court-martialled at Lichfield on 21 February 1945. The local press reported that a colonel was president of the court and the other members consisted of a colonel, five majors and a captain. Lieutenant Wetherby was the trial judge advocate, prosecuting Martinez, who was represented by Captains Dolezal and Wintraub. The prosecution homed in on the "heinous", "bestial" and "sub-human" crime against a helpless old woman. The soldier who carried out the midnight bed check, Sergeant Barnbaum, travelled back from combat duty in France to give evidence at the trial and confirmed that Martinez was the only soldier not in his bed at the time.

Martinez still claimed he had been asleep in the latrine. Under examination, he repeated his story in essence: the house was one he had been recommended to go to before and he had seen soldiers round the house before; Cope was not the woman he had talked to previously, but he thought he was going into the same house as he had been to before. In concluding for the defence, Dolezal ventured that, although Martinez was not drunk, "it was well to assume he was under the influence of intoxicants. It was also apparent that he was not of very high education, and that no doubt explained some things given in his statements." In reply, Wetherby said that "whether the point of education was considered or not, they had to have a guiding stick to stamp out offences of that kind".

The court considered its verdict in session and the president announced that Martinez had been found guilty. In the way peculiar to the military, the sentence would not be disclosed until it was reviewed by the relevant authority. In fact, he had been sentenced to death with the concurrence of all members of the court. In contrast with Smith, whose story was picked up by many local newspapers, the US press barely noticed.

The case was automatically heard again on 29 May before the board of review by Judge Advocates Sleeper, Sherman and Dewey. Having dealt with an error in its records about the presence of Major Chester Mebus in the court on the day of a trial and found it to be immaterial, the board concluded that "every element of the offense of rape is amply proved by competent substantial evidence" and that this was enough to support the guilty verdict. Whilst he had not "inflicted serious bodily injury" on Cope, the board said, he had still committed his act by force and she resisted as best she could, placing the case squarely within the rules the board had discussed in other cases.

The commanding general in the European Theatre upheld the sentence and Martinez was hanged by Thomas and Albert Pierrepoint on 15 June. Like the other US servicemen to face the drop at Shepton Mallet, he was taken to the gallows at 1.00 a.m. "dressed in regulation uniform, from which all decorations, insignia, or other evidence of membership therein have been removed". He was kept on the platform of the gallows for several minutes with the noose around his neck while the charges were read. There would be no calculation of the right drop for his weight that British hangmen carried out to ensure a clean break in the neck without any danger of either decapitation or strangulation. The average time taken from 15 of the 16 hangings at Shepton Mallet was 14.8 minutes from leaving the cell to being pronounced dead. This was also the last time Albert Pierrepoint ever officiated as an assistant; on all of his subsequent executions, he operated the lever himself.

Like all the American servicemen executed in the UK, Martinez was first buried at Brookwood Memorial War Cemetery in Surrey but was reinterred in 1949 at the Oise-Aisne American Cemetery in northern France. He lies in row 2, grave 39 of Plot E, which was designated to the 'dishonoured dead'. In all, 94 of the 98 men executed following General Courts Martial for murder, rape or both in the European and Mediterranean theatres of operations lie there.

A further 43 US servicemen were executed in the three years from 1942 to 1945, with six more in the post-war period, including the Southwest Pacific area, the continental US, Hawaii, Japan and the Philippines. All were performed under the authority of the Articles of War of June 4, 1920, an Act of Congress which governed military justice up to 1948. The US military – though not the Navy – continued hanging and shooting until 1955, with three airmen being executed under different codes and ten soldiers under the original Uniform Code of Military Justice. Some others were still awaiting execution by lethal injection under this code at the time of writing for cases dating between 1988 and 2013.

In September 1945, Shepton Mallet resumed duty as a British military prison for service personnel who were to be discharged post-sentence, if serving less than two years. It was notorious for its severe discipline and was nicknamed 'the glass house'. The Kray twins served the end of their national service in the prison after absconding and met their long-time rival Charlie Richardson there. From 1966, it was again a civilian prison. The gallows were dismantled that same year and the room became the prison library. Later, it became a training prison for men with short sentences, helping them learn skills for the outside world. From the 1980s, however, it began to hold recidivists and from 1991, lifers nearing the end of their sentence.

The prison closed on 28 March 2013, by when it was the oldest prison still in use in the UK. Although conditions had improved since the 1990s, it was old, often overcrowded and unfit for purposes. The US Armed Forces, appropriately, were among those present at the closing ceremony. After much discussion and many plans were rejected, the site's sale was announced in December 2014. Early plans for its conversion to "mixed-used schemes of assisted living units alongside retail and social amenity areas" stalled but in February 2021, Mendip District Council approved a plan to convert most of the site into 146 homes. Parts of the former B Wing are to be converted to a community and heritage space; some other non-listed buildings will be demolished. Whether the gallows building will survive is not clear.

3. "Two men attacked us. I missed them and shot my wife": The murder of Lily Griffiths by Joseph Howard Grossley in New Road, Porthcawl, Glamorgan, on 12 March 1945 and his execution at HMP Cardiff on 5 September 1945

Through *The Great Escape*, a stirring and often repeated adventure film of 1963 that is based around a true story, many Britons still know of how 76 Allied POWs escaped from Stalag Luft III during World War II. Far fewer know that many thousands of German POWs were sent to a network of camps up and down the country after D-Day or that some of them made the largest ever largest jailbreak in the UK. In March 1945, no fewer than 84 German POWs escaped from a camp for senior SS officials at Island Farm in Bridgend, Wales. The number was deliberately understated by officialdom at the time. Unlike the British 'Great Escape', none of the POWs were killed during or after the escape but the murder of a woman during the brief emergency it caused was inextricably linked with it.

Island Farm itself occupied the site of a huge munitions factory established as Britain rearmed in the late 1930s and was known as The Arsenal or the Bridgend Arsenal. It employed some 40,000 people at peak, filling shells for the front line and the Navy. By some reckonings, it was the largest factory ever built in the UK; it was certainly the largest armaments factory. Most of the mainly female workforce, who were drawn from all over South

Wales, preferred to travel to work rather than live on-site. For this reason, the 22 Nissen huts built on land commandeered by the factory management remained almost empty until October 1943, when American forces began to be posted throughout South Wales. The 2nd Battalion of the 109th Infantry Regiment stayed here and General Dwight Eisenhower, Supreme Commander of the Allied Expeditionary Force and future US president, visited once.

Island Farm was vacated again before D-Day, though not before there had been some 350 GI brides among the local girls, according to local estimates. It was then renamed Camp 198 and filled with captured German officers. Many were fanatical Nazis, who proudly shouted "Heil Hitler" as they arrived at Bridgend station and refused to take orders from British NCOs. As officers, the prisoners could not be forced to work. In practice, the camp was controlled by the SS; it was poorly guarded and perhaps the conscript guards were overawed by these confident, aloof men. Beatings were handed out to prisoners who declined to send birthday or Christmas cards to Hitler, or even made casual remarks about the horrors of war.

Escape attempts were inevitable. Two had already been foiled when, on the night of 10-11 March, the 84 men made their way down a tunnel that had been dug from Hut 9 to a field nearby. The escapees had planned with typical German thoroughness, from building a pipe out of condensed milk cans with the ends removed for ventilation, to lining the tunnel with old clothes so as not to come out muddy. Much about how they did it remains unknown. Not until the 1980s, when a casual act of vandalism dislodged some clay from a false wall, did historians work out how the soil they removed was hidden.

It was apparently a second lieutenant who joined in at the last moment that stymied the occasion. He was spotted, covered in mud, near the camp exit. The alarm was raised and by next morning, 14 POWs had been recaptured. The rest followed in dribs and drabs, with some caught by the Home Guard and village bobbies. Only eight got out of Glamorgan, but some fled as far as Castle Bromwich in the West Midlands and Southampton. A story persists that three got away permanently, because a ministerial statement in Hansard after a mistaken sighting in Kent stated that 52 of the 67 not already caught now had been. Probably this was a simple counting error.

For days, however, the immediate area had been agog with rumours and fear about what fugitive 'Boche' might do. In between managing the operation to recover prisoners – a set of swastika map pins was kept in a biscuit tin to mark where each was taken – Superintendent Bill May of Bridgend police took charge of the case. Few locals would have been unduly surprised to hear that two escaped Germans had shot a local woman in the seaside town of Porthcawl on the night of 12 March, barely five miles away from Island Farm, had that story ever got out.

Lily Griffiths was staying in Porthcawl at the time with her 'husband', Bombardier Joseph Howard Grossley. (Alternative versions give his name as Howard Joseph or Howard John; either way, he went by Howard.) Although the two had been living together and had a two-year-old son, they were not married and he already had a wife in his native Canada. Grossley was born in Verdun, Quebec, on 25 September 1907. An intelligent boy, he spoke French and Spanish, as well as English, by the time he left school at 14. He then married Marie Goulet of Burlington, Ontario, when both were aged only 16 and she was pregnant. They never lived together, however, and her family brought the boy up.

At some point, Frank and Clara Viens of Winooski, Vermont, fostered Grossley. He worked in their grocery for ten years, as a drill press operator in Hartford, Connecticut, for seven, and finally as a park supervisor in Montreal, Finally, he enlisted in the Royal Canadian Army (RCA) in July 1940 and was sent to Britain in September. Army records give a full description of him, although no photos are known to exist. He was 5'7" tall and blonde, with blue eyes and a stocky frame that made him look bigger than he really was. His profession is recorded as chauffeur and he worked as a staff car driver.

At some point and by means unknown, Grossley suffered horrific phosphorus burns to his back, for which he had to wear a specially made silk vest. He was in constant pain and no doubt because of this, his Army record was patchy. Within two months he had gone absent without leave (AWOL), for which he received four days' detention and was docked 12 days' pay. Over the next two years, he was admitted to hospital three times. Somehow, he managed to be promoted to bombardier, despite never seeing active service. Initially, the Canadian government paid him a married man's allowance, but this was cut off because he had made a false statement about his marital status and he had to pay it back.

A reference given on 12 January 1943 described Grossley as "somewhat worried about his general state of health and the care of his son worries him … He is now unable to do much for his son. Apart from these problems, he is happy in his work." This pattern of poor health continued over the next two years, with three more hospital stays and six periods of privileged leave. During these years, he was treated for hysteria, 'emotional disturbance' and the more down-to-earth condition of syphilis.

The worries Grossley had about his son probably got worse, because he now fathered another one, Anthony Howard, who was born on 9 December 1943. While attached to the Canadian military HQ in Acton, he had met Lily Griffiths, who was up visiting a sister, and they got involved. She hid from her family the fact that she was in a relationship with a foreigner and had a child out of wedlock. Grossley applied for a married man's allowance but was knocked back because they were not married.

He later applied to leave the Army to take up a civilian job, but this was also turned down. Consequently, Lily, who was not in good health either, had to be the breadwinner.

In the summer of 1944, the couple had a holiday at the home of Ernest and Jennie Blodwin Atkinson and their family at 227 New Road in Porthcawl. On 26 January 1945, having failed to return from his last absence, Grossley was declared AWOL again and was officially recorded as a deserter as of 17 February. In early March, he and Lily arrived back at the Atkinsons' home and asked to take up lodgings on a longer-term basis. She was three or four months pregnant again at the time. Lily brought Anthony down from her sister Catherine Davies' home in Cwmaman a few days later. Although Jennie Atkinson thought they seemed very happy together, appearances were deceptive. Grossley's life had become a haze of debt, pain and mental illness. He had regularly been unfaithful to Lily and he physically abused her.

At about 12.15 p.m. on 12 March, Lily went for a job interview at the Arsenal. It was successful, though she was told she could not start until the following week because of her heavy cold. Later, she took the boy back to Aberdare. At about 6.00 p.m., Grossley was sitting listening to the radio with the Atkinsons and their teenage son, and thus learned about the German escape. The boy said that if he had Grossley's gun, he would go out and look for the Germans. Ernest Atkinson heard this and asked Grossley if it was true that he had a gun. He said it was and the boy asked if he might see it, so he went upstairs, took the service revolver in his possession out of his bag and brought it down to show them.

Atkinson then asked if it was loaded and was surprised to learn that it was. At his request, Grossley unloaded it, then showed them how it worked, took it back, reloaded it and put it inside the pocket of the battledress he was wearing. When he was asked if he intended to carry it when he went out to meet Lily, he said that as a soldier he had a duty to have it always loaded and he would be carrying it when he went out, in case he encountered any Germans. The supposition was that he had decided to use the breakout at Island Farm as a cover to get rid of Lily and did so that very night.

At 6.30 p.m., Grossley and Ernest Atkinson left the house. By about 8.00, they were at the Esplanade Hotel and Grossley talked of selling the gun to a US Army sergeant he knew. After Ernest went home, he fell into conversation with taxi driver William Rhys Thomas, who went on with him to the Victoria. Grossley had drunk a further four pints by closing time at 10.00 p.m. He returned to the house shortly after. By then, Lily was back and was sitting in the kitchen, mending a pair of socks.

When Grossley came in, she asked him where he had been. "Out," he said, in the tone of someone who resented being asked anything, and he took a ring from his mackintosh pocket, which he said had been given to him. Then he walked to the door of their room, beckoning Lily to follow. Jennie thought he did not seem very drunk. Both went upstairs and neither of the Atkinsons saw or heard them until an hour later, when they heard the front door open and close behind the couple as they left.

Exactly where they were in the following 55 minutes is not clear but there is no doubt that during this time, Grossley assaulted Lily. At just before midnight, John Carter Clare at number 175 heard what sounded like a woman's scream, followed by a loud bang. He looked out and could not see anything clearly but could tell someone was standing in an alleyway four houses away. Lillian Elizabeth Harvey heard a similar sound from number 181, as did gas fitter Arthur James Speck at 183, who was repairing a radio with three friends, George Isaac Lewis, Frank Jones and Fred Aston. They looked out of the door and over the wall dividing the two houses.

At this point they could not see anything either, but as Lewis and Speck waited by the gate, Aston and Jones went down the lane to investigate. While they fumbled in the dark towards the source of the sound, they discerned someone holding a torch, then saw a man in a mackintosh, Grossley, standing by a bend in the road in a highly distressed state. All heard him say: "Fetch a doctor, I have shot my dear wife". He asked one to go and tell Ernest Atkinson what had happened.

Speck, walking past him, was the first to see Lily, who was lying on her back on the ground. Grossley fell to his knees and cried out "My darling, what have I done" and Lily said: "Don't worry dear. You couldn't help it." Speck assumed someone else was the attacker and asked her who it was. She said she did not know but Grossley pointed towards the allotments at the end of the lane and said two men had run off in that direction. Lewis heard him say that the assailants were two German escapees, who had demanded Lily's handbag and his clothes. As he tried to wrestle with them, he said, he had pulled out his revolver and tried to get between them and Lily, but it had gone off accidentally during the struggle and hit her.

Lewis telephoned the police, but as it happened, PC Thomas Lewis was patrolling nearby while Sergeant Thomas Nicholas had been at the junction of New Road and South Road when he heard the shot. They both arrived on the scene within minutes. Frank Jones told them what had happened. Grossley seemed very distressed and said: "Oh dear, oh dear, I've shot my wife. Two men attacked us. I missed them and shot my wife". Lily asked for pain relief, to which Jones said that help was on the way. Nicholas then took the gun, an automatic Colt .38, from Grossley. As he was taken to Porthcawl Police Station shortly after, Grossley asked if Lily might die and Nicholas cautioned him.

Inspector William Matthews, who lived on the premises, took over at 12.15 a.m. The gun contained six live rounds and one spent cartridge. Grossley, he noted, was still sobbing hysterically and repeating "I've shot my wife" over and over again. When he had got in control of himself, he agreed to make a written statement and was told he would be detained, pending further enquiries. The last record of him made by the Canadian Army said that he was 'Taken off Strength on being apprehended by Civil Police and held in Civil Custody 23:59 Hrs'.

Dr Robert Hodgkinson had meanwhile arrived at the scene to find Lily complaining that she was in terrible pain from the bullet wound. He administered morphine and had her taken into a nearby house, where he saw what looked like recent bruises on her face and legs. Later at Bridgend General Hospital, he saw more on her arms, legs and lower abdomen that looked like she had been held and kicked several times with considerable force. It was a significant finding, because Shirley Jones, the Atkinsons' niece, who also lived at 227 New Road and called in at 8.00 p.m., was later to say that Lily did not have any visible bruises on her face or arms at that point.

Since Lily was facing a dangerous operation, Hodgkinson suggested she might want to make a statement. She did, and it agreed in essence with Grossley's about the Germans. At 4.00 a.m. on 13 March, she was taken down for surgery. However, the damaged lung had collapsed, and another operation was necessary. When Hodgkinson opened her up again that afternoon, he aspirated two pints of blood and aborted the foetus but the whole area was hopelessly infected. When she came round, she asked how she was. As tactfully as he could, Hodgkinson told her she was going to die and asked if she wanted to make another statement. She said she would.

Detective Inspector Lancelot Bailey arrived at Porthcawl and interviewed Speck about the incident, then the Atkinsons. They were surprised to learn that their lodgers were not married, but Ernest still said that he thought Grossley to be "a good man". In parallel, Detective Sergeant Bill Heap examined the scene of the shooting: he picked up a Canadian Army cap in the garden of 183 New Road and noticed a small hole in the windowpane. Two women who lived there had found a bullet on the settee, while the cartridge was found in Lillian Harvey's garden at number 181. Shortly after, Frank Rowe, an allotment holder, came forward to say he had found the loaded magazine. Catherine Davies was contacted and told the police that Grossley had admitted recently that he had a wife in the US.

Based on all this, Bailey reinterviewed Grossley, who he described as "mild-mannered, courteous and articulate". He started with Speck's evidence that Grossley had indicated that only one man had run towards the allotments, adding that it was odd that no one else had sighted any escaped POWs. (One wonders what might have happened if two Germans had been found in or near Porthcawl that night and Grossley had identified them. Might they have swung for it if they could not prove themselves innocent?) "I still say we were attacked by Germans," Grossley replied.

Bailey then asked in which direction he fired his gun. He was adamant it was down the alleyway. Bailey pointed out that the only bullet fired had ended up in the front room of number 183; in other words, it had clearly not been fired towards the allotments. Grossley cracked now, said that he "must have been crazy to make up the story" and that he wanted to tell the truth now. There were no Germans. Rather, he had pulled out the gun to kill himself, Lily tried to stop him and it went off by accident. He was charged with attempted murder before magistrates at Bridgend and was remanded for seven days after Bailey said that further inquiries needed to be made.

At 11.15 p.m. on 13 March, Bailey, Hodgkinson, Grossley's solicitor, two JPs and Grossley himself came to Lily's bedside. According to Bailey, when he entered the room, she looked at him and asked: "Howard, do you know I'm dying?" He was not allowed to reply. After she was sworn, Bailey read her original statement to her and she said, in a weak voice, "I don't wish to add anything", then "Howard would never hurt me. He has always been good to me". However, when told that Grossley had made a statement that contradicted his original one, she started crying and said: "I can't stand this".

Eventually, she pulled herself round and began speaking. Grossley had been drunk and had already said that it might be best for all concerned if he killed himself, she said. He pulled the gun out and said: "I will finish myself now". They struggled and she tried to take it from him, but he pushed her away, then she heard a loud shot and felt a terrible pain in the chest. He panicked, cried out that he had not meant to do that and went for help. Even before he did, self-preservation had evidently kicked in as he asked her to say that two Germans had attacked them if anyone asked. The statement ended by saying that he had sometimes beaten her, albeit only when drunk, and would have no memory of it the next morning. For the second time, their statements agreed in essence. Now, Bailey thought, it appeared that they were true.

Late on the afternoon of Thursday 15 March, Catherine Davies arrived at Bridgend station. She informed Bailey that Lily was fading fast and had told her a completely different story of the events two nights before. Bailey and Heap went back to the hospital to find her conscious but very weak. Bailey asked if she would like to repeat what she had said to him – and she did. Grossley, she told him, "has treated me terribly these last three years".

When he had returned that night, he was drunk and started hitting her in the bedroom. She told him she was not going to put up with it any longer. He forced her to put her coat on and go outside, where he continued to punch and kick her despite her pleas to him to "be decent". She promised that things would change if he would alter his ways, and that she would speak to him when he was sober. Grossley retorted, "You've turned against me. Now I'll finish it off", shot her quite deliberately, then said he was sorry.

Bailey read the statement back to her. As she signed it, according to Nurse Beryl Edwards, she said: "This is the God's honest truth". At 5.00 a.m. on the following day, 16 March, she died of a collapsed and septic lung. Dr Jethro Gough, who carried out the post mortem with Hodgkinson's assistance, identified numerous marks on her chin, left upper arm and lower abdomen, as well as a bruise to her left eye. All had been inflicted in the last few days, except the one to the arm, which might have been a week old. The bullet had entered her body through the left side of her chest, passed through the left breast, stomach, liver and left lung, before exiting close to the last rib. It had caused the left lung to collapse. This and consequent septic inflammation in the chest cavity had brought about her death.

Grossley made a second appearance before magistrates on 22 March and on 29 March he was charged with murder. After further hearings on 24-25 April, he was sent for trial. Before it began on 11-12 July at the Glamorgan Assizes in Swansea, before Mr Justice Singleton, Hildreth Glyn-Jones QC for the defence argued that Lily's last statement was inadmissible because no magistrate was present when it was taken and the words "Now I'll finish it off" were ambiguous.

'Dying declarations' could be admitted in evidence because the assumed religious awe at the approach of death was equivalent to an oath to tell the truth, but this depended on the specific circumstances. Singleton concurred with the defence and excluded it, but it was to be the last favour he did for Grossley and it is fair to assume that he reluctantly did the correct thing in law while being convinced from the outset that Grossley was guilty and should swing.

Ralph Sutton QC appeared for the prosecution. There were 20 witnesses, including Detective Sergeant Arthur Gordon Thomas, DI Bailey and PC Lewis, the Atkinsons, Shirley Jones, William Rhys Thomas, Drs Hodgkinson and Gough, Nurse Edwards and Lillian Harvey. Catherine Davies gave evidence of identification and about Grossley's wife in Canada. George Edward Lewis Carter, a forensic scientist at the police forensic laboratory in Cardiff, said that there were no scorch marks on Lily's clothing, which led him to think the gun had been at least 16 to 20 inches away from her when it was fired. This rather went against the notion that it went off in a hand-to-hand struggle but did not entirely eliminate that possibility. As the defence noted, she could have been pulling away at the time.

Francis Edward Morton, a ballistics expert from Webley Scott in Birmingham, said that the gun was in good working order despite being 40 years old; required two pulls, the second of 6 lbs pressure; and could not go off accidentally without the finger being on the trigger. Bailey related how Grossley stuck to his story for the first few days then changed it when shown facts that proved it false.

Grossley himself did not take the stand, Glyn-Jones perhaps calculating that it was better to exploit any holes in the circumstantial evidence than let this emotional wreck talk himself further into a hole. In his final speech, Sutton emphasised the evidence of the injuries on Lily's body predating the incident, which could only have been caused by Grossley, his initial false statement and his wife in Canada, so as to blacken his name. Expert witnesses, he said, had shown that the gun was fired from a distance and it was clearly premeditated murder.

Glyn-Jones told the jury that they must be satisfied beyond reasonable doubt that it was not an accident. The second statements of the victim and the defendant, he reminded them, said the same thing. It was impossible for them to have colluded since the night of the shooting and Lily made hers knowing she was dying. What better motive could there be to tell the truth? Singleton summed up hostile to the defence and it seems likely that his knowledge of Lilly Griffiths' last statement had something to do with this. In closing, he asked three questions rhetorically. Why did Grossley take Lily out at night? Why had he taken out the revolver when it had been kept upstairs before? And why had he made a false statement? The jury found him guilty. As Singleton sentenced him to death, he was silent but turned very pale.

Further tragedy ensued on 15 August, which was VJ Day and in the midst of a heatwave. While most of Cwmaman was celebrating, Anthony wandered away from the back of Catherine Davies' garden and accidentally drowned in the Glynhafod Lido, a small area in the course of a stream that had been enlarged for public swimming. This, and a large number of other near-drownings, eventually led to the pool being closed and rebuilt; it is still visible today. Grossley was not told immediately; indeed, the will he made out on 23 August requested that his son be adopted by a Canadian family and given a Catholic education. He made this will after hearing his appeal declined at the Court of Criminal Appeal in London two days previously.

The defence had been confident. Singleton, they said, had failed to remind the jury of the need to find guilt beyond reasonable doubt; the jury did not have to accept that it was an accident, merely that it might have been. Indeed, Glyn-Jones argued, Singleton had dismissed this key point of law when counsel raised it. He had also read out Grossley's first statement but omitted to remind the jury that he was in a hysterical state, then failed to remind them when summing up that Grossley had made another statement, which Lily independently corroborated. Nor had he mentioned the episodes of depression that Grossley suffered because of his injuries; or the lack of motive; or that Grossley had shown the gun to the Atkinsons, which seemed improbable if he were planning to murder Lily with it later that night.

Finally, Glyn-Jones argued, Singleton was remiss in posing the final questions to the jury in the way he did, while not reminding them that the defence had answers to them all. Justices Wrottesley, Croom-Johnson and Slade dismissed the appeal, saying that they had found no reason to intervene. "It is clear and was clear to the jury that the pistol used in the shooting would not go off unless the trigger was pressed," Wrottesley said. The jury had been properly directed and the trial conducted properly.

By 2 September, as a letter he wrote on that day to his wife Marie showed, Grossley knew of his son's death. Next day, he was told the date of his own. He wrote to his foster parents, though he had nothing to say about Lily or Anthony. "Dearest Mother and Dad," he began. "Just a few lines that I will ever be able to send you my dear [sic], for tomorrow at 9 o'clock a.m. I will be no more. Everyone has been kind to me, and the Catholic priest has spent much time with me. He was most kind, like you or Dad would have been to me. I have made a general confession of my life. I feel quite at ease in leaving for the great beyond.

"Believe me, mother and Dad, I am not guilty of this crime – before earthly judge [sic] yes, but not before God, the supreme judge of us all. I feel quite calm now. I have received the last sacraments this afternoon in the chapel. I ask God in his great mercy to be compassionate to me. I am happy to go mother and Dad. He and I would of [sic] like to of [sic] seen you once more. Well, we will meet on the other side. God bless you both for all you have done for me always. You know what my life has been on Earth, so I am glad to leave now. Maybe I will find peace in the next world." The rest concerned his worldly goods and the C$1,000 he believed he was owed by the Canadian government.

Albert Pierrepoint and Steve Wade hanged Grossley next morning, 5 September. Although it was only the second execution in 15 years at Cardiff, very few people were there when the chief warder pinned the death notices up on the gate, signed by the governor, Major Brown, the prison doctor and the chaplain. In a further act of military bureaucracy, Grossley was stripped of the three medals he had earned during his ill-starred service: the Defence Medal, normally given for six months' service in Britain; the Canadian Volunteer Service Medal and Clasp for honourably completing 18 months of total voluntary service, including 60 days outside Canada; and the War Medal, awarded to any member of the armed forces and merchant marines serving at least 28 days.

One minor mystery in the case is that someone with the same name and service number is apparently buried in the Brookwood Memorial War Cemetery in Surrey, having died two years to the day earlier in combat. There has been speculation that this was done to spare his real wife the shame, or that the man hanged at Cardiff was not the real Howard Grossley, but most likely there was a simple mix-up in an office when someone read '1943' for '1945' and automatically added his name to a list. Five other Canadian soldiers had been executed in Britain during World War II, plus one more who had been invalided out of the Army and settled in Ireland. All of them had committed murder, most famously August Sangret, in the 'Wigwam Murder' of his girlfriend Joan Wolfe in 1943.

After the 'Great Escape', all 1,600 German officers were moved to Camp 181 in Nottinghamshire. Island Farm was renamed Special Camp XI and received Germans awaiting trial at Nuremberg, including Field Marshall von Rundstedt, a close adviser of Hitler, who escaped trial because he was medically unfit. It was closed in 1948. Bridgend Industrial Estate was built on part of the site in the 1990s and most of the huts were demolished in 2002. Hut 9 is still there, looked after by the Hut 9, Preservation Group, and is occasionally open to visitors. The group, in 2018 placed a memorial on Lily's and Anthony's previously unmarked graves in Aberdare Cemetery.

The other lasting memorial to these events comes from documentary filmmakers Seanchai, who told the story of the breakout in *The Great German Escape* and *Lily*. The latter tells the story of how Grossley, "a deserter from the Canadian Army, while attempting to capture a prisoner, accidentally shot and killed Lily Griffith, his common law wife ... The truth hides a heart-rending tragedy across three families and two continents," it says, with maybe just a little artistic licence...

4. "I could see Laura's face in front of me": The murder of Dr David Walker Dewar by Thomas Eric Richardson at 176 Beeston Road, Leeds, on 30 April 1945 and his execution at HMP Armley on 7 September 1945

Adultery and casual sex were rife during World War II. Many soldiers were away from their immediate home environment for the first time in their lives, with sexual opportunities they could never have dreamed of before. Back on the home front, wives and girlfriends were working in factories or on the land, making their own money and meeting people they would not otherwise have met. The humble pleasures of life were in short supply and the young in particular grabbed them with both hands, knowing that this might be the last decent meal, the last evening of dancing or the last bout of sex they ever had.

No wonder some couples decided up-front that what happened on tour should stay on tour and that they could settle down to monogamous marriage once it was all over. Such arrangements did not always work out and many marriages that might have succeeded in normal times ended disastrously after the war. A fair few of the men executed for murder in the immediate post-war years were servicemen who found themselves in a love triangle and blasted their way out of it by murdering their rival, their wife or both.

Laura Walker lived at 3 Lady Pit Crescent in the Hunslet area of Leeds and worked as a woodcutting machinist. Her husband, Private A.B. Walker, was away serving in the armed forces in Italy. At some point in around 1942, she started an affair with Dr David Walker Dewar. A Scot who had taken his degree at Glasgow University – his parents, Michael and Janet, still lived in Bellshill - Dewar had his home and surgery at 176 Beeston Road. He had been GP to her family, the Broadleys, since 1931, when he first moved to the area.

Despite being married, Dewar was a prolific womaniser, whose interests in life were not those expected of a professional man in those days. With what sounds like staggering snobbery to the modern reader, the prosecutor at the trial of the man accused of killing him said: "It is with great regret that it becomes necessary after his death to reveal in public court that Dr Dewar's mode of life left a good deal to be desired. He was a man of somewhat intemperate habits and associated with people, if one may say so, of the middle and lower classes and of the greyhound racing fraternity. He was in the habit of frequenting public houses and clubs of the less reputable type, and he was in the habit of remaining in these places quite late at night drinking. That was one side of his nature. And on the other he was unfortunately somewhat over-fond of the opposite sex."

By Laura's account, their sexual relationship was over by April 1945 and they now saw each other only socially. She was certainly not the only 'other woman' in his life. Unfortunately for all concerned, neither was he the only other man in hers because she had at least one more lover.

Thomas Eric Richardson, who appears to have gone by his second name, was the youngest of the seven sons of Harold Richardson and Lily Motson, who had died in 1931. He had won a scholarship to Cockburn High School and was apprenticed as an engineer at a firm of surgical instrument makers called Thackrays in Viaduct Road at 17. Ten years on, he still worked there and lived with his 78-year-old father at 27 Harlech Road off Dewsbury Road. A quiet young man whose main interests in life were cycling and his work, he had never been in trouble with the law other than a 20-shilling fine for failing to stop his bicycle at a 'Halt' sign in 1936.

In his spare time, Richardson had worked to design improved instruments and had recently submitted some drawings for a new type of orthopaedic table that Thackrays were thinking of patenting. His health was erratic. He had a long history of fits, which presumably led to him escaping a military call-up; he then served in the Home Guard from June 1943 to August 1944, when he was discharged on account of dizziness due to vertigo. A doctor diagnosed petit mal epilepsy in October 1943, but he had not complained of any further symptoms again after that.

By his own account, Richardson was a boyhood friend of Private Walker, disapproved of Laura's relationship with Dewar and tried to persuade her to end it in order to save her reputation. In reality, he had been involved with her too for some two years by April 1945. She was the only woman he had ever had sex with. Predictably, jealousy crept in, not helped by the fact that she told him only to come to her house in the dark so as to avoid provoking gossip. During that month, Richardson was off sick from work twice for extended periods, the first time with a carbuncle on his neck, the second from 19 to 28 April with a septic eyelid. Undoubtedly, he was feeling very poorly but it did not impair his ability to carry out a deadly act of violence.

Saturday 28 April was the last day of Dewar's life and it had been busy. He went with his wife to the dog track on Elland Road, returned home for tea and then set out to pick up Laura Walker on Cemetery Road at 8.30 p.m. Before this, she was to say, they had not been out together for "a long, long time". As fate would have it, Richardson saw her in Tempest Road at 7.00 p.m. and she told him that she was going out with Dewar that night – purely socially, she tried to assure him. Despite his attempts to persuade her not to go, she would not be budged. She told him they were only visiting friends and he could come to hers at about 12.30 a.m.

Dewar collected Laura in his car and, in between some patient visits, they had drinks in the Coach & Horses, the Yorkshire Hussar and finally the Spring Hill Tavern on Borth Hall Street, where the licensee was a friend. He dropped her at her home at 12.45

a.m. on Sunday 29 and went home. Richardson was hiding in the dark nearby and attacked with ferocious violence. It was a bright, moonlit night, giving him enough visibility to carry the act through. A passing railway fireman, Dennis Wilson, saw a young, pale-faced man of about 5'7" run past him at just before 12.56 a.m. as he returned from work. This was almost certainly Richardson fleeing the scene, though Wilson said he would not have recognised the man. About 20 minutes later another railway worker, Joseph Freshwater, noticed an object lying beside the car and the gates partly open, but this was not unusual and he did nothing.

Richardson turned up at Laura Walker's house at 1.15 to 1.20 a.m., saying that he had been in bed, and stayed until 5.00 a.m. She noted that he looked "sickly and tired". During this time, she dressed the carbuncle on his neck for him. By her admission, they also had sex. Only at 8.10 a.m. was Dewar's body discovered, when William Ernest Whitaker, an electrician, walked past the end of the small driveway and noticed the partially opened gates, the car and someone lying beside it. Because it was in an odd position to be working under the car, he went to look and saw Dewar lying dead, face down in a pool of blood that ran all the way to the car, with gaping wounds to the back and side of his head. No one responded Whitaker's frantic knocks at the door, so he ran to the nearest public call box and alerted the police.

Dr Hoyland Smith examined the body at the scene. The whole of the back of the skull was fractured and many pieces of bone were lodged in brain tissue. Some parts of the brain, one "the size of a filbert nut", were found on the grass verge. The pattern of blood splashes suggested that Dewar was hit from behind as he opened the car door, then beaten around the head with a sharp weapon as he lay on the ground. In all, he sustained ten or 11 wounds. It had been a quite savage assault, far beyond what was necessary to ensure that he died. Cause of death was recorded as a compound fracture of the skull and laceration of the brain, inflicted by a heavy instrument that may have been an axe. Nothing had been stolen.

Meanwhile, at 8.45 a.m. on the Sunday, Richardson called in at the National Fire Service station next to Thackrays, where the keys were kept when the factory were closed. He asked William Walker, a fireman there, for the keys, explaining that he had left his wages behind. That evening at 8.30, he was back again, this time telling Fred Jones, who was on night duty, that he thought he had left his lighter behind. The reasons for these visits became clearer later.

The police started asking questions locally and tongues began to wag about Laura Walker's serial infidelity. An inquest was opened on 1 May and adjourned until 15 May. Although some 200 interviews had been carried out, the investigation had not progressed very far by 21 May, when Laura herself went to the police. She told them about her affairs with Dewar and Richardson, and how the latter had turned up at her house on the night of the murder. At about 2.00 p.m. the next day, she said, she had seen him at his workplace and asked if he knew about the murder. Richardson said that he had seen some reports in the newspaper. They had lunch together at the Lonsdale Café on 2 May but did not speak about it. He appeared quite normal on both occasions, she said.

However, on 18 May, Richardson encountered her with a sailor at the Imperial Hotel on Cemetery Road. The three had drinks and left together, but once the sailor was out of earshot, he demanded to know who this man was. She told him that he was staying at her home, Richardson grew agitated about this and said she should tell him to leave but she told him that "my people" were staying with her too and he had no reason to be suspicious. When she prevaricated over when they might meet again next, he "got all aerated" and threatened to beat the man up. She told him to go home, which he did.

Next day, they saw each other again on Malvern Road. (It was later stated by the police that she had been away to Plymouth and he called her to see him because he wanted to know who she had been with. Reading between the lines, it sounds highly probable that she was also sleeping with this man.) Laura said that she had been worrying about the murder and Richardson asked her if she had mentioned his name to the police. He said she had not and he then said he knew who had done it. Why had he not told her before, she asked, so she could have told the police? "The fellow that did it had a reason. I did it. I was not going to let him ruin your life," Richardson told her. When she asked what he had done it with, some press accounts later said, he said, "I am an engineer, you know", and walked away with a knowing smile on his face. In other versions, he simply said that he had done it with a hatchet.

On the basis of Laura's evidence, Detective Superintendent James Craig and Detective Inspector Clifford Thirkill of Leeds CID visited Richardson at his home at 12.40 p.m. the same day and brought him in for questioning. Until that point, Craig later said, they had no particular reason to suspect him. By their account, he greeted them with "I have been expecting you"; he then made a voluntary statement, which admitted his antipathy towards the doctor and that he knew where Dewar had been on the night of the murder.

According to Craig, Richardson's interview began at 1.30 p.m. with some questions about his life in general and went on until 3.15. In the statement written down for him, he described how he had been "friendly" with Laura for two years and their meeting in the street on the evening of 28 April when she told him she was going to meet Dewar and, when pressed, said that she did not know exactly when she would be back but that it would probably be about 12.30 a.m.

Feeling "annoyed and grieved", he said, he went home, later going out for about three halves of beer at the Hope Inn and the Templar and returning home to bed. "I was very ill with a carbuncle on my neck and everything was whizzing around in my head. I could see Laura's face in front of me and I began to have nightmares. I knew I had to have the carbuncle dressed and I got up and did it. I could see Laura's face all night and I don't know what I was doing," he continued.

The statement suggested that Richardson went to her house simply to get the carbuncle dressed, something she had done before, "but I was in such a state of mind, I can't say now whether I went to her house or not at that time" – which was, of course, about the time Dewar was being hacked to death. "All I have is a faint recollection of waking up in the morning." He admitted his hostility to Dewar several times, saying that he and Laura had "had words" about her "association" with him and that "I could not understand why Laura was keeping company with the doctor and it made me very unfriendly towards him". When they parted on 28 April, he added, "I was very bitter and I might have said things which I don't remember now."

Richardson added that he had also discussed the murder with her several times since - and it was probably his odd behaviour that convinced her that he was the killer. He tacitly admitted this at the end of his statement, when he said: "If I have killed Dr Dewar, I have no recollection of what I was doing as I was ill and my mind was in such a state". The most damning words attributed to him by the arresting officers came right at the start of his interview at the station. "I know you have got me well tied up. I did it. If you let me see Laura for one minute, I will make a statement." After he had seen her, he obliged. This was more than enough for him to be arrested and charged with the murder.

At a first hearing on 22 May, Richardson was remanded in custody until 30 May. Dr Francis H. Brisby, the medical officer at HMP Armley, examined his school and work records, concluding that he was "a man of good intelligence, industrious and steady". In prison, Brisby noted, he suffered "dizzy attacks" that might indicate epilepsy but were likelier to be vertigo. Richardson collapsed in the prison yard with his jaw clenched and frothing at the mouth on 24 May. He was transferred to HMP Brixton for an EEG examination for epilepsy but the results were inconclusive and the diagnosis was not changed.

Another hearing took place before Leeds magistrates on 8 June, during which the alleged confession was hotly disputed, and Richardson was committed for trial. This was also the first occasion on which Laura Walker had to speak in public about her tangled private life. The papers lapped it up, needless to say. "In a low, almost inaudible voice", she testified to her relationships with both men over the course of three years, how Richardson resented her friendship with Dewar and how she had slept with him on the morning of the murder, when she did not yet know of it. She also stated that Richardson had admitted the murder to her and was never to be shaken from this. At the end, she fainted in the witness box and had to be revived by a police officer.

Richardson was tried at Leeds on the 16-18 July 1945 before Mr Justice Hallett, with Geoffrey Hugh Benbow Streatfield KC, a future High Court judge, prosecuting. He was defended by Charles B. Fenwick KC. Laura Walker was a key prosecution witness. The press described her as slightly built, with short, dark hair, looking "pale and ill" in the witness box and speaking almost inaudibly. Her testimony largely agreed with Richardson's about the early part of the night, in that they had met in the street when she was on her way to meet Dewar and he asked her to stay with him. When he arrived at her house at 1.10 a.m. on 30 May, he seemed ill, but not "wild and excited" and did not come across like someone who had just committed murder, she added.

Then she repeated her account of how he "was just sort of sniggering at me" when he talked of the murder and, as she walked away from him, he said he had done it. She told him she did not believe him and that he must be out of his mind but "he just kept on laughing". Fenwick suggested that the words he used were not "Yes, I done it" but "Would you think any more of me if I had done it?" but she was firm. She sobbed as she gave damning evidence against the man she called the "one of the nicest and kindest men she knew". To compound her misery, she had to admit once again that she had "had relations" with both men.

Further circumstantial evidence came from Leonard Rollitt, the employee at Thackrays responsible for locking it up over the weekend, and from William Walker about Richardson's two visits on the Sunday. The River Aire was accessible from the rear of the factory but not from the road and it appears clear that he was first checking out that he could dispose of the axe unseen and then actually doing so. Craig testified that he asked Richardson "What have you done with the weapon?" and he replied: "It was an axe. I can't remember seeing the water when I threw it in". However, it emerged that they only wrote down these words an hour after he had completed his statement, making it less than satisfactory. The Aire was searched 200 yards either side of the factory over the course of six days but nothing was found. This, the police contended, was not very surprising as it was full of deep holes.

In his defence, Richardson claimed that he was trying to save Mrs Walker from ruin, though in truth he had completed her ruin himself. "You wanted to keep her for yourself, didn't you?" Streatfield asked. "Not for myself alone, but I did not like her going out with the doctor," came the reply. He testified in response to Fenwick that he had gone to bed in his own house at 10.30 p.m. and did not wake up again until 8.00 a.m. the next day; he did not attack Dewar and did not own any weapon that could have inflicted the wounds.

Under cross-examination, Richardson denied saying "I did it" and claimed that he was bullied by Craig and Thirkill, the former saying, "Come on Eric, we know you did it", and the latter, "Come on Eric, tell the truth. I would have done the same if I had found my girl messing about with the doctor". Harold Richardson backed this up, saying he was "practically certain" that his son was at home all night.

Dr Brisby went over Richardson's medical history and said that the attack bore "a strong suggestion of epileptic manifestation". Not all the symptoms were there, however, and some were definitely missing. It was not typical of a major attack and did not show any signs of the 'automatism' that Dr Hoyland Smith would have expected. Fenwick cross-examined, eliciting from Brisby that it was possible for someone to commit an act in a state of automatism and not remember it afterwards. Streatfield then examined again, asking if he had found any reason to suppose that, even if Richardson were epileptic, he had suffered phases of automatism. No, Brisby said, he had seen nothing of the kind.

When Craig took to the stand, he conceded that he knew of Richardson as "a person of hitherto exemplary character", whereas Dewar was indeed "a man who was very fond of drink and fond of the female sex". He gave details of what had happened on 21 May, denying that Mrs Walker was at the station for the purpose of being confronted by Richardson. "I did not know I was going to see Richardson that day," he said. Rather he was fetched at 12.40 a.m., and either he or Thirkill was with him from 1.30 to 4.30, when he completed his statement and was given a meal.

Richardson was not under interrogation during the whole of that time, Craig stated. He denied asking Richardson to make a statement but agreed that before he made a voluntary statement, he had given a complete admission to the murder. He also denied that Richardson protested throughout that he could not have had anything to do with the murder. "Did he tell you he that he was ill on night of the murder?" Fenwick asked. "He told me he had a carbuncle".

"Did he not tell you that he did not leave the house that night?" No, said Craig. "I put it to you that you and Detective Inspector Thirkill told him that you knew everything and that he was lying, and that you told him that several times?" Again, no. "Did you tell him that somebody had recognised him as he was running away from the house?" "I told him he answered the description of someone who was seen running away from the house," Craig said. When asked why he addressed Richardson by his first name and if he always did that, he said: "Not always. It depends."

Fenwick then put it to Craig that Richardson never said that he had done it. "He did say 'I did it'. I am sure he said it," replied. At one point, Fenwick asked Craig if he was aware he had himself just been asked 65 questions in ten minutes and suggested that he must have asked Richardson hundreds during a 90-minute interrogation. In stepped Hallett, ever the establishment man, to say that counsel was suggesting that Craig had bluffed Richardson into confessing. "I suggest that he was questioned into a cocked hat," Fenwick replied. Craig denied this. He further denied telling Richardson that he had "got him tied up", other than telling him that he answered the description of a man seen running away from the scene of the crime, as, he admitted, hundreds of other men in Leeds probably did. Fenwick managed to score some points over the absence of bloodstains on any of Richardson's clothes and Craig's failure to mention it in his evidence.

Thirkill also testified, strongly resisting any suggestion that Richardson had been bluffed into making his statement, or that the questioning had been harsh. On the contrary, he claimed, Richardson had thanked them on the way to be the charge office for "being gentlemen to him". Fenwick challenged Thirkill that he and Craig had spent 45 minutes asking Richardson questions about his life but made no record of it. Was this a "softening up" process? No, Thirkill said.

In his final address, Fenwick spoke once again of the "ungrateful and unpleasant" task of speaking ill of a dead man but described Dewar as "a pursuer of women", whose reputation and behaviour were unsavoury. "A man who follows that course goes in deadly peril, if not of his life of very grievous injury. There must be lots of men in and about Leeds who had it in for Dr Dewar over women." Richardson's opportunity to do so was no greater than many others had. The jury could only convict him if they accepted "up to the hilt" the confessions attributed to him by the police.

Fenwick further pointed to Dr Hoyland Smith's evidence that the killing was carried out "in a maniacal frenzy" by a man of considerable strength, yet Richardson was universally agreed to be "a quiet, inoffensive little man, much given to study and keen on invention", who was also suffering "agony" from a carbuncle at the time. Furthermore, there must have been blood everywhere and the weapon was evidently taken away. This could only have been done under the clothing of the killer, yet no trace of blood was ever found on Richardson's clothes.

This, Fenwick suggested, was "almost of decisive importance" because Richardons did not have time in the 15 to 20 minutes between the murder and arriving at Laura Walker's house to remove all traces of blood from his body and clothing. As for her, she was in a terrible situation and probably close to hysteria after she went to the police. It would be very dangerous to convict a man based on what he was alleged to have said, torn from its context and not properly recorded for more than an hour.

In concluding, Fenwick also told the jury that he had cross-examined Craig and Thirkill "with some strictness". Hallett, as was his wont, intervened again, saying that the defence might have objected to the admission of Richardson's statement in evidence if they believed it to have been improperly obtained, but had not. Fenwick explained that he had not done so because he feared this becoming a trial within a trial in which the judge would have to make a ruling on this issue; instead, he had decided to let the jury hear the whole of the evidence given and form their own conclusions.

Had one part of the evidence been ruled inadmissible, Fenwick said, it would have been necessary to show the jury the "startling and amazing contrast" between the statements alleged to have been made and those actually written down and signed in the documents. The fact that he did not object to the evidence being given did not mean that he accepted that it was all true. Rather the jury, must "ask themselves again and again" if it was properly obtained. It must provoke grave suspicion if the defendant was induced either through overt pressure or genial persuasion by a policeman who addressed him by his first name and showed empathy for him.

Streatfield countered that unless the killer was a raving maniac, he had obviously committed the murder "calculatedly and intendedly". There was nothing to suggest manslaughter. The jury need only be satisfied that the defendant was the man who committed it and that he was not suffering from any defect of reason at the time. Laura Walker, he said, "had made a thorough mess of her life but nonetheless was a woman willing and trying to speak the truth". The two officers, were very experienced, knew the proper methods of interrogation and Mrs Walker's testimony had corroborated them.

Hallett's two-hour summing-up steered the jury towards conviction and echoed Streatfield's praise for Craig and Thirkill. After an hour and 40 minutes of deliberation, the jury of ten men and two women found Richardson guilty but strongly recommended mercy, perhaps because they blamed Laura Walker and Dewar as much as him for what he had done. Richardson stood "white-faced" as he was sentenced to death, the newspapers reported.

An appeal was lodged on 22 July and heard on 22 August, on several grounds: possible misdirection as to there being no possibility of the police being mistaken with regards to Richardson's statement or about insanity; the admission of the evidence about the threats against the sailor, despite the prosecution considering it inadmissible; misdirection by saying that there was no possibility of any mistake by a police officer in regard to the statement, and also as to the proof of insanity; and reliance on the verbal admission to Laura Walker and the written admission to the police, which was not a confession.

In short, it was claimed, Hallett turned the jury's decision into a vote of confidence in the reliability of the police.

Justices Wrottesley, Stable and Croom-Johnson dismissed the appeal without calling on Myles Archibald, junior counsel for the crown. Hallett, they ruled, had correctly directed the jury that they must acquit the defendant if they had any doubts about the reliability of the evidence, adding that what the defence was implicitly accusing the police of would be "nothing short of murder". The time would come, with other police forces, when it could be shown that this is exactly what some of them did. In Richardson's case, they may have been sloppy in their record keeping and they may have put pressure on him, but they had the right man.

The statutory enquiry into Richardson's mental health by Drs Hopwood and East rehashed Brisby's findings. The prisoner was of above average intelligence, quiet and well-behaved and fully aware of his position, though he continued to deny his guilt; there was nothing indicative of epilepsy and he did not have the instability or impulsiveness they would associate with the condition. It was noted that he had said jokingly: "It would be queer if it were a chap like me that had done it".

As often when the defendant was of previous good character, Home Secretary James Chuter Ede received many calls for clemency. Wurzel sent in a petition with 8,104 names on it asking for a reprieve on the basis that the evidence did not prove guilt beyond all doubt and the jury's recommendation to mercy; Harold Richardson sent a telegram to the Queen and the Prime Minister; the local MP Alice Bacon, who was to become a perennial voice against the rope, weighed in; Ruth Ellison wired from a conference of Labour women in Leeds, suggesting that "surely an act of clemency from yourself on the very threshold of your immense duties would act as a signal that Labour takes cognisance of the recommendation of the people".

Richardson himself wrote to beg for a reprieve. He did not admit his guilt, instead listing his achievements and claiming that he had always tried to be a good citizen and never had any impulse to "do a thing of this sort". He had intended to stay at home to take care of his elderly father and deeply regretted the situation the case had put his father and other relations in. However, Chuter Ede decided that the law must take its course. He may well have been influenced by Hallett telling him that he could not throw any light on the reason for the jury's recommendation to mercy. Richardson, by then 28, was hanged on 7 September by Thomas Pierrepoint and Herbert Morris. Only a handful of people were waiting outside the gate for the notice to be posted. Three days later, Dr Dewar's will was published. He left property to a tidy value of £4,186.

Even now, some blame Laura Walker as much as Richardson. One commentator on social media writes: "How sad that one deceitful woman, who in my opinion is the real criminal here, can cause so much death and unhappiness because she couldn't stay true to the basic foundation of marriage, monogamy ... She gave him the axe when she took him to her bed. And she is, also, to blame as she is the reason for the crime, the judge even agreed", to a chorus of approval online.

Hallett may well have agreed. He was an elderly man of his time, after all, as well as being one of the worst judges of his day. And Laura Walker was certainly not a good wife. But no, she is not to blame for the terrible revenge perpetrated by an inadequate, self-important, two-timed man when the woman he wanted to himself did not do what he wanted her to. She told the truth in the witness box knowing what the outcome would probably be. There is even less excuse for playing 'blame the woman' now, but then some things clearly never change. What happened when Private Walker returned home has mercifully gone unrecorded.

5. "The righteous death of a traitor": The murder of Sergeant-Major Wolfgang Rosterg at Comrie POW Camp by Cadet First Class Erich König, Sergeant Joachim Palme-Goltz, Private Kurt Zühlsdorff, Private First-Class Josef Mertens, Corporal Heinrich-Wernhard Brüning and others at Camp 21 near Comrie, Perthshire, on 23 December 1944 and their executions at HMP Pentonville on 6 October 1945

The number of Germans in custody in Britain soared after D-Day, peaking at about 25,000 men in some 160 POW camps. Some, no doubt, were not sorry to be free of the threat of sudden death or serious injury. Others were more dedicated to the cause. From September 1944, well before the 'German Great Escape' near Bridgend that formed the backdrop to [3] Howard Grossley's case, a group of POWs at Camp Le Marchant (or Camp 23), within and adjacent to a former military barracks on the Marlborough Downs near Devizes in Wiltshire, plotted a mass break-out.

At the heart of it, as in Bridgend, were Waffen SS men. The escape was planned for a day in Christmas week, when the camp would be relatively lightly staffed. The start would be a mass breakout through a weak point in the prison defences, then the Germans would seize vehicles, use them to obtain weapons, tanks and even an unguarded plane from nearby RAF Yatesbury. Then, somehow, they would free prisoners from other camps, most notably Moor Lodge in Sheffield. Finally, they would march to the East coast to be rescued by paratroopers and ships sent from Bremen to meet them, notwithstanding the complete control of the sea the Allies had by then. Lieutenant-Colonel Alexander Scotland, head of the Prisoner of War Interrogation Section of the Intelligence Corps, later said that no escape story was "more daring in concept, more fantastic, more ambitious, more hopelessly fanatical".

Trainee American interrogators, who had been sent to Camp Le Marchant to practise their techniques, first learned about the plot in late December. In some versions they overheard *Oberfähnrich* (Cadet First-Class) – alternatively *SS-Unterscharführer* – Erich König, saying: "The arms store is the key". König, 21, was the son of a former professor at the University of Vienna and was the most committed Nazi in the camp. In other versions, they extracted the story from two POWs named Storch and Wunderlich. How much they really could have learned from these men is uncertain; Storch, at least, had his own escape plan and may have been only pretending to co-operate and span a web of half-truths to his interrogators, so bizarre was the detail he gave; Herbart Wunderlich was later to go on trial for the resulting murder.

Meanwhile, the Government Code & Cipher School at Bletchley Park had deciphered a message from the German Supreme Command, who were seeking to recruit English-speaking experts for a 'special mission'. This was actually about the formation of a special unit to operate behind Allied lines at the Battle of the Bulge rather than an uprising in Britain, but the authorities took no chances, not least since initial German success in the Ardennes was raising morale among POWs. On 14 December 1944, B Company of the 8th Battalion of the Parachute Regiment moved in on Camp 23 and took 32 supposed ringleaders out for interrogation in London.

As a direct result, 28 of them were transferred to Cultybraggan Camp, or Camp 21, at Comrie, Perthshire. This housed up to 4,000 Category A prisoners, the most dangerous, notably Waffen SS men, paratroopers and U-boat crewmen. It lay in a remote moorland area and was in practice governed by the most committed Nazis, who were referred to as 'blacks', hence the nickname 'Black Camp of the North'. Anyone who was even lukewarm to the cause was a marked man. Just two weeks beforehand, on 29 November, *Oberleutnant* Willy Thormann had been found hanging from a tree there in a presumed suicide.

The 28 men were also moving from relatively comfortable quarters into Nissen huts in the dead of the Scottish winter and were not happy about it. Among them were Sergeant-Major (*Feldwebel*) Wolfgang Rosterg and a friend of his, who has remained anonymous ever since. The hardened Nazis suspected Rosterg for several reasons. He was notably older than them, at 35, and had memories dating from before Nazi rule; he was a regular soldier, who had joined the Army before the war and was captured in Normandy; and he was not a Nazi sympathiser, which he showed by scoffing at those who looked up at every passing plane and wondered if it was German and had come to rescue them.

Rosterg has been quoted as saying that he had seen enough of the world not to support a system like azism. Perhaps this was because he had come to the UK in the late 1930s to continue his education. As a result, he spoke good English, which earned him an unofficial role as interpreter to Jim Gaiger, camp clerk of works, and brought him into regular contact with the British. In this role, he issued passes from one part of the strictly controlled compound to another, which cannot have made him any more popular. Gaiger himself remembered him as "very thick" (meaning heavy), with pebbled glasses.

Another source names Rosterg as the son of a wealthy industrialist in IG Farben, the chemical conglomerate created by the Nazis, which supplied Zyklon B for the gas chambers. If correct, this can only refer to August Rosterg (1870-1945), majority owner and CEO of Wintershall, a potash works. August Rosterg was a fanatical Nazi. Even before Hitler came to power, he had given the Nazi Party 25 million Reichsmarks to bolster them against a left-wing coup. He wrote articles for a Nazi newspaper and belonged to a group of industrialists that worked to strengthen ties between the party and business. In 1941, he had entered into a contract with his eldest son, Heinz, which enabled him to cash in the family's dividends from Wintershall and capitalise the entire property, an act that effectively disinherited Wolfgang. Unlike Wolfgang, August left the sinking ship, fleeing to Sweden before the end of the war and dying there soon after.

The 'Role Commandant', who effectively ran Camp Comrie, summoned the newly arrived prisoners and interrogated them to prove their Nazi credentials. Rosterg was a marked man. According to evidence given at the trial of some of those who assaulted him but were not accused of his murder, his arrival at Comrie on 22 December was greeted with cries of 'traitor' for supposedly betraying the plot. His bags were searched, which yielded a list of prisoners from Camp 23 and a document describing his activity in France. The former was actually a list of those needing delousing but was taken as more sinister, while the latter was shown as proof that he had given advice and equipment to the French resistance and police. It has also been reported that he translated articles from Scottish newspapers to other prisoners, showing that Hitler's offensive in the Ardennes was failing.

During this 'interrogation', Rosterg was asked if he was a Nazi and he replied, "he most certainly was not". Next morning, at about 6.30 a.m., Rosterg was dragged out of his bed in Hut 4 and subjected to a kangaroo court 'trial', with König holding a rope around his neck. They put a series of allegations to him and repeatedly beat him with iron bars and fists when König nodded. Two of his ribs were broken, one piercing a lung. Shortly before 8.00 a.m., they took him to a hut that the compound leader used as an offic. König had told Rosterg "that if he had any honour, he would hang himself". The rope was put round his neck again and he was pushed outside the office, where a large crowd was waiting.

Unteroffizier (Sergeant) Joachim Palme-Goltz, 20, seized one end of the rope and Rosterg was thrown to the ground. Palme-Goltz, *Soldat* (Private) – or *SS-Mann* – Kurt Zühlsdorff, 20, and Corporal Rolf Herzig, among others, allegedly kicked him and stamped on him, then dragged him via the rope around his neck towards the lavatory. There, Goltz and Zühlsdorff put one end of the rope over a pipe running around the lavatory ceiling. *Gefreiter* (Private First-Class) or *Matrose* (seaman) Josef Mertens, 22, pulled on the other end but could not manage alone and called for assistance. His eyes and tongue were found bulging from his face and he had urinated uncontrollably in his dying moments.

During all this, Rosterg's friend, who had hastily destroyed the anti-Nazi documentation on him, had pretended to support the action while looking around to find a guard to put him into protective custody. He was told at the end that his trial had been postponed for now. In the end, the roll call bell saved him. The inmates were lined up in a field and when Rosterg's name was called out, a voice said that he had committed suicide. Rosterg's friend made bold to say he had been murdered. The body was found and the friend was taken away. It was to be many months, however, before further action was taken.

Whether Rosterg had betrayed the plot is uncertain. The British military authorities definitely knew about it before the suspects were ever brought to London, but the interrogations also brought out some more detail and someone clearly gave them some vital information. They themselves later denied that Rosterg was an informant. In terms of their actions, it makes no difference. If he was not, sending him to Comrie was a horrendous and inexplicable blunder; if he was, he was cynically put in mortal danger.

Scotland Yard and the Combined Services Detailed Interrogation Centre were called in to investigate. The process took a long time because of the SS code of silence and consequent fear among prisoners of reprisals against themselves or their families in Germany. At some point before April 1945, Lieutenant-Colonel Archibald Wilson took over command at Camp 21 and assigned the investigation to Captain John Wheatley, a member of the Judge Advocate General's Department and a future Lord Justice Clerk of Scotland, with Staff Sergeant Herbert Sulzbach, a German Jew who had been interned on the Isle of Man until he volunteered for the Pioneer Corps, as interpreter.

Wheatley had to go slowly. His diary recorded the "extremely violent and threatening" atmosphere, which only the willingness of Polish guards to take action against the hated Nazis could hold a lid on. Even so, another POW was severely beaten up and others begged to be moved because they were so frightened. Slowly he built up the case, focusing on those who could be proved to be present when Rosterg was actually killed rather than those who took part in the 'trial' or the beating. Under Scottish law, the word of one witness would not have been enough to convict anyone and fear continued to deter other potential witnesses. Even when the trial took place under military law in England, the court had to restrict reporting of their names.

Eventually, 12 men were charged with Rosterg's murder, but charges were dropped against four for lack of evidence. Eight – three SS men, three Luftwaffe men, one from the Army and one from the Navy – ultimately stood trial in the drawing room at the 'London Cage' in Kensington before a military tribunal on 2-12 July. As well as König, Zühlsdorff (who had been a grocer's assistant before the war), Palme-Goltz, Mertens and Herzig, they were *SS-Rottenführer* Heinrich-Wernhard Brüning, 22; Wunderlich, also 22; and Hans Klein, age unknown.

Colonel R.H.A. Kellie presided as Judge Advocate, with the civilian C.L. Stirling as Deputy Judge Advocate. Two lieutenant-colonels and four majors were in effect the jury. Major R.A.L. Hilliard of the

Judge Advocate General's Office prosecuted. Captain Roger Willis (later Judge Willis of Bloomsbury County Court) represented Zühlsdorff, König, Wunderlich and Klein; Major R. Evans appeared for Brüning, Palme-Goltz, Mertens and Herzig.

On the first day, the press reported, the defendants were marched "in a military fashion" by an escort of Grenadier Guards into an Elizabethan-style, oak-panelled room, where they halted and faced the window under which six British officers sat. Herzig – "a powerful, typical German" – was wearing three degrees of the Iron Cross, while one of the SS men was also wearing an Iron Cross Second Class. Stirling told them that the court wished them to have a fair trial and to understand what was going on. Two British captains acted as interpreters. "The accused stood strictly to attention during the opening formalities. They replied to questions in short, curt sentences."

Before they were arraigned, Major Evans applied for a separate trial for Brüning on the grounds that the prosecution wanted to call him as a witness in the defence of Palme-Goltz and Mertens and "should not be in the position of possibly convicting himself". The court agreed with Hilliard's objection that any such prejudice was unlikely. All eight then pleaded not guilty.

Hilliard asked the court to inform witnesses that their names would not be published, noting that many were frightened about where the information might end up and whether they or their relatives might suffer. He then described the events leading up to the murder. The prosecution case would be "that some of the men before the Court are actually the murderers with their own hands, but that all of them were present in pursuance of common design … to cause the death of Rosterg".

The first witness, a German POW, testified that Rosterg told him that he could speak six or seven languages and "had been about the world enough not to believe any more in National Socialism". Some of those in the room then said: "All right, we will see all about this fellow". The witness was asked to point out who among the accused had said this and "those named sprang to their feet and gazed back with hard, unflinching eyes. One smiled sardonically." The witness continued that he had heard that something was going to happen, and, out of curiosity, went into Hut 4, where he saw Rosterg. Klein then asked Herzig: "Is that the swine, who came with you yesterday?" Herzig replied that it was.

Using a length of thin rope from two sacks that had been brought in, the witness demonstrated how Rosterg had the noose round his neck and the end was held fast behind his back. König, he alleged, said: "Every time you shout out, you swine, I will pull the rope tighter". Another POW read from a piece of paper found on Rosterg. During this Klein asked: "Did you do that, you swine?" Rosterg was unable to reply because he was groaning. Goltz hit him with a bar, and held hard onto the rope and tightened it, while Klein hit him in the face with a bar from the stove equipment.

The witness heard Rosterg shouting loudly and saw König pulling him by the rope towards the washhouse. When they came back with him, they had tried to wash the blood from his face, but fresh blood was running from it. Someone said: "We will go to the camp leader and have an end of all this." The rope was removed from Rosterg's neck, and he was taken through a crowd to the compound office. After a while, König came out alone and said: "We are doing it all quietly and gently. He has signed something about him to hang himself, but he doesn't know that yet."

As Rosterg lay on the ground, the witness continued, Palme-Goltz knelt on his chest and put his hands round his throat. Herzig, Mertens and others then "came and kicked him ... all over the body". Rosterg was then dragged along an asphalt path with kerbstones, the rope still around his neck, and they "pulled his head against the kerbstones with all their power". Next, they "dragged Rosterg through the mud until he was absolutely black".

The witness claimed that he told his comrades that it was wrong to do this simply because a man had a certain point of view but was told: "You are just as bad a criminal as he is. If you think that, you had better keep your mouth shut." He added that he had first been asked to give evidence in January but was unable to do so until he left the camp; had he tried to give a note to a British officer, he risked being beaten up. In answer to Stirling, he said that Rosterg was alive until he was pushed out of the compound office and was killed outside the office when they knelt on him and kicked him.

On the second day, another POW gave evidence that Brüning had "boasted about the fact that he had taken part in the murder, and that Rosterg had betrayed an attempt to escape and had done something in France". A third testified that, on the night of 22 December he heard screaming and crying, then loud singing from Hut 4. Next morning, he went in and saw Rosterg with the rope round his neck. One man read out a piece of paper in English which had been found in Rosterg's kit, and asked him: "Were you such a swine?" Then various men struck him when König gave them the nod. The paper referred to Rosterg being on the divisional staff in France and being in communication with French civilians and police.

Before beginning cross-examination, Willis asked permission to speak to one of the accused. They all sprang to their feet as he approached and he waved to them to sit down, then spoke in English with one for a few moments. He then asked the witness: "Was it a story which would be discreditable to a member of the German armed forces at that time?" The witness replied: "Any German soldier could have traffic with the civilians in France". He named

König and the man who read out from the paper as the principal actors in the 'trial', adding that König said, "We should let the man go", when they left the room with Rosterg. One witness whose name is in the public domain was Corporal Fritz Hüber, who said he saw König holding the rope. When König cross-examined him in person, he boldly added that König had "used to say there was something fishy about me".

On the third day, another POW said that Palme-Goltz had boasted of pulling the rope tight "on this swine's neck" and stood by this when Willis asked him if he was quite sure, "bearing in mind that a man's life may depend on the answer". The same man told Evans that he had been in the office at Devizes the day before they were moved, when Wunderlich came in and demanded a pass to go outside the ordinary compound. The commander refused and sent him on to Rosterg as his senior in the compound office.

This man did not know whether or not Rosterg had actually given away information to the British, only that he had "deserted". He himself came under accusation from Nazi supporters but managed to convince them otherwise. Even after the murder, angry mutterings continued against possible 'traitors'. Naturally, the witness told Willis, he was concerned for his own safety. During the questioning, the press reported, "a document fluttered from the table of the defending officers. Several of the accused sprang up to recover it".

An anonymous British Intelligence Corps officer, 'Captain X', then testified that Zühlsdorff had admitted in an interview that he had heard that one of the 27 arrivals was a traitor and "helped in the hanging in so far that I held [Rosterg] under the arms and lifted him up". Somebody entered his hut and said that Rosterg was being brought to justice and he helped to pull the rope dragging Rosterg to the latrine in order to speed it up.

He did this, Zühlsdorff had said, because "I understood a traitor had acknowledged, having committed high treason, that he had to expect death. At the same time, I heard about the notes which he had carried with him … During the next few days everybody in the camp talked about the case and, generally speaking, everybody was disgusted that a German was at all capable of betraying his Fatherland." After this, an English translation of Wunderlich's alleged statement was read. Evans asked 'Captain X' if any of the accused had been made to kneel, were threatened or offered inducements to confess. To each, he said no.

Another witness, who had been in Brüning's company in France, testified that Brüning had boasted of taking part in the murder and "stating that Rosterg had betrayed an attempt to escape and had done something in France". He went on to confirm others' accounts of the beating and that he later heard Klein shout: "Now the swine is hanging". Another said that König told Rosterg "that he had committed treason and that he had the lives of many Germans on his conscience". The papers that appeared at the mock trial, he said, "were brought to the camp after an attempt to escape from the camp at Devizes. A lot of people were rushing round, packing their trunks for the invasion of England".

The quarter-inch thick rope used to hang Rosterg was produced during the evidence of the Royal Army Medical Corps major who had been called to Camp Comrie after the attack. He said that artificial respiration was being conducted as he arrived, and he listened for heart sounds. Eventually, satisfied that Rosterg was dead, he stopped. Dr Alexander Rintoul, who carried out the post mortem, stated that in his opinion Rosterg was strangled when being dragged along the ground and was already dead when he was hung up. "The whole head and face were covered with blood and grit was embedded into the face. There were extensive abrasions of almost the whole forehead." These and other marks "were consistent with having been hauled across rough ground face-downwards. There were horizontal marks on the forehead which would have been caused by blunt instrument, perhaps a stick or a bar," Rintoul said.

The defence opened with Brüning claiming that his statement was not true. 'Captain X', he claimed, had said, "You rogue, you swine, you murderer, you have killed Rosterg", and then told him he would be hanged if he did not make a statement". He had then been cross-examined by a sergeant and was "told I had to admit it and that it would be advantageous to me," so he wrote out the typewritten statement that had been put in front of him. Palme-Goltz likewise said "in loud, ringing tones" that his statement had been extracted by inducement. On this basis, Evans asked for the statements to be ruled inadmissible, but Hilliard argued that the prosecution had shown that they were made freely and Stirling ruled that the court could hear witnesses and decide which were telling the truth.

Brüning's statement was then read out. It referred to a paper stolen from Rosterg, in which he said that, when serving as an *Orts-Kommandant* in Russia, he was on good terms with the local people and transferred arms to partisans. In the same role in France, later, the statement claimed that Rosterg had kept a secret register about all the weapons and equipment he had transferred to the Allies; posed as a hostage and murdered Red Cross nurses and female auxiliaries; and informed the Allies about the location of the entrances to the Elbe Tunnel in Hamburg so that they might be bombed.

Before the court reconvened on 6 July, Klein was formally acquitted for lack of evidence and returned to custody. Hilliard resumed his questioning of Zühlsdorff, who, after initial prevarication, agreed that as an SS man he was a Nazi and would want to kill a traitor. He denied that König was the camp leader as the camp was full of Nazis and the leader would be the senior camp leader. "I would have helped in the hanging of Rosterg in any case because he was a traitor, but I should not have taken any orders from König." He had been "disgusted" at hearing that Rosterg betrayed German Red Cross helpers and signalwomen.

As to why he wanted to hang a man who he thought was already dead, it was "because the man was too heavy for my comrades to pull up. I would just as well have helped had this man still been alive. This man had to be found hanging, because that is the righteous death of a traitor." Zühlsdorff also testified that Palme-Goltz had said, "when Rosterg came out, I jumped on him, grabbed a rope and threw him to the ground. Then as he lay on the ground, I kneeled on him". He had also seen Brüning in London and heard his story about being made to kneel before a British captain and write a statement.

On his role in Rosterg's death, Zühlsdorff was unrepentant: hanging was the right punishment and he had enough evidence; 20-30 people in the barracks were saying it, as well as the "notes and drawings" made by Rosterg. Wunderlich then testified, alleging that Rosterg had indeed done everything he was accused of and that when he heard about it, he thought, "that his own father serving at the front might have been shot by one of the smuggled weapons".

At that moment, he said, "I did have the intention to kill him". He went to the office where he saw Rosterg being dragged along by a rope and joined in by helping drag Rosterg to the latrine, grabbing him by the tunic and lifting him up to hang him. That was all he did, he said. Although he had known Rosterg was a deserter while still at Devizes, at the time he was busy planning a mass breakout.

Next up was König, whose evidence continued over to 7 July. He had occupied a bed near Rosterg's in Hut 4, he said. During the night of 22 December, a struggle broke out "and a document was taken from Rosterg, which was likely to make any German extremely angry with him", covering every aspect of his alleged treason. The doors were locked at night and it was impossible for Rosterg to leave. Senior RAF, Army and Navy officers appeared in the court as he gave his testimony.

König admitted telling Rosterg, "If you have a grain of honour in your body you will hang yourself", but claimed that when Rosterg came out of the hut, he protected him. It was clear that Rosterg was going to die, though König skirted around his intention to commit murder. Asked if he was a Nazi, he said, "I am convinced that I need not answer that question" but, when pressed, said he had not been a party member, though he had been in the Hitler Youth. He denied being in control during the 'trial' or that the decision to kill Rosterg was left to him.

On 7 July, Herzig took the stand, telling the court that, although he and Zühlsdorff were "good comrades", they never discussed politics. He denied being a Nazi before being called up, though he too had been in the Hitler Youth. Klein, "who wore the Knight's Cross and whose word, therefore, could not be doubted", had told him about Rosterg's treachery and he remembered an English proverb, 'Right or wrong, my country' when deciding that this man deserved the rope. He had been too ill to take any part in the murder but "Had I been in a proper physical state to have done that, I have no doubt that I should have been led away," and he looked at the body afterwards. Herzig further disputed the evidence of two German witnesses who said they saw him lift Rosterg's body to be hung up, claiming they had said this "through feelings of revenge".

When the court reconvened on 9 July, Mertens testified that he had heard that Rosterg himself had admitted his crimes. "I certainly thought that he deserved the rope and said so at the time ... Anyone who had suffered the aerial attacks at home understood why we were incensed against the traitor." When he saw soldiers dragging a body to the latrine, he knew straight away who it must be and saw that he was dead; all he did, he claimed, was to take hold of the rope, pull it for the last few yards to the pipe and help hang the body up. When asked if he or the others had been frightened of the consequences of their actions, he said that he was not and knew they would be charged with murder.

Palme-Goltz, an SS man since the age of 16, then testified that he was sleeping in Hut 2 when he was woken up and told to go to Hut 4. There, he was shown a paper with his name on it and "a sort of charge sheet, headed 'law suit'". Then he saw Rosterg, with swollen eyes and a rope around his neck, crying 'Help!' several times. "The crowd was very enraged and kept on shouting 'Hang up the swine!' ... I myself became incensed and excited, and at this moment I completely lost my self-control. I became even more incensed when I realised that, through this man, I had been suspected of being a traitor. That was question of my own military honour."

He took the rope, pulled the noose tight round Rosterg's neck, pulled him to the ground, knelt upon him and pulled the noose again; his cries and shouting ceased now. After this, the rope was taken from him and Rosterg was pulled from under him. At Stirling's request and using Mertens as a prop, Palme-Goltz showed how he had done this. "I assumed that at this moment he died", he said and agreed with the questions "You would not have been satisfied merely to have Rosterg's life taken. You wanted him to hang so that other German POWs might see what happened to a traitor?"

On 10 July, both sides made their concluding speeches. Hilliard spent three hours going over the evidence that Rosterg had declared himself not to be a Nazi and consequently the others thought him a traitor. "It might be that the court will think that the finding of this document was also a natural sequence of events," he said. "The prosecution says it is immaterial what the motive was. There was no right to kill Rosterg because he was not a Nazi, or because he was a traitor. Is there any doubt that when Rosterg left that hut the common purpose was to hang him?" König, who in seven months had risen to the most senior Army rank below commissioned officer, was clearly the brains behind what had happened, he contended.

This was not translated for the accused, who reportedly "showed signs of being bored. They yawned, fidgeted and scribbled on their notebooks", but paid much closer attention to defence counsel. Willis first told the court that "it was perfectly clear Rosterg's hanging was something symbolic", like how traitors' dismembered bodies once adorned city gates. Even though Rosterg was already dead, his body must be hanged because he was a traitor. The court could not, he concluded, be able to say they were satisfied beyond reasonable doubt that Zühlsdorff, König and Wunderlich were guilty.

Willis added that his clients had told him a story that he could not prove but which he had reason to believe to be true, of how a British officer betrayed an escape plan at a POW camp in Breslau in 1943 and was hanged by his comrades. The German authorities did not punish those responsible and the accused "did not appreciate why they were being treated differently from British prisoners in Germany". It was a rather weak argument, however ironic beause what the German authorities did in a parallel situation was not relevant here. König, Willis added, was the last surviving male in his family; nine others had been killed in the war. Zühlsdorff had once been captured by French partisans and forced to dig his own grave; he was only saved when American troops arrived.

Evans followed suit for Brüning, Palme-Goltz, Mertens and Herzig. There was no disputing their motive, he said. All 900 POWs at Comrie had the same motive "if they were true to the loyalty of their uniform". If the court accepted that Brüning's story of the forced statement was true, there was not enough evidence to convict him. For Palme-Goltz, he asked for a verdict of manslaughter. "Goltz is a man who has been brought up with certain loyalties and traditions, and he is very jealous of his honour as a soldier." It would follow from that that the others had, at worst, abetted an act of manslaughter. None of the four, he argued, "was of sufficient strength of character to be able to instigate the murder. Their act might be looked upon as an act of war, which they could justify their own consciences as military necessity."

Stirling summed up. "I am going to suggest that from the German point of view Rosterg was not a good soldier, and that he would have deserved and received from any good German contempt and dislike," he said. "You will probably think he deserted from the German Army, not merely by leaving it so that he might spend his time as he liked, but deserted to the enemy, the British." The court was a military court, not a court martial; the authorities had "wisely and properly" ensured that it was no easier to convict a German POW than a British soldier and the burden of proof was on the prosecution. The court would close to consider its findings and continue thereafter if needed.

On 12 July, Wunderlich was acquitted but the other six were convicted and sentenced to death. The Judge Advocate General upheld the sentences on 23 July. The Geneva Convention dictated that the executions could not be carried out for three months while a full review took place and they appealed. During this process, Herzig's sentence was commuted to penal servitude for life. In late August, Wunderlich, Klein and four others, were again tried at the London Cage for causing grievous bodily harm to Rosterg.

The War Office posted notice of sentence on the remaining five on 5 October. The following morning, between 9.00 and 10.30 a.m., when the notices were posted on the gate, they were hanged at HMP Pentonville. Albert Pierrepoint officiated, assisted by Steve Wade and Harry Allen, a Manchester man who had been added to the list alongside Wade, Harry Kirk and Henry Critchell but had dropped off for a few years due to war service and now returned.

Secondary sources disagree on how the executions were carried out, variously positing two double hangings and a single one; a triple and a double; or five singles. The LPC 4 form lists them in a 1-5 order with their age, height and drop length as follows: Zühlsdorf (20, 6'3", 6'11"); Mertens (21, 5'7½", 6'7"); Palme-Goltz (20, 5'8", 6'3"); Brüning (22, 5'10", 6'11"); König (21, 6'2", 6'0").

Mertens alone expressed regret for his actions. Defiant to the end, König shouted *"Alles für Deutschland!"* as the noose was placed round his neck. This all took place under military jurisdiction, with Lieutenant-Colonel F. Forbes, Deputy Provost Marshal for London District, replacing the under-sheriff and signing the notice of execution, and Army chaplains attending the condemned. There had been very little publicity since the trial and the only people at the gates at 9.00 a.m. were "two police officers and a little group of press men and photographers".

Whilst plenty of spies had been hanged or shot during the war, these were the first German POWs to be executed for murder. Allen wrote in his journal: "It was a foul murder, they had staged a mock trial, kicking him to death and dragging him by the neck to the toilets, where they hung his lifeless body on a waste pipe. ... [They] are the most callous men I have ever met so far but I blame the Nazi doctrine for that. It must be a terrible creed."

Rosterg is buried at Cannock Chase War Cemetery in Staffordshire in Section 4, Row 15, Grave 207, alongside Willy Thormann. The hanged men were buried in unmarked graves in Pentonville, as per normal practice, and British authorities later said that the location of the graves had been lost. The rope used to strangle Rosterg is still in the British National Archive. Camp Le Marchant reverted to being a barracks before being redeveloped for housing; the land where some of the camp stood beside it was a county council depot for many years but is also to have housing built on it.

Cultybraggan Camp was later an Army and cadet training centre. Among those who passed through as a boy was Bill Jones, who, like many others, noted its eerie atmosphere and the lack of information about its history. In 2018 he published a fictionalised version of the case, *Black Camp 21*, written from the point of view of Rosterg's friend. The case also attracted two full-length non-fiction accounts and appeared in an episode of the Channel 4 series *Secret History* in October 1999, in which Rosterg's friend spoke with his face blacked out and under a pseudonym. For decades, he said, he had lived in fear that a Nazi sympathiser might assassinate him.

As the only preserved World War II POW camp in Scotland, Cultybraggan has been designated a Unique Heritage Asset of International Value by Heritage Scotland and is open to visitors. Hut 4, however, is gone. There was a more positive post-script from another former 'black' prisoner, who was already at Camp Comrie when Rosterg was murdered and stayed until he was transferred out in spring 1945 to work on nearby farms.

Heinrich Steinmeyer was a Waffen SS man and a hardened Nazi but was greatly moved by how well the locals treated him. After his final release in 1948, he stayed on in Scotland until he returned to Germany to look after his mother. "The Scots saved my life three times. The Scottish people showed me mercy," Steinmeyer told *The Scotsman*. "When I was brought to Scotland, I realised the Scots were no different from us. We should never have been fighting each other. I love Scotland very much." He died aged 90, in 2013 and in his will, he left an estate worth £384,000 for the assistance of elderly people in Comrie.

6. "There are six more I have got to kill, then I will kill myself": The murder of Vera Guest by Ronald Bertram Mauri at 105 Denecroft Crescent, Hillingdon, on 11 July 1945 and his execution at HMP Pentonville on 31 October 1945

Most of the capital cases of the months immediately after the end of World War II played out one way or another in its shadow. Two American GIs were hanged for crimes committed under US military codes of law enacted into UK law [1], [2]. A Canadian deserter used the occasion of an escape by German prisoners of war to explain away the shooting of his girlfriend [3]. Two sets of German POWs murdered suspected collaborators when other planned escapes failed [5], [7]. People were caught in love triangles that would not have happened but for the way war moved men and women out of their home environments [4], [14], [15]. One soldier shot another, drunkenly mistaking him for a third soldier he had fallen out with over a girl, herself in the forces [10]. Three men swung for acts of treason or treachery committed over the course of the war [8], [12], [13]. Two British deserters killed a Canadian officer in a street robbery [11].

Others, more indirectly, later found their marriages irrevocably changed by war. All these men went to their deaths in circumstances that would almost certainly never have come about but for the war. With the murder of Vera Guest by Ronald Bertram Mauri, however, there occurred the first entirely 'civilian' murder for which the perpetrator went to the gallows after VE Day. The circumstances were strange and also bring into question, like many other cases after it, the way insanity and other mental health issues were assessed in murder trials in 1940s Britain. However, the war did not enter into the equation for the simple reason that Mauri did not serve in arms. We can be sure of this because he was in one of the toughest prisons in the country in 1941 when his name first surfaced in the press.

Mauri's genealogy has been amply documented online by a man who shared some common ancestry with him. He was actually named Rinaldo when he was born on 23 March 1913 in Southampton, the youngest of three sons born since 1909 to Tobia Mauri (1872-1929) and Kate Effemy (1873-1959). His father was of Italian origin, though relatively little is known about him. The couple also had a daughter, Eileen, born in January 1915, and one of the older brothers was called Bernard. Rather unusually, Tobia and Kate were not married while they were having all these children; they were also probably not living together in 1911, when she lodged with their two older sons at the home of a 35-year-old clerk, Percy Thornback, in Alexandra Road.

Also rather unusually, Kate was 40 years old when she gave birth to Ronald, a very advanced age in those days and less than two years before her first grandchild was born. She previously had three daughters by her first husband, a railway guard called Charles Henry Tegues, between 1893 and 1898. Tobia and Kate finally married in the St Pancras district of London in 1921 and he died eight years later. In September 1939, she was recorded as still living in that area, at 74 Cleveland Street near Tottenham Court Road. Ronald, described as a 'single motor driver', was living with his mother at the time. His year of birth was given as 1915 in that record, but if his sister was born in that year, the likelihood is that this was an inaccurate transcription and that he was indeed born in 1913 and was 32 at the time of his crime, as the secondary sources state.

An undated photo shows a swarthy, thick-set, rather thuggish-looking man, whose part-Italian ancestry appears obvious enough. A later description from Scotland Yard had him as about 5'7" tall, with a stocky build, straight, fair hair parted to the side, hazel-coloured eyes, a fair complexion and clean shaven. He weighed 194 lbs and was described on hid LPC4 form recording his execution as 'stout and strong'. Descriptions of him at the time of his crime said that he had "a cast in the right eye, a scar on the left cheek and a broken nose". This was enough for one Australian newspaper to dub him 'Scarface' and British papers to refer to him as 'the man with the scar', though whether the first, rather predictable soubriquet was ever used by anyone else is not certain. There is nothing to suggest that he really was a gangster, but there was plenty of evidence of a volatile temperament that cost an innocent young girl's life.

Mauri had a long criminal record. In May 1936, he and two others were charged at Bedford magistrates' court with breaking and entering into a garage at Eaton Socon on two occasions between 23 and 26 April and stealing five car tyres to the value of £13.3s. He was also charged with receiving two fruit machines that his co-defendants had stolen from a café in Huntingdonshire and which were found in his room. At his trial at the Bedfordshire Assizes, he claimed that the others had assured him that they were legitimate. This seems rather implausible, but he was acquitted for lack of evidence and discharged.

In October 1937, Mauri was charged with stealing a car worth £90 from outside the house of Gertrude Fuller, a nurse, in Bedford. From the press reports of the case, it is clear that he had other previous convictions. It also stated that he was working as a boxing manager under licence from the British Boxing Board of Control and had been handing out bills about a forthcoming bout around the town while looking for work there. In 1939, according to his mother, he got married in Brixton to a woman called Renée.

The following June, Mauri and William Oseman, a 28-year-old motor driver, were remanded at Marylebone on charges of stealing an ambulance car belonging to London County Council and handbags containing money and other property to the value of about £67 from at least five different women. Their technique was always the same: to drive the car up to their targets, stop and get out, pretend to ask for directions and snatch her bag. One woman, Ionia Alice Boulton, resisted when they stole her bag on 11 June and received a punch in the mouth for her pains, but she managed to note down the number of the car. Another victim was pushed away; the rest did not resist. The police followed the pair to Hampstead, where their car collided with a street refuge and they ran away. A patrol officer stopped Mauri shortly afterwards, Oseman was picked up later and they were charged.

Although there is no record of his sentence, it was almost certainly because of these crimes that Mauri found himself in HMP Dartmoor. Reopened as a civilian prison in the 1920s, Dartmoor was severe, almost impossible to escape from because of its remoteness on the moors. It housed some of the country's most troublesome prisoners. Here, on 14 January 1941, two other inmates, Jack Delaware Lorraine, a 38-year-old former seaman and persistent housebreaker, and Ronald Holdsworth, a 26-year-old bricklayer of Canadian origin who had served sentences for robbery with violence, attempted suicide and attempted murder, attacked Mauri.

This was apparently a long-running feud. At the time, Mauri was sitting on some hot water pipes in the cockpit of the punishment room, to which he had been sent – by his account – for refusing to return from the hospital wing to the hall. Lorraine struck and wounded him in the left eye, causing a serious injury that temporarily blinded him and required operating on. Holdsworth then chased him as he fled and slashed at him with a razor blade. This blade and a chip from an earthenware mug were found in the punishment room later.

The pair were tried at the Devon Assizes in Tavistock on 6 March, charged with "feloniously and maliciously wounding" Mauri, with the intention of disfiguring him. Mauri and a prison officer, S. Brogden, both testified to this effect at the trial. Defence counsel F.S. Laskey conceded that the attack happened but said that Mauri had expressed support for the Italian forces at a time when they were suffering setbacks in North Africa. He put it to Mauri that he had said, "Wait and see what is really going to happen when the Italians set about the British", then that he was pleased by the air raids on Coventry.

Mauri denied both, saying he had lost relatives in air raids himself. He tacitly admitted that he had fights in the yard, saying warders would not stop prisoners doing this if they fought fairly but that they would be punished afterwards. At the trial, Holdsworth also stated that there was a code of honour among prisoners that they never gave evidence against each other and the punishment for this was to be beaten up, while Lorraine claimed to be the ringleader. It was also cryptically said that others had told lies, which appears to allude to Mauri. Lorraine and Holdsworth were found guilty and, on 25 June, were given only 20 and 18 months of additional time respectively. Significantly, perhaps, Mr Justice Wrottesley said in passing sentence that he "considered there had been a certain amount of provocation" and that the crime was therefore "comparatively light".

This slashing was clearly the source of Mauri's disfigurement. Was it also the source of his bitterness and rage towards the world? He must have been freed not long after this, because by late 1945 he had a four-year-old daughter called Yvonne, though he had separated from his wife and was living in Nottingham. Although he was ostensibly looking after the little girl himself, his work as a lorry driver for a haulage contractor called A. Buttolph & Son meant that he must have been leaving her with others at least some of the time. Mauri lodged with a colleague, Arthur Robert Barnaby, who lived with his wife and her orphaned 18-year-old sister, Vera Guest, at 1 St Leger Terrace in the Mapperley area of town.

The handful of photos of Vera in life show a rather sombre-faced young woman, with long, dark hair in the 1940s style. She met Mauri while working as a machinist in a local factory and a relationship began. However, she might not have been quite as devoted to Mauri as he liked to think; Barnaby later said that she had a boyfriend in the US paratroopers and was waiting for him to come back on leave from the Netherlands so that they could get married, until her head was turned. According to press reports, Mauri was very "fond" of her, but there were also rows, during which he sometimes "slapped her face one or two times".

In April, ignoring her sister and brother-in-law's advice, Vera went with Mauri and Yvonne to stay with his sister Eileen, now Mrs Lake. The Lakes lived at 105 Denecroft Crescent in Hillingdon, a generic street on one of the many generic suburbs developed in the 1930s as the arterial roads out of London and the rise of the motor car made the city's expansion possible. The house itself is a typical 1930s construction, not far from the A40 and RAF Northolt on one of the main Western approaches to London. Eileen herself worked at Fairey Aviation in Hayes, one of many aircraft factories in the area.

On 3 June, Mauri was charged with the theft of nearly 200,000 cigarettes in cartons and 101 lbs of tobacco with a total value of £1,158 from Buttolph's factory on Bluebell Hill Road in Nottingham and taking a lorry without the owner's consent on 30 May. He was recorded at the time as of no fixed abode but originally from St Ann's Valley, in the north-western suburbs of Nottingham. His alleged co-conspirators were Cyril Topham, 42, the licensee at the Grandstand Hotel in Derby; Topham's brother Walter, 31, who worked for the cigarette manufacturer John Player; and their brothers-in-law, Harold Pearson, another lorry driver aged 50, and Noel Pheasant, a 32-year-old clerk. A network of other 'receivers' was also supposedly involved.

Nottingham magistrates heard evidence about this and remanded Mauri, Pearson and Pheasant for a week. A special court heard more details about the case on 20 June. The defendants were given bail, Mauri's mother paying £26 for his. Mauri returned, with Vera and Yvonne, to Hillingdon on 2 July. The case clearly played on his mind and he asked Eileen to look after Yvonne if he was jailed. He was due to take the train to Nottingham to stand trial on 11 July and told Eileen he was going there as she left for work. He did not go, however, and an arrest warrant was issued for failing to surrender to his bail and appear in court. And during the day, he murdered Vera. At some point, neighbours heard screams coming from the house and a man in a uniform was seen walking away from it. They went to check and found that the doors were locked.

As Eileen made her way home from work, she was surprised to see Mauri outside the Billington Arms pub. When she asked him why he was there, he told her: "Can you stand a shock? I've done something terrible. I'm a murderer." "Don't be silly, who would you want to kill?" she asked. "I've killed Vera. She's on the bed in the front room," came the answer. Not sure what to believe, she asked him to come back to the house so that she could call the police. "I can't, I've got to get away. There are six more I got to kill and then I'm going to kill myself."

Perhaps beginning to take it all in, she asked who he meant. First, he said, would be his sister-in-law Emily, who he believed was cheating on his brother, Bernard, then away on active service in Burma; next were Renée and a neighbour of Eileen's who he blamed for what had happened. "Isn't one enough?" Eileen pleaded. "Come back to the house." Mauri walked with her a few yards but then said he had to get away and was going to London.

When Eileen went inside the house, she found a letter, reading, with bizarre understatement: "Don't go in the front room as Vera is dead in there and she don't look a very nice sight". It was all too true. Vera was lying dead under a blanket on a bed-settee in the front room with a silk scarf pulled tight around her neck. Eileen's screams brought a neighbour round. The dead girl's lips were drawn and her eyes were half closed. She had also sustained a lacerated, crescent-shaped wound to the back of her head, which Home Office pathologist Dr Donald Teare said, would have been enough to stun but not kill her. Cause of death was asphyxia due to strangulation.

Detectives found three more letters Mauri had left behind, fully showing his paranoid nature. One was to his employer, asking them to pay off the bail his mother would forfeit because he had not turned up to court, "as she is an old woman, and it would kill her if she got sent to prison over me, and as she has not got 25 pence in the world, let alone £26". Another to Eileen read: "I have done Vera in. You can tell that fat cow over the road that she was responsible for Vera's death. I loved her very much, but she didn't want to live without me, so I had to kill her. Yes, I am going to kill that fat cow and that little rat of a husband of hers, and there is one more person I have got to kill in Nottingham before I take my life. But first of all I have got three victims down here I must do in before I come up to Nottingham."

The second, after warning Eileen not to enter the room, asked her for forgiveness. "Vera asked me to kill her as she didn't want to live without me. There are six more people I have got to kill, then I shall have to do away with myself," it continued. "The police are to blame for this as they framed me for the job in Nottingham, so what is the good of living when I am hunted wherever I go?" He later claimed that the police had fitted him up by putting words in the mouths of witnesses. Reiterating his plans, he added, with characteristic bombast, that the police thought they were smart but he would show himself smarter still; he would stay in London and kill the first three, then go up to Nottingham to kill the others. This contradicted a detail in the other note, which mentioned only one planned victim there.

Concluding, Mauri asked Eileen to bring up Yvonne, let her take the name Lake "and don't let her know what I was like". As a postscript, he said she was welcome to give his life story to the papers but should make sure they paid. To his mother, he wrote: "Please try to forgive me for the way I have treated you. I know I have been a bad son to you, and now I must finish my life like this. Perhaps in the next world I shall be better. I should have been all right if the police had left me alone. I have got a nice gun with me and I shall shoot any copper who tries to arrest me ... So good-bye, mother dear. From your broken-hearted son, Ron."

On the following day, Walter Topham and Pheasant were convicted and jailed for four months in connection with the theft of the cigarettes back in Nottingham, while Cyril Topham and Pearson were acquitted. There was never any other suspect but Mauri for the murder of Vera Guest. Scotland Yard, in the guarded language of police suspicion down the ages, announced that they believed he could assist them with their enquiries and put out a description to the press. Suspecting that his mother was harbouring him, plain clothes police carried out an all-night vigil behind curtained windows commanding the approaches to her road in Soho. She was interviewed by the press the next day and said that she thought Mauri must be dead, as otherwise he would have got word to her.

Meanwhile, Nottingham police kept watch on the railway, bus stations and the house at St Leger Terrace, fearing that the Barnabys might be among his intended victims in Nottingham, although it was also possible that he was after those he believed to have fingered him for the cigarette theft. Mauri, however, did not go to either location. Instead, a manhunt ensued that was reported in breathless detail and uncertain accuracy in newspapers across the world. He was first spotted driving what was believed to be a stolen car at Nutbourne near Chichester in Sussex on Friday 13 July, but the policeman on duty had not seen his photo or description and let him go, only realising his mistake when he returned to the station.

Mauri then headed west, by his own account travelling over 500 miles and passing many police stations. It was claimed that he intended to hide out in the Black Mountains of Wales. When his car ran out of petrol, he called in at a farm at Sollers Hope in Herefordshire, then drove off without paying. The man he spoke to there, Fred Gittoes, was also a part-time special constable. Noting that this man looked like the one police were looking for, Gittoes wrote down his registration number, FUJ 499, and telephoned them. At Huntley in Gloucestershire, Mauri asked a couple in a car for directions and snatched the woman's handbag, which contained £80. He was also spotted at Newent, Dymock and Ross-on-Wye at different times.

Acting on Gittoes' information, three policemen tried to block his way at Wilton Bridge where he crossed over the Wye and, they said, he tried to run them down. Mauri sped on towards Wales. At the Dixton crossroads, just outside Monmouth, he turned right and headed for Buckholt Wood, where he abandoned his car. Further calls from the public brought armed police to the scene and Mauri ran into a wood near the River Monnow, just above its confluence with the Wye. He first hid behind Haddon Lodge and made his way to the riverbank near a clergymen's retreat called The Chantry. (Both buildings still stand; the first is a business address, the latter a retirement home.) A young cleric staying there, Reverend J. Orde, heard shots and saw a man crouching behind the bank and the police calling him from the opposite bank to give himself up, which he refused to do.

The banks were steep and thickly wooded as they still are today. The accounts the police gave of what happened make it evident that they were covering up the fact that they shot an unarmed man, though no doubt they believed him to be armed as well as dangerous. By some clearly incorrect newspaper accounts, Mauri crouched behind a bush and fired his revolver, narrowly missing a policeman. PC R. Walbyoff of Monmouthshire Police, who played wing three-quarter for Newport RFC, raised his revolver and called on Mauri to surrender from the opposite bank. They pursued him back towards Monmouth hiding behind hedges as they went.

Walbyoff ducked behind a tree, as Inspector I.R. Bishop and Sergeant A.M. Sutton continued to crawl, commando-style, towards Mauri from opposite angles, urging him to give himself up. They thought they had lost sight of him until they heard what sounded like a revolver being fired from inside some rushes. Mauri, shoulder-deep in the water now, was clutching a submerged tree root because he could not swim. "Keep back, or I shall let you have it," he bellowed. "You're not going to take me alive. I have a revolver with three rounds – two for you and one for me."

When challenged again, he laughed and said: "Keep back, I've done one murder and I'll do some more.

I'll shoot to kill. You bastards will only use blanks." Bishop retorted that he had live ammunition and fired once into the bank two yards from Mauri to prove it. Mauri remained defiant. "What a bloody shot! Come on, let's shoot it out, I'm quicker on the draw than you," he called. Bishop left cover and returned with a 12-bore shotgun. Still Mauri taunted him to shoot, then parted the foliage to show something shining in his hand. He later said, according to Detective Sergeant Cripps, that this was a cigarette case and he had lost his gun earlier.

"This is it," Mauri called. Bishop sighted his gun and fired. The bullet hit a tree, fragmenting into pellets, one of which hit Mauri in the temple. He fell into a deeper part of the river and was pulled out, half-drowned, and put onto a ladder, bleeding from the head. As they gave him first aid, Bishop said, Mauri asked him: "Are you the inspector? Will you do something for me? Tell my mother and sister this is the best way out and say I'm sorry for all the trouble I've given them." He asked for the money in his trousers to be sent to his mother and claimed once again, that he was framed for the cigarette theft "and it made me mad". Of Vera he said: "The girl was dead when I tied the stocking around her neck. She wanted to die." He even urged them to write down everything he was saying correctly and to remember to caution him.

The police PR machine, such as it was, was wheeled out to say that they had shot to stop him harming others, not to kill. It was all a tad unpersuasive to modern eyes. Mauri was taken to hospital in Monmouth, where he was kept under armed guard while he recovered. Detective Sergeant Atkins from Abergavenny, who stayed at his bedside, noted that he seemed to be enjoying all the attention and commented on all the calls the press seemed to be making. When he was fit enough to be moved, he was taken to Lydney for enquiries into the £85 in sodden notes that were recovered from his trouser pocket.

On the afternoon of 17 July, Cripps, Detective Inspector Howard and Detective Sergeant Gibson of the Metropolitan Police CID saw him in the hospital, where he smoked and chatted with them for some time. Gibson told him he would be taken to Uxbridge and charged, to which he did not reply. Later when the charge was read to him and he was cautioned, he said "Yes" and made a statement, full of the paranoid rage that had sustained him all along.

Next day, he appeared at a police court in Uxbridge, where he was remanded in custody for eight days, charged with the murder. The press reported that he was wearing a blue sports coat and an open neck grey shirt, had wound marks on the right side of his forehead and was being kept under close guard. Permission was given for his sister to visit him immediately. Asked at the end of formal evidence if he had anything to say, Mauri said only that he wanted to apply for legal aid, which was granted. The press also reported that there was a large crowd waiting outside, mostly women and some with babies in prams, who pressed right up to the police car that took him back to prison.

A further remand took place on 26 July. After another hearing on 6 August, at which his letters were read out, he was committed for trial. This opened before Mr Justice Tucker at the Old Bailey on 20 September. Tucker soon after presided at the trial of [12] William Joyce but this was the last capital murder trial for the judge best known until then for the libel case of Her Serene Highness Princess Stephanie Hohenlohe-Waldenburg-Schillingsfürst versus Viscount Rothermere in 1939. This sensationalised trial pitched the Austrian-born princess and Nazi spy against the press baron who had been Hitler's chief supporter in Britain for breach of contract in allegedly failing to pay for her safe passage to the US. *Time* magazine said that Tucker presided in "his kindly, dawdling fashion". He was appointed to the Court of Appeal two years later.

Mauri's trial lasted a mere four hours. Lawrence A. Byrne KC, soon to be a High Court judge himself, prosecuted; Henry Curtis-Bennett KC defended. The defendant sat impassively as the police gave their evidence for the prosecution but when Arthur Barnaby testified that he had once seen Mauri hit Vera in the jaw, Mauri stood up and shouted: "You dirty little rat. You dirty little liar." His solicitor prevailed on him to sit down, which he did, still shouting: "He should be in the dock, not me".

Eileen Lake also testified about the relationship between her brother and Vera and what he had said and written to her after the murder.

Mauri's own story had evolved a bit by then. Even before this had all blown up, he claimed in the statement that was read out in court, he tried to break the relationship with Vera off, because he was being framed by the police and would go to jail. He told her that he did not want to see a young girl throw her life away, but she said that she would stick by him, no matter what happened. On the morning of 11 July, he claimed, he told her that he intended to take his own life but was "going to settle a few debts first", starting with killing his sister-in-law, Emily.

Vera, he claimed, said "Ron, if you do that, please take me with you", and he said: "No, Vera, I couldn't do that". She repeated: "If you are going to kill all those people, please kill me first". When he refused, saying she was young and had a life to live, she threatened to kill herself. She became hysterical, claimed Mauri, and started throwing herself around the room until she hit her head on the gas stove and knocked herself out. He was under the impression, he claimed, that she was already dead, but to save her from further suffering, he put the scarf around her neck and pulled it tight, then carried her into the next room. He had not at any point planned or intended to kill her. His mind was "a muck-up" because he was so depressed at the prospect of another long prison sentence; he remembered writing some letters but little more, he claimed.

Curtis-Bennett submitted that the killing was an act of manslaughter because Mauri had believed Vera Guest to be dead at her own hands when he strangled her but Tucker directed the jury that there was no case for manslaughter. The letters impressed the all-male jury more than Mauri's bizarre story and they returned with a verdict of guilty after just 13 minutes of deliberation. The press reported that, as sentence was passed, Mauri "was perfectly composed and did not hear his sister's heartbroken sobs a few yards behind him".

The appeal was heard and dismissed on 15 October. Mr Justice Wrotteseley, who had encountered Mauri before, said that his claim to have strangled Vera to spare her further suffering proved that he knew she was still alive and it was therefore murder, even if the attempted suicide was real. Mauri was hanged at HMP Wandsworth on 31 October by Albert Pierrepoint and Harry Kirk. Home Secretary James Chuter Ede later said the decision not to grant a reprieve came out of considerations of Mauri's long criminal record and highly volatile nature, which would make him dangerous for many years to come.

There is no doubt whatsoever about Mauri's guilt, but what impelled him to kill a young girl who was apparently infatuated with him is impossible to know. That he might want to die himself because of a robbery accusation against him, whether true or not, and the odd precision of the vow to kill six people make the case hard to understand, however obvious it is that he was terrified of the prospect of being in prison again. He was definitely abnormal. Much must have been going on in his life that we do not know about since the justice system of the day was not terribly interested, beyond ruling him sane enough to stand trial for what he had done. No one was terribly interested in the young victim either and she is now little more than a name in the documents.

7. "I am a German soldier and as such have had no interest in politics": The murder of Sergeant Gerhardt Rettig by Sergeant-Major Emil Schmittendorf, Corporal Armin Robert Franz Kühne and others at Lodge Moor POW Camp near Sheffield on 24 March 1945 and their executions at HMP Pentonville on 16 November 1945

The German prisoners-of-war (POWs) who planned the abortive mass breakout from Camp Le Marchant near Devizes in Wiltshire that ultimately led to the murder of [5] Wolfgang Rosterg apparently hoped to link up with their confederates from another large camp, Lodge Moor, near Sheffield. Together, they and other escaped POWs were supposed to liberate many other prisoners and march to the East Coast of England to be rescued by the German Navy.

How far POWs in different camps managed to communicate with each other to coordinate their plans through the 'bush telegraph' is uncertain, but even if there was no really strong link between this murder case and [5], there are plenty of parallels: a discovered escape plot; the identification of a regular soldier as the 'traitor'; a savage mass lynching by the committed Nazis among them; a scrupulously legalistic investigation by the British military authorities; and the rope at HMP Pentonville for some of the ringleaders.

Lodge Moor itself had been a POW camp during World War I. Among those detained here towards the end of that war was Admiral Karl Dönitz, the future head of the German Navy and briefly Hitler's successor at the end of World War II. As the commander of a U-boat, he might have faced prosecution, which he evaded by shamming mental illness until he secured a transfer to Wythenshawe Hospital in Manchester.

In 1941, as POW numbers started to grow, the site was put into service again. It was officially named Camp 17 and was also known as Redmires. Lodge Moor was essentially a holding prison, according to a historian of the POW experience. Vast numbers passed through it as the Allies swept through France in the summer of 1944. The Nissen huts filled up and many had to sleep in tents, which offered them little comfort in a drenched September on high moorland.

Most were German, though a few hundred were Italians, who were allowed out to work on farms or in factories because they were seen as lower risk. The location was remote enough that escape seemed unlikely anyway – which did not stop some trying. Seven prisoners tried to escape in December and on 14 March 1945, a man was shot and fatally injured making an attempt. At that stage, a much larger escape was already being planned.

As at other camps, British categorised the German POWs as pro-Nazi 'blacks', anti-Nazi 'whites' and the 'greys' in the middle, who made up the majority. The 'blacks' at Lodge Moor were led by *Feldwebel* (Sergeant-Major) Emil Schmittendorf, 31, and *Gefreiter* (Corporal) Armin Kühne. Little is known about Schmittendorf's background other than that he had been a regular soldier since 1934 and was married with children.

Kühne was born in the town of Gera, near Leipzig, in January 1927, making him only six when Hitler came to power. He was one of 12 children of Hermann and Helene Kühne. He had joined the Hitler Youth at nine and left home at 12, never to see his parents again. He was educated in political schools, where the focus of study was National Socialism and the life of Hitler. Despite being only two months over 18 at the time of the murder, Kühne was sardonically nicknamed 'Doktor Göbbels' in the camp because of his fervent support for Hitler. A picture of him shows the archetypal blonde Aryan *ubermensch*, yet one who was still really only a boy.

The inmates at Lodge Moor dug a tunnel over the course of many months during the hours when their outnumbered captors thought they were sleeping. It was almost complete when a British sergeant found it; he had apparently been tipped off about its location. There have been assertions the British authorities knew about the tunnel almost from the outset but deliberately let the POWs carry on because they would be less trouble while they were focused on digging it. Whether or not the plot had actually been betrayed, the Nazi mentality required someone to blame. And it was common British practice to plant a man among the prisoners to source information.

Unteroffizier (Sergeant) Gerhardt Rettig was perfect for the role of scapegoat as far as the most zealously Nazi prisoners were concerned. Like Rosterg, he was a regular soldier but was not a Nazi and was living in a camp full of Nazi supporters. He had been seen talking to guards near the tunnel entrance and was spotted passing a note to one of the guards through the wire on 24 March. Shortly after, this Rettig spoke to the German camp leader or *Lagerführer* – who reportedly did not think he was an informer – and let it be known that he feared that he might be suspected. As a result, arrangements were made for him and a friend of his who shared his outlook to be transferred immediately to a different camp. They were sent to pack up their kits but never had the chance to move.

The 5.40 p.m. roll call sounded. As Rettig walked out of his hut to attend it, he was chased back in by an angry mob of 20 to 30 men who, his unnamed friend later testified, were led by Kühne and *Unteroffizier* Heinz Ditzler. They beat him until his face was covered in blood and his eyes were half closed. He was then chased outside the hut and cornered at the washhouse. By now, the mob was about 100-strong and grew to anything from 300 to 500, according to different accounts, though no doubt the vast majority were watching rather than participating. Some among them yelled "Beat him to death!" and "Hang him!"

At one point, a British guard drew his revolver to try to keep the mob back. When a German Red Cross sergeant tried to help Rettig, they yelled "Knock him down! He is trying to help the traitor!" As Rettig lay on the ground, it was alleged, Schmittendorf raised his head up by the hair and kicked it twice, then poured a bucket of cold water over Rettig. This revived him enough to get up and run into a passage between the kitchens and the dining room where waste was disposed of.

British troops moved in to try and restore order, the cry of "The Tommies are coming!" went up and the crowd of POWs melted away. Rettig was found there by a medical orderly between the arms of the bins "crumpled up and unconscious with severe head wounds". He was driven to a hospital near Sheffield but died in the ambulance on the way, without regaining consciousness. At the trial of the perpetrators, the time of death was recorded as 7.45 p.m.

Rettig's skull was not actually fractured, but the blows had damaged it so badly that coma and death inevitably followed. His upper lip was so badly split that teeth showed through it. A German doctor, who had been on duty at the camp hospital when Rettig was brought in, said that he had severe abrasions to the face and his head and face were so swollen as to be unrecognisable; the British civilian doctor who carried out the post mortem said that an implement must have been used to inflict the wounds as Rettig could not have died from the fist blows alone, although he noted that the skull was thinner than normal. The immediate cause of death was asphyxia from inhaling blood.

Rettig's friend named the ringleaders as Schmittendorf, Kühne, Ditzler and *Soldat* (Private) Jürgen Kersting. Schmittendorf, he alleged, had previously labelled Rettig a traitor for voicing the view that Germany had lost the war. This was supported by testimony from another man at the later trial, who stated: "At Doncaster, I said that if I were questioned by a British officer, I would tell the truth – that Germany had lost the war. Schmittendorf then pointed me out as a scoundrel and a criminal. I have been threatened secretly."

Other witnesses said that Schmittendorf had later told them, "the whole affair has been very successful"; one added that he later said: "The man has got so many blows from me that he will not think of treachery a second time, but we will have to take care because there are spies among us." Another stated that Kühne confirmed that Rettig had given away the location of the tunnel, yet another that Schmittendorf had spoken volubly about the need to punish traitors. Schmittendorf and Ditzler, together with three others, actually managed to escape by crawling under the wire two days later and tried to get to the coast to find a ship on which to get back to Germany, but they were recaptured and brought back.

The four accused came up for trial at the 'London Cage' in August, where they pleaded not guilty to "committing a civil offence, that is to say, murder".

The London Cage was an MI19 POW facility located below 6-8 Kensington Palace Gardens, three requisitioned luxury mansions within a gated street that was nicknamed Millionaire's Row. It was one of nine 'cages' set up in 1940, one for each of the UK's command areas, in which prisoners were subjected to 'special intelligence treatment' by officers trained by Lieutenant-Colonel Scotland in order to break their will to resist before being sent to POW camps. The London Cage was actually next door to the Soviet embassy and sometimes interrogators dressed up as Soviet officers to play on German fears of their most ruthless enemy. Ten officers and about 12 NCOs served as interrogators and interpreters. There was space for about 60 prisoners at any one time.

Some very prominent Nazi war criminals passed through the cage before it finally closed in 1948. There were persistent allegations of torture and mistreatment of prisoners here that eventually led to rows between MI5 and MI6. An early version of Scotland's manuscript, *London Cage*, detailed some clear breaches of the Geneva Convention, including threats of execution and beatings. The sanitised final version denied that violence was used but admitted mental torture, like making prisoners exercise naked or urinate in their clothes. Some Germans, including 18 accused of murdering Allied prisoners after the escape from Stalag Luft III, also alleged that they were tortured there. Conversely, the treatment meted out to them also brought some Nazi war crimes to light.

The trial took place on 7-13 August in the very last days of the war; the atom bombs were dropped on Hiroshima and Nagasaki on 6 and 9 August, then VJ Day was declared on 15 August. Colonel W.H.E.L Fox Pitt was president of the court, while Major A.M.S. Stevenson was deputy judge advocate. As in the trial of the German POWs in [5] the month before, Major R.A.L. Hilliard led the prosecution. Lieutenant Alexander Brands appeared for Kühne and Schmittendorf, Major Nigel Robinson for Ditzler and Kersting. "Standing stiffly to attention, they answered their names smartly," it was reported on the first day, when Hilliard detailed the events of 24 March.

As in the Rosterg case, all of the German witnesses were allowed to testify anonymously for fear of reprisals. Their names remain out of the public domain to this day. Among them was the aforementioned German doctor. On the second day, after the prosecution case concluded, Brands asked the court's permission for a further adjournment so that he could analyse the answers of a potential alibi witness for one of the defendants, who, he said, was in hospital in Yorkshire with pleurisy. A two-hour adjournment was granted but nothing more came of this witness. When the hearing resumed, multiple witnesses accused Schmittendorf of punching and kicking Rettig. Kühne and Ditzer were accused of punching him on the head, and the former was also accused of saying afterwards that it had been done because he gave away the tunnel's location.

All four defendants called witnesses when the court resumed. Unlike their counterparts in the first trial, they did not exult in their actions but simply denied them. By then, they already knew what the consequences of admitting the fact would be, however much they thought what they were doing was right. Questioned by Hilliard, Schmittendorf said that the tunnel was discovered by a British sergeant "who appeared to know where to look for it". After this, he went into a hut where he was told who the 'betrayer' was. "I said 'I am in this, too'. I saw that a beating-up was taking place. A man was being struck from one side to another by blows on the face. When he came to my side, I hit him, too," he testified.

However, Schmittendorf added, this man was not actually Rettig, who was being beaten by another crowd in the hut at the same time. He had not hit Rettig himself. Any witnesses who had said he did were either lying or mistaken. However, he agreed that he had spent many nights working the tunnel over the course of four months and had hoped to escape using it. All of those who worked on it were very angry at the betrayal, he among them, and almost all of the prisoners knew of its existence.

Asked if he was a Nazi, Schmittendorf said, "I am a German soldier and as such have had no interest in politics". He denied any knowledge of there being any pro-Nazi organisation within the camp. "I cannot think that such organisation existed," he added. However, letters he had written to other witnesses were read out that contradicted this claim. One of them stated: "It is important that you saw me in the hut", which is where he claimed to be while Rettig was being murdered. Schmittendorf admitted that he wrote this.

Kühne, described in the press as "a diminutive figure with a large Red Cross armband", took the stand on 8 August to deny taking any part in the attack. Under questioning by Brands, he said he had been in his hut when about 20 men rushed in, knocking beds over as they went. "I straightened my bed and went to the end of the hut to escape the turmoil," he said. Asked if he had heard witnesses saying that he had run into a hut behind Rettig and struck him on the neck and head, he said: "Yes, but it is not true". As a member of the Red Cross, he had no involvement in the tunnel and claimed that he and some others treated its discovery "as a joke".

As to politics, like Schmittendorf, he said it was not relevant. "Why should I be interested in politics? I am not interested whether a man is a Nazi or anti-Nazi. When one is a soldier, one has nothing to do with politics", all of which was palpably untrue in his own case. Kühne too was found out through his writings, with one letter being translated thus: "It is only a matter of two points. During the beating up, I was in the hut and secondly, I fetched the rations. Six comrades of mine from Camp 21 have been condemned to death and the same thing is going to happen to us. If you can give testimony accordingly, I would be very grateful. Please do everything you can." The letter also referred to cuts on his hands and how he was ordered to hold out his hands for inspection by the court. It concluded: "Things might go wrong. Please destroy contents when read. If you cannot, then please remain silent".

In response to Brands, Kühne claimed that when he was brought to the London Cage for interrogation, he was ordered to kneel stark naked and have his hands examined. Ditzler likewise denied being part of the beating-up of Rettig. He had been involved in digging the tunnel for about four days, he admitted, and was angry at the betrayal. Indeed, he claimed to have been betrayed many times before in his escape attempts. "Once I was standing right at the barbed wire, but a traitor was standing next to me," he told the court, and admitted escaping at a time when he knew Rettig was dead. He asked the court's permission to make a statement to the court to help Schmittendorf and Brands was allowed to speak to him, but Schmittendorf refused the offer. Almost nothing is known of Kersting's alleged role. He too denied being part of the murder.

When the court reconvened on Monday 13 August, it announced that Ditzler and Kersting had been acquitted for lack of evidence. Brands now addressed the court for the remaining two, saying that a large crowd of men had been involved. Identification evidence had to be accurate to convict and he observed that the only witness who alleged that Schmittendorf had kicked Rettig was not sure who he was when asked to identify him in court.

Schmittendorf, he noted, was a man in a very difficult situation; he knew no more about his wife and children than that they had been in Berlin and that he had been in the German Army since 1934. In the circumstances, anger towards a possible 'traitor' was surely understandable.

"To escape is not a dishonourable thing but to prevent your comrades escaping is in the minds of most of us, I think, a beastly thing to do," Brands said. He then spoke of Kühne's hothousing in Nazism from a young age. "Having spent his formative years in those unnatural surroundings, is it strange that he reacts to treachery to the *Führer* in the way he was trained to act over the years?" It was a good try but hopeless in the face of the evidence. Judgment on Schmittendorf and Kühne was initially reserved but, to anyone who knew military justice, that meant that they had been convicted and sentenced to death.

This verdict was kept quiet until it was promulgated on 15 November 1945 and six military policemen kept watch on the two throughout the following night. Despite Kühne's youth – he may have been younger at the time he committed his offence than any other man to be hanged in Britain in the twentieth century – he and Schmittendorf were executed at Pentonville the next day by Albert Pierrepoint and Alexander Riley. It is unknown if this was a double execution or two singles. Compared to the very swift processes that could bring a British murderer to justice within three months, it was a remarkably drawn-out affair, such was the care taken to follow the law.

Rettig was buried at Cannock Chase War Cemetery, like his unfortunate fellow victim, Wolfgang Rosterg. Schmittendorf and Kühne, like the five POWs who went before them two months earlier, were buried within the grounds at Pentonville. After the war, the German War Graves Commission asked for permission to remove them to Cannock Chase as well but was told that the British authorities could not find the exact location of the graves.

This was the last execution of German POWs in the UK. Meanwhile, the US Army had hanged 14 of them in a converted warehouse elevator shaft at the United States Disciplinary Barracks in Fort Leavenworth, Kansas, in three batches in July and August 1945. All had been convicted by general court-martial for the murders of fellow Germans believed to have been informants to the American authorities. They were buried in the adjacent prison cemetery.

An eerily similar case in Canada reached its denouement in the following year, when four German POWs were hanged on 18 December 1946 for the murders of two fellow POWs at a giant camp in Medicine Hat in 1943. Once again, the camp was divided between 'blacks', 'greys' and 'whites'; once again, the most fanatical Nazis ran the camp on a day-to-day basis because the guards were so outnumbered; once again, there was vicious hostility to anti-Nazi POWs.

Two were lynched in the summer of 1943. The second, Karl Lehmann, a Communist teacher, was accused of undermining morale because he translated Canadian newspapers that made it clear that Germany was losing the war. He was lured to a classroom after hours on false premises, subjected to a kangaroo court trial, then beaten up and hung by the neck from a gas pipe. The four ringleaders who were executed in what was the largest mass execution in modern Canadian history bitterly protested against not being tried as soldiers and for having a paedophile murderer hang alongside them. This is believed to be the last case where German POWs were put to death for murdering others. As for Lodge Moore itself, a few concrete slabs still remain from the foundations, but otherwise the site has completely disappeared.

8. "That little guttersnipe": The execution of John Amery for treason at HMP Wandsworth on 19 December 1945

That the son of a member of Winston Churchill's war cabinet had decamped to Nazi Germany, made radio broadcasts urging Britain to side with Hitler and tried to recruit British prisoners of war into a fifth column, before being captured by Italian partisans, sent home and hanged for treason would seem too ridiculous for fiction. And yet it is absolutely true.

Leopold 'Leo' Amery (1873-1955) was a barrister and journalist from Devon gentry stock. Indeed, he turned down the editorship of *The Observer* in 1908 and that of *The Times* in 1912, having just been elected as Conservative MP for Birmingham South. This made him the only British man ever to decline the editorships of two national papers. Amery was a friend of the Astors and the Duke of Westminster among many others. On 14 March 1912, his wife Florence 'Bryddie' Greenwood (1885-1975) gave birth to their first son, John in their home at their home behind the Chelsea Embankment. John was christened in the crypt of the House of Commons, with godparents from high society. A second son, Harold Julian, was born in 1916.

In 1922, Leo became First Lord of the Admiralty and the family moved into Admiralty House in Whitehall. From 1924 to 1929, he served as Colonial Secretary. His rise during John's childhood was meteoric and continued in the 1930s, but there was a time bomb lurking within the family that would explode on them during World War II. There had been something deeply, obviously wrong with John Amery from an early age. As a toddler, a nanny described him as "a very hard child", who threw terrible tantrums. At five, a teacher described him as "an extremely abnormal boy, with a fixed attitude of an abnormal type and a tendency to live inside himself". He went through a long succession of private tutors and shocked his nannies by drawing pictures of naked women and leaving them around the house.

John followed his father to Harrow School, where his reports were unanimously dreadful. He resented any form of discipline, stole from shops and other boys, and sneaked out to go to London nightclubs, where he lost his virginity at 14. He was highly promiscuous and drank heavily from his early teens. A housemaster called him "without doubt, the most difficult boy I have ever tried to manage", while the headmaster, Cyril Norwood, considered him to be "morally imbecile". His parents took him to a psychologist, Dr Maurice Wright, who concluded that John had "no moral sense of right and wrong". Finally, he was sent to a school for English boys in Switzerland. This went no better: he contracted syphilis from prostituting himself to men and had to go home.

John Amery was certainly not stupid. Indeed, he won a place at Oxford in 1929 but instead became an assistant film director to a small company. His brief career in film was punctuated by flops and bankruptcies, notably the £100,000 adventure feature *Jungle Skies*, which he persuaded his family and friends to back. It ended with the entire crew stranded in Africa.

As a young man, Amery would carry his teddy bear around with him like Sebastian Flyte in Evelyn Waugh's *Brideshead Revisited*, even buying it drinks and comics. He also carried a gun at all times to frighten off his many creditors. By 1932, he had racked up an astonishing 74 convictions for motoring offences. Next year, he caused a minor society scandal when he announced his intention to marry Una Eveline Wing, although he could not actually do this without his parents' consent, because he was not yet 21. Wing described herself as an actress, but she was well known to the police as a prostitute in Piccadilly.

Amery was almost addicted to using prostitutes and all three of his wives were sex workers in different ways. When hid family used their connections to hamper his plans, the couple moved to France. They married legally in Athens, but Amery was soon wanted for issuing a false cheque to pay for some diamonds. Again, his father bailed him out. He was finally declared bankrupt in 1936, owing the enormous sum of £6,000, but he continued to sponge off his father and others, pawned heirlooms and acted as a male prostitute, while also indulging in sadomasochism with prostitutes.

So far, Amery had been just an overprivileged waster – "that little guttersnipe", as future Prime Minister Neville Chamberlain called him. On the continent, however, he became drawn into extreme right-wing politics. The key influence on him in these years was Jacques Doriot, the French fascist leader, with whom he travelled widely to see fascism in action. He claimed to have fought with General Franco's Nationalists during the Spanish Civil War; won a medal while serving as an intelligence officer with Italian volunteer forces; and seen Communist torture chambers in Barcelona. In reality, although some have cast him as a gun runner taking arms France to Spain, he probably only visited Spain once, briefly, in 1939. This was long enough, however, to apply for a certificate of naturalisation that would figure later on in his story.

By 1941, the Germans occupied northern France and ruled the southern half through the puppet Vichy government. Amery soon got into trouble with Vichy and was forced to live in the Grenoble region. Having failed to interest Italy or Finland in his services, his luck changed when the local German armistice chief, Graf Ceschi, took him under his wing. After some difficulty, Amery secured permission to leave in September 1942 and went to Germany with his new French wife Jeannine Bard, another former prostitute. That October, they met the German English Committee in Berlin and Amery first suggested the creation of a British anti-Bolshevik legion.

This idea did not fly but he came to the attention of the German High Command after writing a letter to a French newspaper criticising British bombing raids. Amery was taken to meet Hitler. The *Führer* was no doubt delighted to have the scion of a British cabinet minister in his hands – Leo was now Secretary of State for India and Burma – and he allowed Amery to make nine propaganda radio broadcasts in November and December.

The main thrust in these was that the alliance with the Soviet Union would destroy Britain, morally and politically. Germany, Amery said, was preventing "world domination by Jewry". Naturally he met [12] William Joyce, but they were not friends. To Joyce Amery was yet another posh English boy who looked down on him and was better paid to boot. They also differed in their approach. Where Joyce berated the British public for their stupidity in fighting Germany and was virulently anti-Semitic, Amery posed as a patriot motivated by love of country and empire. Although he threw in some anti-Semitism for good measure and particularly vilified the Jewish Lord Mayor of London, Bolshevism was the main target of his ire.

"For two years living in a neutral country I have been able to see through the haze of propaganda to reach something which my conscience tells me is the truth," Amery said on 19 November. "That is why I come forward tonight without any political label, without any bias, but just simply as an Englishman to say to you 'A crime is being committed against civilisation. Not only the priceless heritage of our fathers, of our seamen, of our Empire builders is being thrown away in a war that serves no British interests'." There were plenty on the right wing of the Conservative Party at the time who agreed with the last sentence.

The broadcasts had little effect and listener numbers plummeted rapidly, thanks to Amery's "drawling, squeaky, aristocratic voice", as author Adrian Weale described it, and the nonsensical content. And seeing that the tide of the war was just turning at Stalingrad, his judgement was as poor as it was morally defective. The Amery family, now living at 112 Eaton Square in Belgravia, sat together in horror listening to one of the broadcasts. His mother refused to believe it was him. Shortly after, Leo disinherited John and offered to resign from the cabinet, while Julian, a captain in the Special Operations Executive, did the same. Both offers were refused.

John's usefulness did not last very long. Lodging in a top hotel at official expense, he continued his dissolute ways and sent the bills to Hitler's private office. An MI6 report on him at the time said that he was drinking "a whole litre of gin in a single night" and was "so dissipated, both physically and morally" that he was not a serious security concern. In 1943, Jeannine suddenly died, probably from choking on her own vomit, and Amery narrowly escaped a charge of manslaughter. Within weeks, he took up with another prostitute, Michelle Thomas, in Paris.

Whether the Germans sent him back or he chose to go is not clear, but in January, he visited Doriot and his career took an even more sinister turn. Inspired by the example of the *Légion des Volontaires Français* that fought on the Eastern Front, Amery proposed something similar. Hitler was enthusiastic and the Legion of St George was proclaimed. Amery appealed to interned British subjects in the name of 'British National Representation' to "answer this call to arms in the defence of our homes and children and of all civilisation against Asiatic and Jewish bestiality". The Legion would be non-political and would fight only against Communists, he claimed. Leo called this "undoubtedly his most heinous offence". In truth, it never got off the ground. For all John's efforts touring camps, he only managed to recruit 30 men at any time and they never saw action. One doubts whether his affectedly aristocratic demeanour cut much ice with working-class troops. In October, the Waffen SS cut ties with the Legion, renaming it the British Free Corps.

Amery was less active in 1944, but he did get sent to various occupied territories and was prepared to speak on 'Jewish Influence in the English Ruling Stratum' at a planned congress in Krakow, alongside other allies of the Nazis. The event was cancelled as the Soviets drove the Germans back. That September, he was sent to Italy, where German forces were propping up the Salò Republic. Mussolini reportedly viewed him as "the perfect English gentleman" and he made some broadcasts on Radio Rome.

It all ended on about 29 April when Amery and Michelle were captured by Italian partisans near Como, trying to flee to Switzerland. On 2 May, he was interviewed in the San Vittore jail in Milan by Reuters correspondent Roberta Allen and claimed to have been seeking to surrender to Allied troops rather than partisans. The couple were handed over to British forces, led by the future broadcaster Alan Whicker, who was attached to the Film & Photographic Unit. Looking pale and still clad in a black shirt, Amery said: "My God - an Englishman ... Thank God you're here. I thought they were going to shoot me". Whicker himself mentioned it in his war memoirs, saying that he believed the subsequent process was not something the British legal system should be proud of. Michelle was not arrested but chose to stay with Amery anyway.

Once in custody, Amery seemed to think that all would be well now, because "my father would see to it". Scotland Yard detectives who interrogated him at an internment camp reported him to be mainly concerned with his missing possessions, particularly his teddy bear. Two Sundays later, on 13 May, the *Sunday Mirror* splashed his picture on the front page, hailed the "closing chapter in the life of a waster" and described him as "looking like the hang-dog cur he is", while stirring in some more dirt on his past life for good measure. This was to be the first shot in a seven-month battle of words.

On 30 May, a Labour MP asked Foreign Secretary Anthony Eden in the Commons if he could "tell us what is being done with Mr John Amery, about whom there still appears to be a blackout". Eden ducked this by saying this was a matter for the home government. By 10 June, speculation was rife, some noting that Amery seemed to have disappeared and that the Home Office was denying claims that he had been charged with treason. Five days later, the rumour was that he was in a camp in Brussels. One wonders what might have happened had the Home Secretary at the time of Amery's trial been one of Leo's Tory colleagues. The British Communist Party's newspaper, the *Daily Worker*, was certainly suspicious: its 21 June edition reported that Conservative Central Office refused to confirm if they would proceed with John's trial if they won the general election on 5 July and noted that Leo and Julian were both standing. Eight days later, it asked why the trial was still being delayed.

In the event, Labour won by a landslide, Leo lost his seat and Julian was not elected. Two days later, John was flown back under military escort, still dressed in full fascist garb. Detective Inspector Jones arrested him on arrival at 7.50 p.m. and took him to Bow Street Police Station. There, he was charged with high treason, in that between 22 June 1941 and 25 April 1945, "being a person owing allegiance to His Majesty, he adhered to the King's enemies elsewhere than in the King's Realm ... contrary to the Treason Act, 1351", and cautioned. Asked if he had anything to say, he said he would like to wait until he could obtain legal advice.

On 8 July, Amery was taken to Bow Street Magistrates Court under heavy security. The crowd of about 50 outside was considerably fewer than Joyce had attracted. First to arrive had been a young Scot, Thomas Macfarlane, who left his home in Clapham soon after 5.00 a.m. "to make certain of his seat in the Courtroom". Amery was described as "slightly built, wearing a Navy-blue double-breasted suit ... very tanned, and clean shaven". Prosecutor R.L. Jackson asked for a three-week remand, because the next session at the Old Bailey was due to start in eight days and Lawrence Byrne QC, who would appear for the Crown, was occupied with a similar case and so could not guarantee to be here at any time during the next session. In addition, there would be many witnesses, most of whom would have to come from different parts of the continent.

When the magistrate, Gerald McKenna, observed that "Those are not the reasons which have been given wide publicity elsewhere," Jackson answered, "I know the reasons to which you refer. They do not even approximate to the real reasons". Jones than gave formal evidence of arrest, during which Amery "sat in the dock with his legs crossed and his hands folded, his glance slightly averted towards the floor". The remand was granted and the proceedings were over in five minutes. It was announced about now that he would be defended by Gerald Osborne Slade KC, who was also to defend Joyce.

At this stage, Amery's health became an issue. Three days later, it was reported that he and Joyce were both in the hospital wing at HMP Brixton and that the medical officer, Dr Hugh Grierson, had seen him three times during the night and called in a Harley Street specialist. The governor, the reports added, had told Amery that a large sum of money had been made available for his defence – presumably from his long-suffering family – but unlike Joyce, he took little interest in his own case.

In the event, Amery did come to the second hearing on 30 July. Here, Byrne showed the court the proclamation he put out when the Legion was set up. The other offences were propaganda speeches and broadcasts. Byrne then read out a long statement by Amery on his political activities in Europe from 1936 to 1945, which tried to put a different spin on what he had done. He claimed, for instance, to have been in the south of France winding up some business matters when the French Army collapsed, trapping him there. When the Germans invaded the USSR, it was his "considered opinion ... that Europe was in the greatest period of Communist invasion and that nothing could stop it unless the different countries pushed through a social revolution which would spike the guns of the Communists. It was also our view that the Jewish race was mixed up and working hand in glove with Moscow."

Following the "very great shock" of Britain and the USSR becoming allies, Amery said that he thought "that the people responsible in London were acting in a manner that no longer coincided with British imperial interests. I went therefore to Vichy, to see what was going on, determined to do what I could to create a situation whereby a united front of nations might be organised against Russia. I found that there was no intention whatsoever of carrying out any social revolution, that, in a word, Vichy was an ultra-reactionary government of priests." He claimed that his fight had been solely against Communism and said: "I defy anyone to find in my speeches one solitary word against my country".

In another statement, Amery described his activities in Belgrade and Norway. Byrne then held up a large, red-bordered poster written in Italian with a photograph of him in the centre. It read: "Italians, if you do not believe our propaganda, you will believe the words an Englishman – John Amery, son of the British Minister for India, who let loose the war which caused your sufferings, the gang of people who threw our Empire into this criminal and ridiculous war, who ordered the indiscriminate bombing of women and children. Churchill and his gang did not hesitate to drag the flag and the fair name of England in the mud."

Royston Francis Wood had been interned in a camp at St Denis when Amery visited on 21 April 1943 and made a speech in the visitors' hut. This, Wood told the hearing, asserted that many in England wanted to end the war and that a fully equipped bomber had flown over to join the League. Those who joined would serve under German officers, but their NCOs would be British. The internees were hostile to Amery, Wood added.

Another witness, Wilfred Brinkman, said he saw Amery speak at the same camp on 5 March, where he saw British National Representation posters with Amery's name on them. After he had finished speaking, Amery asked Brinkman, a former employee of the American Consulate in Nice, to stay behind. He stressed that he was acting on behalf of the Vichy government, asked him not to say anything about him in the camp and extended his hand. "I looked and said I was not in the habit of shaking hands with traitors. I then walked out. When Amery left the camp, the internees booed him." Finally, Dorian May Carter gave evidence of a broadcast Amery made on German-controlled radio in November 1942 and he was committed for trial.

Given the mountain of evidence about his actions since 1941, there could be no doubt whatsoever that, if he was a British subject, Amery had committed treason. There could only be two lines of defence: insanity or that he was not actually British. His family desperately pursued both. Leo commissioned the psychiatrist Dr Edward Glover to write a report on his son.

This duly concluded that, throughout his life, John had shown "all the symptoms of psychopathy of a type which borders on the schizoid (psychotic) character and which under ordinary circumstances ends in compulsive delinquent and anti-social conduct ... The whole picture is completely characteristic of severe psychopathy, negativism, unteachability, fear of attack of a paranoid type, antisocial behaviour, delinquency, lack of moral feeling and conscience, sexual abnormality. And so on. No element is missing." As such, argued Slade, John was not fit to stand trial. The prosecution would not accept this, meaning that an enquiry into his mental state would be needed. An EEG test, carried out after his condemnation, would find no abnormalities in his brain.

On 12 September, Slade applied at the Old Bailey for the trial not to be heard in the current session on the grounds that Amery might be a Spanish citizen, having been naturalised there. "You appreciate allegiance is the essence of defence of treason in this charge," Slade told Mr Justice Tucker. "In other words, if Amery became a naturalised Spanish citizen before the recent war broke out, he would not owe allegiance to His Majesty. If that is the case, it is obviously of the utmost importance to the defence"; enquiries needed to be made. Tucker said that he did not understand how Amery might not have known this before now. Slade explained that Julian Amery was in Spain now, having been unable, as an election candidate, to go any earlier. This was agreed.

The trial was again postponed at the defence's request on 17 October because enquiries were still going on. Slade explained that the original documents relating to naturalisation might have been destroyed or that Franco might not have had power to grant it at the time when it was purportedly granted, which might raise legal questions over the way the case should be handled.

Mr Justice Hallett granted a second delay "with very great reluctance ... because in this country the disposition is so strong that no person charged should have any possible ground for complaint which may appear to anybody to be reasonable". However, if the defence was not ready to proceed soon, the case would have to go ahead. The answer came on 26 November. The Spanish government confirmed that, while John had taken the initial steps, he had never been "inscribed in the Register of Nationalities" and thus did not have any of the benefits of Spanish nationality.

Amery came to trial at the Old Bailey two days later, on 28 November. *The Times* described how his "long black hair, curling up at the back, was carefully brushed ... [he] appeared most of the time to have a half-smile on his face." The authorities were prepared for the long haul, even if the public had largely lost interest. The Attorney-General, Sir Hartley Shawcross KC, had been flown from the Nuremberg Trials to lead for the Crown. The court commenced an hour late: Slade spent 25 minutes with Amery, then there were discussions between counsels and the Director of Public Prosecutions.

The reason, it emerged, was because Amery had decided to plead guilty. When he did, the press reported: "A sense of electric tension spread immediately throughout the court up quickly to the dock to look at the man who had confessed himself a traitor. Amery showed no outward signs of emotion except a twist of the lips now and again and a little smile. He placed his hands on the ledge of the dock, leaned forward, always keeping his eye on the judge." Mr Justice Humphreys – described by Rebecca West as looking "small in the depth of his red and purple robes, a very old man, with wit on his tongue and a fiercer wit on his face" - said that he never accepted a plea of guilty on a capital charge "without assuring myself the accused thoroughly understands what it is he is doing and that he is in accord with his legal advisers".

Slade duly assured him of this and the plea was recorded. Asked if he had anything to say, Amery replied: "No, thank you, sir". Humphreys gave him another chance to speak, which he again declined, then told him: "I am satisfied that you knew what you did and that you did it intentionally and deliberately after you had received warning from ... your fellow countrymen that the course you were pursuing amounted to high treason. You have forfeited your right to live. You now stand a self-confessed traitor to your King and country." Amery continued to smile and look at Humphreys. "After sentence of death, looking self-possessed, he bowed deeply to the judge and walked down to the cells without any sign of emotion," the press reported. It was over in eight minutes. Shawcross never spoke.

West saw it all as Amery's last fantasy, casting himself as a martyr for his views, "a crazy harlequin enmeshed in unfortunate adventure". Another witness said: "He was like an insect that falls on a hot stove and is withered, and what he did felt like an act of cruelty to the whole court. It was quite clear that he was morally satisfied and that he was congratulating himself on having at last, at the end of his muddled and frustrated existence, achieved an act crystalline in its clarity."

In a later edition of *The Meaning of Treason*, West suggested that Slade, "who always believed his clients to be innocent, not in the highly technical sense with which lawyers must hold that belief, but with the Wordsworthian simplicity which is privilege of the layman", encouraged Amery to plead guilty on the basis that he was more likely to be spared if he did, something that Shawcross told him squarely was wrong. Had he pleaded not guilty and testified, she thought, he might have convinced the world of his insanity, though she herself saw him as neither sane nor evil but "like an automobile that will not hold the road".

Leo Amery still hoped to save his son. On 5 December, the Home Office was reportedly considering a report from a Harley Street specialist who just examined John at the request of the prison authorities. It was claimed that John was very ill with tuberculosis and if this was verified, he would not be hanged. Julian visited him on 7 December and his parents the following day. "I understand that he asked for forgiveness, and there was a reconciliation following years of estrangement," wrote a *Lancashire Evening Post* reporter.

John, the report continued, was emaciated and unable to eat solids. "To all appearances he is a dying man and he does not show any will to live." However, Julian contradicted this two days later, saying that John, while clearly ill, was healthier now than he had been in 1940-1. By 17 December, he was said to be in better health and no longer in bed all day, though still under medical supervision. A petition for a reprieve in Birmingham garnered a meagre 27 signatures, though Field Marshal Smuts in South Africa pleaded the case to Prime Minister Clement Attlee.

John kept his aristocratic insouciance up to the end. Leo said that he acted with "unwavering serenity and even cheerfulness" throughout the last three weeks of his life. On 18 December, Chuter Ede declined a reprieve and said the execution would go ahead as scheduled the next day. That night, the *Daily Mirror* reported, Leo went to the Commons with a bundle of papers, asking MPs to use their influence to save John on the grounds that he was dying of tuberculosis. It was to no avail; John was still smoking heavily, as he had for years, but the coroner's inquest confirmed that he did not have TB.

Albert Pierrepoint, who had only just come back from hanging Josef Kramer and 12 other Nazis, including three women, for the atrocities committed at Belsen, officiated on 19 December, assisted by Henry Critchell. The story that Amery greeted him with the words "Mr Pierrepoint, I've always wanted to meet you, but not, of course, under these circumstances" began in an unpublished newspaper article of the time and has circulated ever since. It is, however, contradicted, by a report from a Prison Commission official who said that Amery extended his hand and said "Oh! Pierrepoint", as his hands were strapped but no more. Pierrepoint certainly described him as one of the bravest men he ever hanged. He gave Amery the 7'8" drop required for a small man of 5'7" and 10 stone.

An Australian newspaper stated that only several soldiers and a group of workmen stood outside in light drizzle, but a man and a woman waited in a car in nearby Heathfield Avenue for several hours and drove away at 9.15 a.m. once notice of execution was posted. The man was believed to be Julian, who had spoken with John the night before; the woman was in tears. Both refused to say who they were or why they were there.

Some believed Amery pleaded guilty to spare his family the shame of a trial. Playwright Ronald Harwood, whose *An English Tragedy* covered the last weeks of Amery's life, with Geoffrey

Streatfield playing Amery, on BBC Radio in 2010, disagreed. In his virulent anti-Semitism, Harwood suggested, Amery was revolting against his own background. Leo's mother, Elisabeth Johanna Saphir, was from a Hungarian Jewish family that had converted to Protestantism. Although he had helped draft the Balfour Declaration, which paved the way for the founding of Israel, Leo hid his own Jewish heritage in case it affected his political career. Indeed, it may be why he anglicised his name. This was no doubt wise, because anti-Semitism was rife in Britain at the time, not least among the upper classes.

For John, raised as an upper-class Englishman, it would have confused his very identity to learn this. Certainly, his horrible ideology was genuine and sincere, whatever his reasons for adopting it. Falsely adopting this creed and sticking by it as its proponents went down to defeat was not the conduct of a cynical chancer. Amery was later, albeit loosely, the model for the character of James Deveraux in an episode of the British TV crime drama *Foyle's War*. The character's background and actions are very similar, and he is also sentenced to death, but dramatically freed when it turns out he was an MI9 spy all along.

Julian Amery was eventually elected to Parliament, for Preston North (1950-66) and Brighton Pavilion (1969-92), serving in many ministerial roles. On his retirement, he was ennobled as Lord Amery of Lustleigh and of Brighton. A member of the

Monday Club, he was a strong imperialist and staunchly on the right of the Conservative party on almost all matters but the death penalty. He voted for abolition in the 1960s. "I lost my brother twice," he once said. "When he went over to the Germans and when he was hanged." Their mother reputedly never smiled again after John's execution. She died in 1975, 20 years on from her husband. In 1996, shortly before his own death, Julian was allowed to have John's body exhumed and cremated. The ashes were scattered in France.

9. "It was me and I want to get it off my chest": The murders of Frederick Benjamin Lucas and Cissie Clara Lucas by John Riley Young and 'Cranham', Undercliff Gardens, Leigh-on-Sea, on 6 June 1945 and his execution at HMP Pentonville on 21 December 1945

On Friday 21 December 1945, two men who had been convicted of murder crashed through the floor to their deaths in the execution suite at Pentonville prison, separated in time by 90 minutes. They would have been aware of each other in the condemned cells, even though they were kept apart at all times. Indeed, they had committed their murders only five miles apart on opposite ends of Southend-on-Sea. Otherwise, nothing links the two crimes, which were radically different in nature that calling both murder seems misleading. [10] James McNicol accidentally shot a friend in a drunken rage, for which he was consumed with remorse; John Riley Young callously murdered two people in order to cover up a poorly planned act of embezzlement.

Young, a 40-year-old bachelor, had been one of seven children. His parents were both dead by 1945, his mother dying at 48 from a sebaceous cyst, his father at 61 from a stroke. He worked in the building trade all his life, which probably accounted for his powerful physique. In 1928, he had been convicted or housebreaking and larceny at the Gloucester sessions. Since 1933, he had lodged at Kathleen Orford's house in Belmont Road in Ilford and there are indications that they were very close and probably lovers. He was also involved with his brother's wife, Iris Maud Young, which had caused the couple to split.

According to the *Daily Mirror*, Young spent freely on women and impressing people. Some took him at face value, others "put him down as a romancer", a police report later said. He boasted about his many conquests and his "Hollywood acquaintances", and he was said to resemble the "dark-haired and moustachioed" Leo Carrillo, a Spanish-American actor and comedian who had a prolific film career between 1927 and 1950. Young was certainly able to charm women: Ilford garage owner Ann Watmough, who had also known him for about four years and said he was "a perfect gentleman ... docile and kindly". As it turned out, he was able to convince some men who should have known better too.

Together with Charles Edward Moore, Young ran a small building firm called Moore & Young. It had no regular staff and seldom employed more than a dozen men. By late May 1945, the firm was more than £1,500 overdrawn at the bank because, in the words of a police report, Young, who had sole control, "was playing ducks and drakes with it". He needed cash urgently. Casting about for a solution, he convinced an acquaintance called James Scott to let him sell some jewellery for him. On 26 May, he met Albert Charles Caldwell, a cartage contractor in Chadwell Heath, told him that he had three valuable diamond rings to sell and asked if he knew anyone who might like to buy them.

Caldwell had known Frederick Lucas, a 52-year-old travelling jeweller and wartime special constable, for some years. Indeed, just two weeks before, he had transported Lucas' goods when Lucas and his wife Cissie Clara (née Finch), 50, had moved from Hainault Road in Leytonstone, East London to their new home in Essex. This was a rather run-down coastal bungalow called 'Cranham', with no floor coverings bar some rugs and the hall carpet. It stood almost on the cliff edge in Undercliff Gardens, which runs alongside the coastline in Leigh-on-Sea, a suburb of Southend.

They had three daughters: Mona, 30, who was away serving with the WAAF in India; Doreen, 24, a sergeant in the ATS, who was married to a Regimental Sergeant-Major in the Canadian Army called Thraves; and 17-year-old Eva Rosemary, who still lived with them and worked as a hairdresser at Bearman's on Leyton High Road. Like many jewellers, Lucas dealt in cash and he carried unset diamonds in his jacket pocket, but he was far from rich.

Two days after meeting Young, on 28 May, Caldwell called in at the office Lucas shared with Herbert Francis Smith at 3 Albemarle Way in London and told him about Young's rings. According to Young, Lucas rang him and arranged to come and look at them but said "No! Too dear," when he asked for £280. Whether he ever did and where truth shaded into fantasy are both unclear, though the rings were real enough. Young further claimed that their conversation continued and Lucas, "a cheery, jocular, very nice sort of chap", said that he would pay him £4 in cash for any gold sovereigns he could find. This seemed quite high, he thought, but Lucas assured him he could sell them on for £5.10s each. After that, he said, he heard no more from Lucas.

More probably, however, it was Young whose plausible blarney convinced Lucas that a contact of his called 'Neal' could secure him some gold sovereigns that he could sell on at a profit. 'Neal' did not exist, but Lucas was taken in. On 1 June, he called on Sidney George Gray of Barkingside and mentioned that he was doing a deal for the purchase of 837 sovereigns. Lucas made several phone calls to Young's home in the following days. Also on 1 June, Young called Caldwell asking for Lucas' address, and he also returned the rings to Scott, told him that Lucas had offered £190 for them. It appears his intentions had been to skim some from the top but he now had bigger fish to fry. And, as ever, he was talking too much.

With characteristic grandiosity, Young now bought a car, presumably to impress Lucas with his standing. On 31 May, he approached garage proprietor Francesco Salvadori outside his house in Ilford and asked him if his Cord Sedan was for sale. Salvadori said that it was and a deal was rapidly struck. Next day, after a test drive, Young wrote him a cheque for £1,333 drawn on the business account. It was crossed but opened at Salvadori's request and Young wrote 'Pay cash' on it. The car was delivered next day.

On 3 June, Young went with Moore's wife Ivy to Cranham, where he told her he had some business to do. She waited outside and when he came back half an hour later, he took off his jacket and told her to keep it on her lap "because there's a lot of money in it". Mrs Moore never saw any money but did notice the pockets were bulging. On the morning of 4 June, Lucas called on Hugh Harbour, a pawnbroker in Pentonville Road, and told him he had agreed to buy 1,000 sovereigns for £4,000 and had given him £1,000 as a deposit but had taken no receipt. The deal was due to be completed the next day, he said.

Shortly after, at 11.00 a.m., he asked to borrow £2,400 from Harry Davies to complete a £4,000 deal he was doing on some old gold. Davies could only spare £1,500 and Lucas borrowed the rest from Paul Palestrant, a jeweller in Hatton Gardens. Meanwhile, Young had been putting £500 in notes from Lucas into a newly opened account at Barclay's Bank in East Ham. He told the manager, Thomas Knight, that a Mr Street was investing in the business, and informed him of the cheque he had written to Salvadori and said he would be putting in enough money to cover it later that day. On the strength of that, the cheque was accepted when Salvadori presented it shortly afterwards.

Young then went to Albemarle Way and asked Smith after Lucas, who had not yet arrived. Eventually, they met up and had a drink at the Coach and Horses in Finsbury. Young claimed later that Lucas offered to give him the remaining £900 now and that he initially refused because he was about "to make a clean breast of things" but Lucas insisted. At length, they agreed to meet at Young's office at 4.00 p.m. to meet 'Mr Neal', who would bring the rest of the sovereigns.

Lucas kept the appointment; 'Neal', of course, did not. Despite that, Young claimed, Lucas insisted on leaving the money with him and Young took him to his house, where, as Mrs Orford later agreed, they had a cup of tea and went for a ride in the Cord. Lucas also expressed interest in having Young renovate the outside of his bungalow and build a greenhouse, something that Eva Lucas would later corroborate. They parted on the understanding that Neal would come to his office at 11.00 next morning.

That evening, Young went to Knight's private address and got him to put £550 more into his private account. Next day, 5 June, he went to Ann Watmough's garage to hire a car but she did not have one available that day and he said he would take one on 6 June instead. Perhaps he wanted the crime he was planning to be attributed to someone with a different car to the one he had ostentatiously bought two days previously. Before leaving, he asked if could put some money in her safe as he did not have one. He took out several bundles of £5 notes wrapped in brown paper and asked her daughter Grace to guess how much money there was; Grace said £1,000 and Young said it was actually nearer £2,000, which he had acquired in a business deal. He would pick it up first thing next morning, he said.

Young clearly wanted people to know about the deal, though whether it was part of a plan or just boastfulness is uncertain. Lucas kept the appointment at 11.00 and Young told him that Neal could not get there before 4.00 p.m. He was now worried and looking for an opportunity to confess, he later claimed, though his conduct suggests otherwise. Young drove Lucas to the Old Kent Road and on the way back, to give his story some colour, rang Lucas' office, told Smith he was Mr Neal and could not come until 11.00 a.m. next day.

Lucas was getting worried now. At noon, Albert Caldwell rang him and warned him about doing business with Young. "Thanks for ringing, Albert, but I think you're a bit late, I've already parted with £4,000," Lucas said. This was a huge sum, twice the value of the house he had just bought. At 1.30 p.m., Young claimed, he rang to say that Neal could not be there till the next day, and Lucas suggested he should come to Cranham, take down the particulars for the building work, then drive him and his wife up to London to meet 'Neal'.

Young even engaged with another local builder, John Francis Cooney, to go with him for that purpose. And still Lucas tried to convince himself and others that all was well; in the afternoon, he showed Harbour a receipt for £3,000 on a billhead from Moore & Young. That evening, he told Eva that a man was coming down next day about the decoration, that he had "a smashing car" and she should come too. Thinking this would make her late for work, she declined.

Young was trapped in the web of lies he had spun. That night, he said later, he could not eat or sleep. He had decided to confess all to the Lucases and for this reason, decided not to take Cooney with him. Next morning at 7.15, he collected a Ford Prefect, from Ann Watmough, called Cooney with a story about his car not starting so as to postpone the visit and set off for Cranham alone. Young arrived at about 9.00 and Lucas showed him where he wanted the greenhouse built.

Once he had been admitted inside, Young said that he confessed that the whole scheme was fraudulent. Lucas angrily called him a "twister" and threatened to call the police. "All right, Mr Lucas," he said and made as if to go, but when Lucas grabbed hold of him, he saw red, threw him across the room, then picked up a chair, wrenched off a leg and battered him at least six times about the head, so hard that it broke. "I must have been absolutely crazy," he said later. All this is uncorroborated, of course. Most of the blows were inflicted while Lucas was standing or sitting but one to the left side of his face could have been while he was lying helpless on the floor.

The little finger of his left hand was broken, probably as he tried to defend himself; his skull was fractured and his brain lacerated.

Then Young heard a noise and saw Cissie Lucas, who he struck her three times on the left side of the face and the back of her head, probably from behind. Her skull was also fractured and her brain contused. Cause of death was later put as shock and asphyxia, the latter being the result of blood from her brain injuries flooding into her throat and choking her. Young said that he went into the front room, horrified at what he had done but still furious. There he saw a roll of notes and a pouch of gems in Lucas' pockets. He picked them up, together with a waistcoat watch, a gold cigarette case and some other watches from the roll-top desk but put some of it down again.

The milkman, Bert Dowling, heard people moving about inside but no voices at 9.30 when he passed down the passageway separating Cranham from Alice Stephens' house, Sunnybank. Both Dowling and postman Richard French, who called shortly after noticed, the couple's pet cocker spaniel – which others had heard howling shortly before – was sitting outside at the time but, unusually, was not barking. This was probably the last stages of the killings; Young agreed that he heard the letterbox rattling. Two letters were delivered, which he took with him.

On the way out, according to Molly Lefebure, secretary to the pathologist Professor Keith

Simpson, Young paused to take a swig of milk from a bottle on the doorstep. This left behind a perfect set of fingerprints for Superintendent Fred Cherrill, Scotland Yard's fingerprint expert, had such evidence actually been necessary to convict him. In what the police saw as a badly thought-out attempt to create an alibi, Young knocked on Mrs Stephens' door at about 10.00 a.m. and asked if she knew where the Lucases were. He had a 9.30 appointment with them but was late because the car had broken down, he said. When Stephens said she did not know, he asked her to say that Mr James had called but could not make anyone hear and would come again in the evening.

According to Young, he did this because he thought he thought he would "like to be seen" but when a "very dear old lady" answered the door, he felt unable to alarm her with the truth and made up the story. Stephens noticed him again, knocking at the back door, at this time. (Young later said that he went back because he felt bad about the dog and took it with him, fed it on sandwiches in the car and left it where he knew it would be found. This was, of all places, Barking.) It was only now Young claimed, that he decided to stage a robbery and went back to take some of the items. One of them was a ring from Cissie's finger that he dropped on the way out; a ten-year-old girl found it in the gutter the following evening.

The police later concluded that he had indeed gone back inside and dragged Cissie Lucas by her feet into the hall then, as there were no bloodstains where the body was found. He did this, they surmised, because he had no idea that the couple had a daughter living there and he was trying to prevent the bodies from being discovered too soon.

As he drove back, Young said, his mind was "tortured by the terrible thing he had done". He got back to Ilford at about 11.00 and rang the solicitor who had sent one of the letters, asking Lucas to call on them on 6 or 8 June. Lucas, he told them, would not be able to oblige because he was stricken with pleurisy and might be away for a week. This was presumably another attempt to cover his trail. Finally, he hid the loot in an empty tank in his office, alongside some of Lucas' money. He was back at his lodgings by 1.00 p.m. Kathleen Orford noticed nothing unusual about him when she returned a few minutes later.

At 6.45 p.m., Young called on his sister-in-law Iris at the home of Gladys Bell. It was Bell's birthday and he had taken around a dressed crab for her. Later, he met with her and her husband at the Dick Turpin pub. Unable to refrain from showing off, he showed them the gold cigarette case and a single-stone diamond ring that he said he had bought. Then on the way home, he brandished some £5 and £1 notes at Bell, perhaps to proposition her. She said she was not interested. Between 11.00 and 12.00 that night, he rang Cooney and said that the job was all off because the people in Southend had gone off in holiday.

Meanwhile, Eva Lucas had returned home at about 6.40 p.m. The front door was locked and all the windows were secure, bar a casement window in Cissie's bedroom through which she managed to get in. As she went into the hall, she stumbled over her mother's blood-soaked body, lying on an eiderdown with a coat over her head. Cissie was already cold to the touch and there was a large wound to her left temple. A neighbour heard Eva's cries for help and called the police. Richard French, who had returned with the parcel, went with her to the sitting room, where her father was lying on his back against the door, covered by hearth rug and with a green cushion on his head, his face covered in blood. Both rooms were "littered with smashed glass and damaged furniture".

A police surgeon, Dr Norman Newman, who happened to live nearby, confirmed that this was murder and the local constabulary soon called in Scotland Yard. Chief Inspector A.H. Philpott and Detective Sergeant David Hislop were summoned to the scene, where they found clues from fingerprints on smashed glass bottles and a ring found on the doorstep. Glasses were found that had contained whisky, suggesting that the murderer had been a guest; moreover, there was no sign of a forced entry other than the one made by Eva. Several bloodstained heel prints, with the letters DARD clearly visible, were found in the dining room and scullery.

Professor Simpson arrived at 12.30 p.m. the next day and carried out the post mortems with Dr Newman. From taking body temperatures, he estimated that Frederick had been dead for over 24 hours but Cissie for no more than 20, putting her death in the time frame of 4.30-6.30 p.m. She had lain dying for many hours. Frederick's watch face was smashed and stopped at exactly 9.00 a.m. It seemed likely that this showed the time he was being attacked because there were scratches and bruises on the back of his hands where he had tried to protect himself. He had suffered severe brain lacerations and probably died soon after this time.

Writing it up later, Philpot and Inspector J.B. Thompson concluded that the murders were "carried out with cold-blooded savagery, as the concluded act of a confidence trick ... It is obvious that Young hoped by disposing of Mr and Mrs Lucas to escape his obligation and prevent his being prosecuted, that the brutality of the crime was not sufficient, he was callous enough to rob both of their personal belongings while they lay dead or dying."

A telegram was found in Frederick Lucas' coat pocket reading 'Ring Ilford 2347, 10 a.m. Young', showing that Young had an appointment with the Lucases that day. They called at his lodgings on 7 June but he was out. When he called at 10.00 a.m., Kathleen Orford told him of this and he said he would return within 30 minutes but he did not. Instead, at 11.20, he rang Lucas' office posing as his solicitor and asked for Lucas. It was thus that he learned that the bodies had been found.

Young went next to his bank to sign a credit slip for the amounts he had already deposited and paid £550 more into his business account. By now, he claimed, he was so stressed that he decided to kill himself. He went back, kissed Orford goodbye at 12.15 p.m. and returned the car to a garage in Barking, saying it had failed to start and he would send a mechanic round in the morning. At 1.30, he went to 217 Morley Road in Barking, where his sister, Joan Eileen Weeder, lived with her sister-in-law, Mary Ann Weeder, and Mary's brother Arthur, who was also temporarily without a place to stay. Both their husbands were away on war service.

Young asked to stay for a while, lying that he had had an argument with Orford and Iris Young, he was tired of their nagging and wanted to get away from them. A big business deal was about to come off, he said, and he would "see her all right". No doubt she had heard these wild tales before. The police regarded this as a move to keep off the scene while still being able to find out what was going on. Joan noticed that he seemed worried and complained of a headache and a sore throat. At 8.30 p.m., she accompanied him to a telephone box to make a call, in which she overheard him give his name as Mr Staines and say: "I mislaid your number but Mr Young gave it to me". She did not know or ask who the call was made to.

Young's house of cards was about to topple. At 10.00 p.m., he rang Kathleen Orford and she told him two police officers had been round looking for him again. Now he knew the game was up and he scribbled out a will in a pocketbook. In it, he left everything to Orford, "the finest and best little woman in the world who has always tried to guide me in the right way" and signed off: "Goodbye everybody. It is better this way. John R. Young". That night, as he slept on the kitchen floor with Arthur Weeder, he attempted to kill himself by blocking up the chimney with Joan's clothes and turning the gas on. There was not enough pressure. Next, he tried putting his head in a pillow with the gas on. That failed too. Weeder was woken up and he told Young to pull himself together.

Instead, Young went for a walk and slashed his wrists with a razor in an Anderson shelter but succeeded only in losing a lot of blood. Next morning, 8 June, Joan later said, her brother continued to act in a "queer" way and she noticed that his wrists were bandaged. He said he had cut them on the fence in the back alley. At about 11.30, he went back into the house and tried to gas himself again by breaking a pipe in the back bedroom and sticking it in his mouth. Joan's daughter Mary Ann found him and Weeder carried him to the back garden. Inspector George Smith and Sergeant Barr arrived to find him lying there semi-conscious. Barr carried out artificial respiration and a search found £114.10s in notes and Frederick Lucas' business card.

Young was taken by ambulance to Oldchurch Hospital in Romford. After he left, Weeder found another rolled-up bundle of notes in the wardrobe. Dr Hedyatollah, the senior casualty officer on duty, noted that Young had three long wounds on his left wrist and one on his right, possibly inflicted with a pocket knife. While there, he made another attempt to kill himself by drawing a pair of scissors in this throat. Barr had to come running when the call of 'Police!' went up and found Young struggling with four nurses. He succeeded only in making three or four scratches to his throat.

At 9.00 a.m. on 9 June, Philpott, Detective Inspector Harris and Detective Inspector David Hislop of Scotland Yard went to the hospital again to interview Young. As they approached his bed, he blurted out: "I've been expecting you. It was me and I want to get it off my chest". Both his trousers and shirt were covered in dry blood, they noted. Young's wounds were dressed again and he was taken to East Ham Police Station to make a characteristically verbose statement. The police visited his business premises, where they found a bundle of 79 £5 notes, 21 rings in a suede poach, the gold cigarette case, six bags of gemstones, two gold pocket watches, two gold wristwatches and other goods traceable to the Lucases in the tank.

When Philpott noticed a cut on Young's left index finger and a missing piece of skin on another, he said: "I got those at the bungalow". Of a large bruise on his right temple, he added: "I got that when I tried to do myself in". After he made a further statement, Harris told him that he would be taken to Southend to be charged and he said: "I'm terribly sorry it happened. I'm at a loss to understand how it happened." There, he gave a third statement and Harris charged him with murder. Once again, he said he was bewildered at what had happened. Young's shoes matched the prints at the scene and it was soon established that he had left several more clues, including his hair on Frederick Lucas' shirt and cuff links and a button from his own trouser fly.

That afternoon, Young appeared before a specially convened magistrates' court to hear evidence of arrest and be remanded. He was granted legal aid. The *Southend Standard* described him as "stockily built and dark-complexioned … dressed in a well-cut brown pinstriped suit with a light brown open-neck shirt". He was clearly in quite a state, with his bloodshot eyes, his wrist in a bandage and bruises on his forehead. His next hearing was before magistrates at Southend again on 11 June, when Eva Lucas had to give evidence of how she found the bodies. Further appearances took place on 15 June and 6 July, when pieces of broken furniture wrapped in transparent paper were exhibited and Eva was ordered to look at him to see if she could identify him. She turned her head slowly, then said: "Dad had so many friends, I cannot remember seeing him before".

Young appeared yet again on 17 July and 30 July, when the local press reported 'sensational evidence' was heard, possibly relating to the attempted suicides. There was certainly a moment of low comedy, when Mary Ann Weeder was asked if the £50 found in the house might be hers and she said: "I wish it was". The defence also tried and failed at this stage to get Young's statement describing the murders ruled inadmissible on the grounds that he had not been cautioned before he made it and was in no fit state to make it anyway, since he had attempted suicide, lost a lot of blood and had little sleep or food before being subject to medical procedures and then being brought to the station. Eva Lucas reportedly fled in tears as the horrific details were read out.

Once again, on 7 August, Young appeared in court in Southend, "with his right eye covered by a black shade and his left arm in a sling". His statement was read out and Philpott described what he had found in the bungalow on 7 June and his encounter with Young at the hospital. After a ten-minute adjournment when Young "showed signs of fatigue", he was committed for trial at the next Chelmsford Assizes. Mr Justice Lewis presided at the trial on 8-9 November and John Flowers KC led for the prosecution. No attempt was made to deny that he had committed the killings. Instead, it was argued, in the legal terminology of the days before diminished responsibility was recognised in law, that he was "guilty but insane".

After the prosecution evidence established the facts, Young's counsel J.P. Eddy KC called him to the witness box. "This is the happiest day of my life. All I want to do is admit the crime. I want only to fight the slur on those who will bear the name after me," he began in his weirdly grandiose way. "I want you to believe that the man who stands here charged with murder and admits that murder is not the man who committed it. It is the frame of a man into whose body a demon had been created as the result of the struggle between us."

Describing the killing, he said that he had told Lucas of his swindle and Lucas flew into a temper. "I felt an impact at the back of my head. I went into a frenzy; I cannot express what happened inside me. I am not really a murderer. He struggled and I kept hitting him. He fell to his knees. Blindly, I struck him again. I felt as though I was striking an army. I am a man whom cruel fate had changed for a few brief moments through a series of circumstances to a person who had no control over himself." And what about Cissie Lucas, one might ask?

Young went on that this was "the finest day" for him, after months of mental agony, that he was not afraid of death and he "concluded his passionate utterances with an expression of thanks for 'very fine, fair British justice'". It was a bravura performance but cross-examination soon exposed the sordid motive. "Did you realise that you had battered Lucas to death?" Flowers asked him. "Yes, but it was all so hazy," Young answered. "It started when I felt a hit on the back of my head. Someone seemed to be pulling my hair."

Evidence was brought forward of repeated suicide attempts, a violent attack on his sister-in-law and a history of mental illness in his family that had affected four close relatives. As a teenager, it was stated, Young suffered two head injuries, one at school and one when he was hit by a tramcar in the street. Dr J. Lovell Barnes, a Harley Street specialist in nervous and mental disorders was brought to the stand after – extraordinary though it seems – examining Young during the lunch break. His opinion was that Young was temporarily insane at the time he committed the crime and would not have had control of his actions.

Lewis, however, replied, "The law does not say that because a person loses control, he is insane" and when Flowers asked, "This man lost his temper?", Lovell Barnes could only agree. Home Office psychiatrists said that Young was sane and two prison medical officers who had supervised him in prison – Dr R.G. Lyster at HMP Chelmsford and Dr Hugh Grierson at HMP Brixton – both said they found no evidence of insanity in his behaviour. Young "seemed perfectly normal, and was rational in his conversation", they agreed. After final speeches and a 45-minute summing up on the second day, the jury, who had to make the decision based on Young's mental state at the time of the murders, were sent out. They found him guilty after one hour of deliberation.

Now that the system was apparently ready to oblige him, he said, "Thank you, sir" and smiled at the court after Lewis sentenced him to death. Despite this, he lodged an appeal on 16 November. The Court of Criminal Appeal dismissed it and a medical panel found that, although he was emotionally unstable, he was neither mentally deficient nor insane in law. The Home Secretary, James Chuter Ede ruled that Young may not have gone to the house with the intention of murder but that his act of killing Cissie Lucas to eliminate a witness and the actions he took to evade detection, however ham-fisted, suggested that he was sane.

Young was hanged by Albert Pierrepoint, assisted by Steve Wade, at 8.00 a.m. on 21 December. Alexander Riley – or Herbert Morris, in alternative accounts - was also apparently there, probably because two men were being executed in quick succession. The main road outside the prison gates was reportedly deserted when a few minutes later, a warder came out and put up the usual notice on the prison wall that Young had been "executed according to law". It was signed by Sir Adam B. Ritchie, High Sheriff of Essex, the prison surgeon, Dr H.P. Young, and the chaplain. More people were waiting 90 minutes later, when McNicol followed him to the gallows.

After the murder, Charles Moore, not surprisingly, changed the company name to Charles Edwards & Sons and carried on in the building trade. He lived on until 1976 and his much younger wife lived to 2002 but they never mentioned the matter to their two sons, who were respectively born shortly before and after the murders took place. Many descendants of both murderer and victims still lived in the area in 2009, when an online chat board put them and in touch with each other. One of Moore's sons, Steve, moved with his family to a house a very short distance from Undercliff Gardens in 1979.

Eva Lucas later married and had at least two children. She was still living in 2009, aged 83. Her youngest daughter, Joy Middleton, stated at that time that her mother "still mourns", as well she might, given the trauma she went through on that awful day when her parents were so brutally taken away from her. Another local man recalled in that year that, "when I was a little kid … we used to call it the haunted bungalow and dare each other to open the gate and walk down the steps and then onto the boarded walk, and very scary it was, too."

10. "This is the first mistake he ever made in his life": The killing of Sergeant Donald Alfred Richard Kirkaldie in a hut at the AA gun site at Thorpe Bay, Essex, by Sergeant James McNicol on 16 August 1945 and his execution at HMP Pentonville on 21 December 1945

Two men went to the gallows at HMP Pentonville in North London on Friday 21 December, who had killed at opposite ends of Southend-on-Sea in Essex. The first was [9] John Riley Young at 8.00 a.m. for a double murder in Leigh-on-Sea. His body was then removed, the trapdoors were reset and the gallows prepared for James McNicol's execution at 9.30. Hanging them separately rather than side by side was a matter for the sheriff in charge to decide. It was not unknown for two men sentenced for different crimes to be hanged together for the sake of convenience and why it was done or not done in any given case was never publicly disclosed.

One hopes McNicol had been removed from his cell and allowed out somewhere for exercise so that he could not hear the booming sound that echoed around the prison as Young plunged to his death. Beyond the fact that they were both tried at Chelmsford and executed at Pentonville, there was nothing much in common between the two cases. Young had callously slain an acquaintance whom he had swindled of £3,000 in order to stop him from going to the police, as well as the man's wife, who would have been a witness. McNicol, though certainly guilty of manslaughter at the very least, was arguably the victim of very harsh justice. Extensive research by his great-niece, Elaine Merrilees, has brought much of this back to light after it had faded from memory.

McNicol was a working-class lad from Dechmont Street in Motherwell, near Glasgow, with three brothers and two sisters. He was born in 1918 and grew up in poverty during the depression of the 1930s. Both of his parents were dead by 1945. His oldest brother, Robert, had helped him to get a job with Motherwell Bridgework, where he worked as a welding inspector, and generally played the father's role.

Before and during the early stages of the war, James had a girlfriend called Alice Barrett and some of her letters to him have survived. He was keen on marrying her, but there was an obstacle. She was from a Catholic family, while his family were not just Protestants but heavily involved in the culture of masonic lodges and the Orange Order. Even though he was prepared to convert to Catholicism, her parents were implacably opposed to the match. Alice, while fond of him, had misgivings based as much on his temper as his background; indeed, he was once in trouble with the police for an altercation with Alice's father, which cannot have helped his cause.

The war taking him away gave her the occasion to tell him to take time to think over things. She still wrote to him. Revealingly, one of her letters reads: "One girl in the factory said I was a fool to have gave [*sic*] you up. I know I was. She always said I looked so happy whenever she saw me with you and she would like to get hold of a fellow like the one I had. A lot of the girls at the factory think you were a nice fellow, but they don't know what a temper you have, do they?" The relationship eventually fizzled out.

McNicol signed up at the start of World War II, aged 21, and served with enough distinction in the Royal Artillery at Dunkirk and in West Africa and Burma that he was promoted to sergeant in August 1944. At some point after this, he contracted malaria and was invalided out of service. By August 1945, he was serving in a heavy anti-aircraft battery at St Augustine's Avenue, on the site of what is now Thorpe Bay Gardens on the outskirts of Southend-on-Sea. This was the northernmost of a long string of batteries overseen by the 37th AA Brigade running north from Dagenham on the Thames Estuary. They guarded such key sites as the ammunition stores at Purfleet, Coryton refinery and Tilbury docks. This particular battery was manned continuously until 1946, although the brigade there changed often. The officers and troops associated with it are now commemorated by a memorial at St Augustine's Church.

At the end of the war, the 494th AA Battery was posted there. McNicol shared one of the Nissen huts with five others, including two of the same rank: Leonard William Cox from Hornsey in North London and Donald Alfred Richard Kirkaldie from

Ramsgate in Kent. The three were on friendly terms with each other, at least at the outset. Kirkaldie, also 27 at the time, was born in September 1918 and served with the Royal Artillery 143 (M)HAA Regiment. Before the war he had worked for Alfred Olby, a builders' merchant, and served in the Territorial Army but had not been called up for medical reasons and served as a sergeant-instructor instead. He married Irene Griggs in late 1939 and they had a four-year-old daughter, Patricia.

While less well remembered than VE Day on 8 May 1945, VJ Day on 15 August, commemorating victory over Japan, was also a joyous occasion that prompted celebrations all over the country. Everyone who had served in arms could now expect to return home to normal life. At Thorpe Bay, like many others, the commanding officer, Captain Edmund Roxby, gave permission to hold a bonfire followed by a dance in the evening.

McNicol, alas, was not much in the mood. The night before, he had had a tiff with Private Jean Evelyn Neale of the Auxiliary Territorial Service (ATS), who he had been seeing casually for a week. They had been up together the previous night until 4.30 a.m. and he had asked her to go into an empty ATS hut for what was coyly described in court as a "flirtation". When she refused, he threw her handbag on the floor and said: "Well, go back to the hut". "That's the last of you," she told him.

McNicol began drinking at the Halfway House pub on the Southend esplanade during the afternoon of

15 August, along with Cox and three others, then carried on in the evening. They may each have sunk as many as 17 pints of beer by the time they returned to camp at about 10.00 p.m. Some more was apparently brought back with him. Exactly how much McNicol had to drink is uncertain, but it was enough to make him riotously drunk and prone to irrational behaviour because of his internal rage at being rejected. It also means that Cox's police statement, taken the day after, might be drawn from an impaired memory.

During the bonfire, McNicol asked Neale if she was going on to the dance and she said she did not know, but in the end she did go. Trouble duly ensued at about 11.00 p.m., when Cox and Leading Aircraftsman Gerald McKay, who lived locally and had been invited along, left the sergeants' mess. They had taken the remains of the six quarts the first group had bought from here and moved on to the NAAFI, the recreational hub for the junior ranks. Here, Cox and McKay met and danced with Neale and another ATS girl, 'Ginger' Searle.

McNicol was angry at seeing 'his' girl with another man, who appeared to be a 'civvy' because he was not in uniform. He threw a glass of beer over them both as they stopped to let him pass by. McKay challenged him to explain why he had done this and McNicol said: "I threw it. Do you want to make something of it?" Neale told Cox, who came out and also asked McNicol why he had done it, and McNicol allegedly replied: "I don't like him and I don't like you. I never have done." Cox retorted that "if I wasn't frightened of losing my chevrons [i.e. being demoted], I would do something about it". Others intervened to stop a fight but McNicol said he was willing to go outside and sort it out later.

Finally, after the dance ended, McKay and Cox walked Neale and her friends back to their huts. Cox then went to his own hut at about 12.30 a.m. Kirkaldie and two others were already in bed. He found that his bed had been overturned and his blankets thrown around, no doubt as a childish prank. When McNicol came in, Cox challenged him and further threats were exchanged. However, Cox refused to go outside and fight and McNicol would not fight inside. Instead, McNicol went back to the mess. Shortly after, he sent Bombardier Alley with a message to Cox, asking him to come for a drink.

Cox went but declined the drink, said he would see McNicol in the morning, then returned to the hut, with Kirkaldie. They tied the door handle to the bedsteads with some rope to ensure that McNicol could not open it and went back to bed. McNicol's own account of the altercation was similar but he added that during their stand-off, it was Cox who told him that he disliked him and always had done. In addition, he claimed, it was Cox who was up for fighting in the dancehall and had later told him that he (Cox) would kill him if he had not been due for discharge in three weeks. McNicol added that either Cox or Alley called him a "mad bastard" when he went to find matches to light a cigarette, and that

Cox and Kirkaldie found him and continued the abuse.

Not long after, the occupants of the hut were woken by a door rattling, followed by the sound of a window being broken. Then the light was switched on from the outside. Two shots were fired, the first hitting and slightly wounding Cox in the chest. The second struck Kirkaldie in the throat and passed right through his neck. The others inside were roused but in the chaos McNicol escaped. Captain John Owen arrived at the hut at 3.15 a.m. to find Kirkaldie slumped in a half-sitting position on his bed, his lower jaw shattered by the bullet. Cox was lying on the floor, a second bullet close by him. Inspector Hemson was called to the scene of the killing at 3.45. Cox was taken to Southend General Hospital in a serious condition but later recovered. Kirkaldie was stone dead.

Another soldier who spoke to Elaine Merrilees anonymously, backed up most of the details of McNicol's account in terms of the dispute with McKay, who, he also said, left the dance soon after it, and about Cox's aggressive behaviour afterwards. McNicol, he told her, was trying to avoid confrontation with Cox but even as he went to leave, Cox said: "You had better let your family know that you won't be coming home and sleep with one eye open, as I intend to finish this later". This supported McNicol's own claim later that Cox had sworn at him and said he would kill him "if I hadn't another three weeks to do in the Army". That appeared to be an implied threat to kill or injure McNicol that riled him into another set of fisticuffs, which Kirkaldie and others broke up.

McNicol stormed off, the anonymous soldier's account continues. He found McNicol in the mess and calmed him down, only for Cox to come in and confront him once more about the overturning of his bed. This time, McNicol invited him to step outside to fight but Cox retorted that this was not the time or place and said he would file a complaint with the commanding officer in the morning. He then slammed the mess door so hard on his way out that it came off its hinges. This man, who gave statements to the police and officers, was not called to testify at the trial, added that McNicol was certainly not one to shy away from conflict but also said he was "a genuine nice chap and his actions that night were hard to believe".

Fearing at least being beaten up in the morning or not wanting to appear afraid of Cox, McNicol later said that he decided he would have to "have a good hit at him that night or the men would think I was afraid of him". While wandering about, he entered the command post and saw some Lee Enfield rifles, took one and returned to camp. This post was not as secure as it was meant to be and most of the troops knew as much. Any sergeant could access the key, which was kept in the front office. McNicol knew where to find a gun and he had a clip of five rounds of ammunition on him, which was against rules. He had also taken a short bayonet from his kitbag in case Cox "got nasty" again and had fixed it to the rifle. Unquestionably, he was armed, dangerous and spoiling for trouble.

"I had no intention of killing him but I wanted to wound him," McNicol claimed later. "I broke the window and could not draw back. I tried to shoot Cox in the leg. I tried the rifle two or three times. I was dazed then. I knew I had done wrong" – though at the time, he always claimed, he was not aware of exactly what he had done. In a daze, he walked away, buried the rifle in a field behind the coastguard station, where it was found a week later using a metal detector; its bolt was drawn and the breech and magazine were full of soil. He headed to the seafront, where he washed his face and his cut hand and threw his boots over a hedge for no reason he could explain, then slept fully clothed in a bed in the sergeants' hut at another gun site by Butler's Farm in Rochford.

The police found him wandering on the esplanade at 5.40 a.m., cautioned him and took him to the Southend Central Police Station. At the time, Hemson said later, he seemed to be "in a normal condition", though he must have been dreadfully hung over. At any rate, he was allowed to sleep some more before Detective Inspector Harris interviewed him. He declined to wait when offered, saying: "I had a good sleep this afternoon, and I want to tell you all about it now". He then made a statement. When charged with the murder, he said: "All I say is I didn't know I had killed Kirkaldie".

He made his first appearance before magistrates on 18 August and was remanded in custody for ten days.

Poignantly, Irene Kirkaldie, who had seen her husband for the last time the previous weekend, was in London to witness the VJ Day celebrations and returned home to Ramsgate on 16 August to have the news broken to her. The following Monday, 20 August, she received a letter from him that had been delayed in the post. In the interim, police surgeon Dr H.P. Hiscocks carried out a post mortem, establishing that the bullet had penetrated Kirkaldie's mouth from side to side, via the floor of the mouth below his tongue. The lower jaw had been blown to pieces. There was also a wound between the thyroid gland and the lower jaw. Death was due to shock and haemorrhage. It was probably instantaneous. Kirkaldie was buried at Ramsgate cemetery on 23 August. Six sergeants from his unit were the pallbearers and a large crowd looked on as the coffin, covered with a Union Jack, was carried to the grave. Among the tributes, the press recorded, was a basket of flowers inscribed 'To my darling daddy, from his little Pats'.

According to Elaine Merrilees, the McNicols were not worried at the first reports they heard. His brother Robert knew that James could never handle his drink, was prone to getting into fights when drunk and had spent the night sleeping off a hangover in a cell more than once. When they heard the full details, they were stunned. The name

Kirkaldie was familiar to them from James' letters describing him as a good friend. While McNicol awaited trial, Robert and his other siblings visited him.

Aided by money from his masonic lodge and other local sympathisers, Robert spent much of his time going back and forth to London. James, according to Elaine Merrilees, "could barely contain his remorse for what he had done, for the shame he had brought upon his family, nor his own grief for Donald Kirkaldie, a man who for the past two years had been his loyal friend and confidant". Robert also wrote to Irene Kirkaldie to express the family's sorrow about what had happened and she apparently replied with a "kind" letter. Others in the regiment were also sympathetic, despite their own grief at Kirkaldie's death, one sergeant describing McNicol as a "damn good soldier."

McNicol was tried for murder and attempted murder before Mr Justice Lewis at the Essex Assizes in Chelmsford on 13-14 November. Press reports at the time described him as "a short, sturdy figure in uniform", "a stockily built man, with his fair hair brushed back from his high forehead". Cecil Havers KC appeared for the prosecution, Tristram Beresford KC for the defence. Cox, by then demobilised, and Neale both appeared as prosecution witnesses. They gave accounts that did not materially differ from McNicol's, other than that Cox denied making any threat to kill, whereas

McNicol said that he had, and he agreed "that there was a lot of unpleasantness".

Describing the moment when he was shot, Cox said: "I saw the muzzle of a rifle put through the window. Then I heard an explosion. It felt as if I had been kicked by a horse." No doubt mortified at having to talk about her sex life in court, Neale told the story of their brief courtship and how it had ended; McNicol, she said, had no reason to be jealous of either Cox or Kirkaldie on her account. A bombardier testified that he did not think McNicol looked drunk at the dance, though he "had a strange grin on his face", while Hemson said that he appeared to be recovering from the effects of drink when found on the esplanade and seemed "quite self-possessed".

Answering questions from Beresford "clearly, in a firm voice", McNicol recounted his version. He claimed that he had found the door locked at the hut and became angry – this is why he fired the second shot, he said. Both shots were "fired wildly" into the hut, with no intention to kill. Under cross-examination, he admitted he intended to shoot Cox, though not to kill him; that he had both ammunition and a bayonet; that he intended to use it if he could find Cox; that he had been feeling "very angry against Cox"; and that he only found himself at the armoury by chance when the idea came to him to take the rifle in case Cox started anything.

How would he do that, asked Havers. "By firing at his legs?" McNicol said. "Why did you switch on the light?" "So that I should not hit him in a dangerous spot?" And why had he fired a second shot? "To scare the others in the hut." Havers homed in. "You deliberately fired a shot into a hut in which there were six men?" Yes, McNicol admitted. "Didn't it occur to you that you might hit one of them?" No, he replied. All this was completely implausible and cannot have made a good impression on the jury.

Beresford asked for a verdict of manslaughter on the grounds that McNicol was too drunk to form any intention of killing anyone. Lewis's summing-up was favourable to the defence and he noted that there was no evidence of any hostility from McNicol towards Kirkaldie. Nonetheless, the jury of ten men and two women convicted him of murder. The strain clearly told on one of the men, who collapsed and had to be helped out of court. Lewis duly sentenced McNicol to death. "Thank you, my lord," he said in a firm tone of voice, then turned smartly around and ran down the steps to the holding cell.

McNicol was kept at HMP Wormwood Scrubs, which was not a hanging jail, while he lodged an appeal on 16 November, the same day as Young. This was heard before three Lords Justices of Appeal in Ordinary on 5 December. Counsel reiterated the defence that he was so far under the influence of alcohol as to be incapable of forming any intention to murder. Mr Justice Humphreys agreed that McNicol clearly was drunk and motivated by his quarrel with Cox. Nonetheless he had plainly gone to the hut intending to do someone an injury and this had caused a man to die, which was murder in law. Thus, there was no misdirection of the jury and no grounds on which to overturn the conviction.

The McNicol family now swung into action. His sisters Mary and Ann stood in Motherwell High Street seeking signatures for a petition for clemency, younger brothers Richard and Andrew did the same in Wishaw and Robert and a school friend went door to door throughout Lanarkshire every night after work. Despite the sectarian divide in the region, some 20,700 people signed it, about half of the population of the burgh of Motherwell & Wishaw. They included the provost, magistrates and councillors of the burgh, ministers, businessmen and professionals, his schoolmates and his work companions.

All the officers and men of 494th HAA Battery signed it too. The petition cited multiple grounds McNicol's "unassuming and blameless character" before joining the Army; the attack of malaria in the Far East and the possible accentuation of the effects of alcohol by the quinine he had taken; his very drunken state on the night of the killing, so much that "he was temporarily near to insanity"; that Kirkaldie was a friend of his, so that premeditation was not a factor; that he was "a war hero and much loved and respected in his hometown and within the ranks of his regiment"; the sorrow it would cause to his family and friends; and, the fact that it occurred on VJ Day, "when some indulgence in alcohol was general". The local MP, Alex Anderson, was particularly active and went with W.E. Currie of the Scottish Union of Ex-Servicemen & Women to meet Home Secretary James Chuter Ede to ask for the case to be reviewed. He remained a friend of Robert McNicol afterwards.

McNicol himself wrote a moving petition to Chuter Ede, saying that he was well aware that he was "guilty of a terrible tragedy and must in some way be punished", and that nothing he could say or do would alter the sufferings of Kirkaldie's loved ones. Drunkenness, he agreed, was "no defence in law for what I did", but "had I been my usual sober self, nothing would have been further from my mind than to harm any living soul, least of all this, my great friend", with whom he had no quarrel.

"Indeed, I must have been in a hopeless state prior to the incident and have little or no recollection of what happened. I must have been in a very fuddled state of mind, and quite irresponsible. In that abnormal state of mind, I must have taken a rifle and fired it into the hut. The shouts and screams after the incident made me run away, and it was some time before I sobered up and realised that something was wrong." He begged for a reprieve "so that I can in some small way atone for the past and bring some compensation to the innocent persons whom I have wronged. If this reprieve was forthcoming, I swear that during the years of my imprisonment I would do all in my power to rehabilitate myself, and thus to atone for the past. I therefore fervently hope and pray that you will spare my life so that I can be given the opportunity to prove to all concerned that I can be a decent and law-abiding citizen."

Chuter Ede looked in detail at both petitions and the grounds Anderson set forth but wrote on 18 December that he could not find sufficient grounds for a reprieve. An article in the *Motherwell Times* asserts that McNicol made a last, desperate attempt to die on his own terms. Together with Young, he was scheduled to be transported to Pentonville after dark on Thursday 20 December, the day before the execution. Just after lunch, he asked for permission from the guard who was with him at all times to go into the attached toilet cabinet. While the guard stood by the half-closed door with his foot in the entrance, McNicol sprang to the top of the cistern, six feet off the ground, so as to fling himself head first to the concrete floor. A slight noise alerted the guard, who jumped inside the cabinet and "was only just in time to grab the frenzied man's legs and save him from at least inflicting grave injury upon himself and most likely killing himself. McNicol fought desperately while being dragged to safety."

When this was relayed to the governor, he decided to transport McNicol to HMP Pentonville straight away "where he could be kept under even closer guard during his last hours". This story shows as well as any the bureaucratic horror of the death penalty in action: a prison warder, on pain of disciplinary action, had to act to stop a man from killing himself so that the state ccould do it instead the next day, and the authorities reorganised their plans to ensure that this happened.

That same afternoon, Robert McNicol visited his brother for the last time. Elaine Merrilees wrote that he "seemed to have accepted his fate and said that he hoped his execution would bring some solace to Donald's family. He again apologised for the shame he had brought upon the family and once again begged forgiveness, he had written letters to each of his brothers and sisters reconciling any and all disagreements they had had in the past". According to the *Motherwell Times*, McNicol "remained restless" all night but "had calmed considerably" by 9.30 when he was hanged by Albert Pierrepoint assisted by Herbert Morris (or Alexander Riley in some accounts) and Steve Wade.

Most of the family remained in Motherwell but Robert stayed outside the prison, alongside his brother-in-law, Private Robert Wardrope, who was wearing khaki battledress. When the notice of execution, signed by Sir Adam B. Ritchie, High Sheriff of Essex, the prison surgeon, Dr H.P. Young, and the chaplain, was put up, Robert "showed signs of deep distress". He turned to the reporter and said: "This is the first mistake he ever made in his life, and this is what they have done to him. I tried to see the Home Secretary in a last effort to save my brother's life, but I was told this was impossible. More than 20,000 people in Motherwell signed a petition asking for a reprieve."

Robert knocked at the door, his eyes filling up with tears, and asked if he could see the chaplain to know James's last words. The warder who answered said that this was not usual and the chaplain was not available. Wardrope added that in his view: "The English law is all wrong. I feel sure that if my brother-in-law had been tried in Scotland, he would not have been condemned to death for something that he did after he had been drinking heavily ... I fully expected the jury to bring in a verdict of manslaughter." They then walked away.

It was not until ten days later, 31 December, that the *Motherwell Times* learned of a report that was commissioned by the defence but came too late to be used in the trial. This confirmed that malaria sufferers were known to suffer mental blackouts if they mixed too much alcohol with their quinine. In early January, the McNicol Petition Committee posted an ad in the *Motherwell Times*, thanking those who "gave so much time and sympathy" in the fight for a reprieve on behalf of the relatives and friend, particularly noting Stirling and the men of 494th AA Battery.

According to Elaine Merrilees, Robert McNicol gathered the family together on his return home, said they were never to speak about James or his crime, then destroyed all the photos of him in the family album. He had personally promised his mother that he would look after his siblings before she died and felt he had let her down. He spent much time walking alone with his thought or at his mother's grave in Motherwell cemetery. Although he remained a patriotic royalist, his faith in British justice never recovered until he died, aged 79, in 1994. On another note, a Southend psychic attempted a 'psychological investigation' at the supposed site on the seventy-fifth anniversary of the murders, seeking to speak to Kirkaldie's spirit. It is all on YouTube if you like that sort of thing.

11. "The other one hit him when I was holding him": The murder of Captain John Alexander Ritchie by Robert Blaine and Charles Connelly in Bourchier Street, Soho, London on 14 September 1945 and the execution of Blaine at HMP Pentonville on 29 December 1945

Like a lot of servicemen waiting to go home after the end of the war, Captain John Alexander Ritchie, 41, of the Canadian Army would have relished a good night out in London in the late summer of 1945. He had survived the conflict unharmed and there was a whole life to look forward to once he was back home. Soho was a natural choice. Despite the privations of war, it was still home to many restaurants, pubs, theatres and cinemas that kept the nightlife going after the market stalls had packed up for the day. The Windmill Theatre, later immortalised in the feature film *Mrs Henderson Presents*, famously remained open throughout the war, offering static, tastefully posed nudes to sex-starved men of all ages.

For those who wanted to do more than look, Soho was also the place to go. Wartime always creates a boom in prostitution and the number of prostitutes in London had probably been growing even before this. The London School of Economics' New London Survey of Life & Labour estimated that the total grew from about 3,000 in 1931 to 6,700 in 1946. Working girls were effectively free to parade on the street – mainly in and around Old Compton Street – right up until 1959, when the Street

Offences Act made life harder for them. Compared to the women who were 'making do and mending', the well-dressed, highly made-up prostitutes must have seemed exotic indeed, not least to the American GIs who could readily afford their services.

Such an area also brings dangers. The 'Blackout Ripper', Gordon Cummins, plied his dreadful trade in and around the district in 1942; one of his victims, Evelyn Oatley, was murdered in her own flat in Soho. There were several more murders of prostitutes around the area during the war that police attributed to soldiers, usually American, which were never solved. The years after the war saw a spate of murders of prostitutes, none of which was ever solved. With prostitutes came pimps, as well as volatile young men and villains of every type. Assorted spivs and black marketers were also rife in an area that had been one of the murkier parts of London for centuries. Not that Soho was massively more dangerous than the streets of many other large cities, but it was also a place that had more than its share of serious crime in the 1940s. What drew Captain Ritchie in that night will remain unknown; it has been suggested that his intentions were homosexual in nature. Either way, they are unlikely to have been entirely respectable.

Ritchie himself originally hailed from the tiny settlement of Roseisle, Manitoba, and had later moved to Morrisburg, Ontario. His parents, Alexander H. Ritchie and Euphemia Gibb, were first generation Scottish immigrants. They had borne tragedy before. Their first son Thomas, who was born in Scotland in 1895, served in 2nd Battalion of Canadian Infantry Eastern Ontario Regiment in World War I and was lost without trace in an attack west of Passchendaele on 6 November 1917, aged 22. He was later listed as 'presumed dead' and is commemorated at the Menin Gate Memorial in Ypres, as well as on the memorial at Roseisle.

An undated photo of the younger Alexander Ritchie in uniform shows a round-faced, rather stern-looking man, seemingly well into middle age. After the war's end, Ritchie was stationed in Hampshire. He travelled up to London on 13 September and stayed at the YMCA Officer's Club on Leinster Place. The next evening, he went out to dinner with friends at the Criterion. Part of a lavish complex of restaurants in a late Victorian neo-Byzantine set of buildings facing Piccadilly Circus, this was one of the smartest restaurants in London in its day.

North American officers were among relatively few with enough cash in their pockets to afford to eat there at the time. At about 10.00 p.m., Ritchie and another Canadian officer, Lieutenant James Alexander Findlay, split from their dining companions. Ritchie said that he was going to Leicester Square to meet a friend who had failed to turn up the previous night. That may indeed have been his intention, but before he got there he had a fatal encounter with two British men who were also in battledress.

One had been born Reginald Douglas Johnson but was now known as Robert Blaine. If a petition he was later to write begging for clemency is to be trusted – and nothing in it is verifiably false - Blaine had a childhood of almost unrelieved hardship. He said he was born in County Tipperary on 8 August 1921 when his father was a sergeant-major in the Lincolnshire Regiment. His father was discharged because of deafness, returned the family to his home town of Boston, Lincolnshire, and began a window-cleaning business.

His mother deserted the family many times, during one of which his father sold the business to go looking for her, leaving him and his older brother to look after the four younger children for some weeks. Later, his father worked as a street corner newspaper vendor and moved the family to a smaller dwelling of three rooms, while Blaine himself collected rags from the homes of the better off to sell at a small profit. After a few months, he managed to set himself up as a market trader in rags. He was in the top class at school and worked on the land in school holidays until he left at the age of 14, briefly worked for a printer and continued to do odd jobs and sell papers in the evenings.

After his mother disappeared one last time and his father brought her back from London, it was decided that they would all move to London to escape the small-town clacking tongues. Blaine recalled the whole family of seven sleeping on the bare floor of their rooms at one point. He himself always found work, first in a shoe factory in London and then in a hotel kitchen in Brighton, but his father struggled to find anything. Before long, two of his younger brothers were put into Dr Barnardo's homes. His mother deserted them again and the rest of the family dispersed to other parts, leaving Blaine behind in Brighton, where he went through various jobs as a kitchen porter, errand boy and 'houseboy' at a college.

After nine months in his last job at a hotel 11 miles from Brighton, Blaine had to leave in the "slack season". He walked away unsure which way to go when he walked out but, he claimed, but while he was waiting for a bus to Brighton a man pulled up his car opposite and said he could give him a lift as far as Croydon. It was a decision he later regretted, although he continued to find work in London. For the first time since the age of ten, he now fell in with other lads of his own. It came about that in December 1938, the other two boys he was with were both out of work, they were all "practically starving on my wages" and had to leave their lodgings.

One morning, after sleeping out in Hyde Park, he stole two bottles of milk from a doorstep in Piccadilly but a policeman saw them and ran them to ground in an underground station. For reasons Blaine did not understand, Bow Street magistrates gave the other two three months hard labour while he was discharged. This was his first criminal conviction and he vowed not to repeat it. However, during his next job on night shifts in Farnborough, he fell in with a crowd of navvies who introduced him to alcohol. "I have been drinking ever since," he said. Turning up drunk for work got him the sack from this job but he continued to seek work wherever he could.

When war broke out, Blaine tried to join the Army but they did not want him. A second conviction followed on 8 June 1940, when the crowd he was with dared him to steal a hat from a man outside a pub they were drinking in. This earned him three months' hard labour, presumably because of being a repeat offender. After his release, Blaine worked on building air raid shelters and clearing rubble during the Blitz.

For whatever reason, he had adopted his new name by the time of his second conviction and all of his later convictions, which came thick and fast in the multiple opportunities the Blitz afforded, were as Robert Blaine: stealing shirts and hosiery from a bomb-damaged shop in November 1940, which earned him eight months' hard labour; being a 'suspected person', which essentially meant loitering with intent around some unattended cars, in June 1941, leading to another three months' hard labour; two more months for the same offence with intent to pickpocket in September 1941; five days for being drunk and disorderly a week after his release; then warehouse-breaking and stealing 25 coats worth £154.18s.2d with a gang of others at the London Sessions in January 1942.

This earned him a three-year sentence in Sherwood Borstal, where [57] Kenneth Strickson committed the murder that took him into the gallows nearly seven years later. The report from HMP Feltham at Blaine's sentencing in 1942 described him as "A mature youth who has a most unsatisfactory record. Since June 1940, he has served for terms of imprisonment and there would seem to be little hope of him leading an industrious life." Blaine was released early and told to report for military service but went drinking instead. He lived rough until another conviction for shopbreaking with intent at the London Sessions in August 1943.

Following his release on 17 April 1944, he was called up his father's old regiment and was later transferred to others. During his training, he said, he twice used - and overstayed - his leave to look for the family he had not seen in seven years but could not find any of them and served several periods detentions as a result. Following the last of these, a medical board re-examined him and found him unfit to serve because of "bad nerves". Secondary accounts saying that he had "served with distinction" are clearly wrong, because he never served at all.

On 18 August 1945, Blaine was discharged and returned to live at 101 Borrett Road in Walworth, south London. It has also been said that he was diagnosed a psychopath, but this would have been very unusual and no evidence of epilepsy or insanity in him or his family was ever found. Pictures taken of him in custody in 1945 show a tall (5'10½") young man with a long head, pronounced nose, dark wavy hair and skin pitted by acne. It is known that he was treated for diphtheria while living rough.

The other man in the alleyway that night in September 1945 was Charles Connelly, a Scot who Blaine predictably knew as 'Jock'. It has been suggested, in view of how the case panned out, that there was no such person, but Connelly was real enough. He was – or at least Blaine thought he was, from the absence of any military decorations on his battledress – a deserter and appears to have been known to some of Blaine's other acquaintances. The two had met in a pub and had been drinking together on and off for the previous three to four weeks, sometimes in the Alfred's Head by Elephant & Castle, sometimes in the Duke of York in Goodge Street.

According to Blaine, they left the Duke of York at 10.30 p.m. on the night of the murder and had a late supper in a café across the road before heading off down Wardour Street towards Piccadilly Circus at about 11.00. Both were quite drunk. On the way, Connelly picked up a loose brick from a pile at 2 Sheraton Street, broke it in half and handed it to Blaine, saying "Cop that" and telling him to keep it safe. Assuming that his partner was planning a break-in, Blaine hid it inside his tunic and gave it back to Connelly when asked as they turned into Bourchier Street.

This was an undistinguished back street running east-west towards Dean Street in the heart of Soho that was well known at the time for the alleyways off it, where prostitutes touted for clients. It was a desolate place with a demolished factory on one side and waste ground on the other. Opposite numbers 7-11 on the southern side, the street opened to form a yard where goods had formerly been loaded for the factory. The diagrams drawn by PC George Pannell do not actually show a public urinal in it as Blaine described but it is fair to assume that the poorly lit area was widely used as one. Even today, Bourchier Street is known to some as 'Piss Alley'; Stephen Fry mentions this in an autobiographical work.

According to Blaine, Connelly went into the urinal area while he waited outside. Connelly came back out and said: "Give me that and clock out". Blaine did as he was told and Connelly went around a corner. Blaine then heard a shout and the sounds of a scuffle and ran round the corner. "I saw him on top of this geezer, hitting him on the head with a brick. I was up against them." To the police, Blaine said that he told Connelly to 'turn it in' and taken the brick from Connelly's hand. He later claimed to have said "Don't be silly, you might kill the man", to which Connelly replied: "It's all right, he's only knocked out and he was trying to pick my pockets in the urinal". Blaine stated: "I saw him going through his pockets and I knelt down and went through some as well. I dived down his battledress. I heard nothing. The geezer was spark out." He took some papers, which was all he could find, and stuffed them into his clothes.

Their luck was out. As they made to leave the scene just after 11.45 p.m., two plain-clothes police officers from 'C' Division, Sergeant John Dimsey and PC Charles Pearce, approached the entrance to the passageway. "We got up and Jock walked over to the passage. He said, 'There's two laws coming down', so we walked down the bottom of the passage and he started running, so I started running," Blaine's account continued. Suspecting that the two had just left a prostitute behind in the alley, Pearce shone his torch down and saw Alexander Ritchie lying on his back with his head in a pool of blood. A broken, bloodstained brick and his khaki beret lay beside him. He was probably already dead or very close to it.

The policemen turned round and gave chase to the two soldiers, who sped off in different directions. Blaine was too drunk to get far and Dimsey ran him to ground in a shop doorway on Romilly Street, a short, two-block street running parallel to Bourchier Street. "What do you know about the soldier in Bourchier Street?" Romsey asked. Blaine replied: "I don't know what you're talking about. What soldier?" "I'll take you round and show you," Dimsey said. Pearce, meanwhile, chased Connelly through the streets but lost him into the night near Cambridge Circus. He returned to find his partner with Blaine. The three turned into Dean Street, Dimsey gripping Blaine's left arm, and Pearce made to leave him again to stop a private car. This seems an odd choice to make when they were holding a man suspected of a serious assault or worse.

As he did this, Blaine put his free hand into his right pocket and Dimsey shouted at him not to. Pearce rushed back to grab his right arm and found a penknife in the pocket. "What's this for?" Pearce asked. "I wouldn't do anything to you boys," Blaine answered (according to them; he denied it). The three then returned to the alleyway, where Dimsey continued to hold Blaine while Pearce examined Ritchie's body. "The man's dead. His head is bashed in with a brick," Pearce said, to which Blaine allegedly replied: "I didn't do it. The other one hit him when I was holding him." Both policemen were later to say in court that these were the words he used and they were to become significant. Blaine then took out a wallet from his left-hand blouse pocket and said that "the other bloke" had given him this. At this stage, he was not using Connelly's name.

Dimsey and Pearce took him to West End Central Police Station. Dr William Kennedy, the divisional police surgeon who examined him at 1.15 a.m. on 15 September found that he was not drunk and there were some recent abrasions and dirt on his right hand, notably on the knuckle of his right ring finger. Blaine readily admitted under questioning that he had been involved in the attack and that he had gone through Ritchie's pockets – he could hardly do otherwise, given that Ritchie's bank book and cheque book were both found on him, along with £5 – but he continued to deny being the killer.

When Detective Inspector Robert Stevens cautioned him at 3.15 a.m. and told him that he would be charged with murder, Blaine said: "I'm in dead trouble. I thought it would only be a GBH job. Jock Connelly gave me the brick, which I put in my blouse. I've got some of the gear from the bloke." He then made a statement describing the events of the previous evening. It concluded: "Jock clouted him. I didn't see if there was a fight. I heard a holler and went up to them. I only took some gear. That's all I know. I can't say anything else. That's the truth."

At 7.30 a.m., Detective Inspector Percy Burgess passed by Blaine's cell when he asked to have a word. Under caution, Blaine said he had been "thinking things over" and had some other things to disclose. First, he claimed that he and Connelly had attacked a Canadian Air Force corporal at the end of Dean Street on the night before the attack on Ritchie; this, he said, was where he got the £5 found on him. Secondly, he implied that Ritchie might have propositioned Connelly, though he did not know for sure. "I stood outside the urinal and Jock went in. I don't know if he chatted to anybody in there, but I think he did and was asked to go round the corner. I didn't touch [Ritchie] and the first time I saw him, he was laying out on his back. This is when I went down his pockets, after I had seen Jock clouting him. The only stuff I got was what seemed to be papers."

It is hard to judge what the truth of this is. Blaine may have been introducing an element into his story that he thought would disgust the police and he was clearly attempting to distance himself still further from the attack, probably unaware that it made no difference in law. When charged with murder, he was bemused. "I didn't do the geezer," he said. "I can't understand it. I had nothing to do with it." Blaine appeared before magistrates and on 19 September was remanded in custody at Marlborough Street Police Station. Meanwhile, Home Office pathologist Sir Bernard Spilsbury recorded the cause of Ritchie's death as a fractured skull caused by a violent blow behind the right ear with a hard object. There had also been injury and haemorrhage around the brain, as well as abrasions to the face and the inside of his lips that were consistent with having been punched in the mouth.

The police nearly caught Connelly but for a bureaucratic bungle. A photo was found and printed in the papers. Connelly was described as 5'10" tall, with blue eyes, wavy brown hair parted down the centre, and speaking with a strong Scottish accent. His age was given as 19 and 21 in different accounts, and he was said to have absconded from Borstal. After giving PC Pearce the slip, he made his way to the coast and stowed away on the Europa, a ship returning troops to the US.

On 13 November, it was reported that Scotland Yard wanted to speak to a 19-year-old who immigration officials at Plymouth believed to be him. This man had been arrested on arrival in New York, where he gave his name as Kelly, and was sent back to Plymouth on the liner Argentina on 14 November, the day before Blaine's trial started. When it docked, 'Kelly' was brought ashore in handcuffs. However, according to the *Daily Sketch*, because he was a British subject against whom nothing was known at the time and the shipping company did not want to prosecute him, he was released. "Normally, a secret list of men and women who are to be detained or carefully scrutinised is kept by port police officers and a man whose description has been circulated usually has little chance of landing unwanted," the *Sketch* said.

For whatever reason, the dots were not joined up. Only when Connelly's photo and description were released did immigration officials recognise him as 'Kelly'. The police and American military police searched the West End but found nothing. As late as January 1949, it was reported that Scotland Yard detectives were seeking information on a man called Charles Connelly they believed had been sentenced for larceny in New York State, possibly using a different name. The state police there said that they had no record of a man of that name being held on such a charge. Whatever the case, he was never found. He is believed to be the only man in a British murder case ever to remain permanently at large while an accomplice was executed.

From prison, Blaine wrote to one Joe Mills of Walworth Road asking him if he had seen 'Jock' lately and if he did, to tell him to give himself up "so I can get out of here as I would do the same for him if I was guilty and he were in my position". Connelly did not resurface and Blaine's trial was not going to be delayed on account of a missing accomplice. It took place at the Old Bailey before Mr Justice Humphreys on 16 November. Lawrence Byrne KC led for the prosecution, Frederick Levy KC for the defence. Most of the evidence came from the police, with Stevens, Burgess, Inspector James Wray, PC David Prichard, Pannell, Dimsey and Pearce all giving evidence. Further testimony came from Spilsbury and Dr Kennedy.

Dimsey repeated that, when he was informed that Ritchie was dead, Blaine had told him: "I didn't do it. The other one hit him when I was holding him." These words were not in Blaine's statement and, when he was called to the stand, he denied saying them. He admitted robbing Ritchie but claimed he had not done him any physical harm. As to why he did this, Blaine said that he thought that Ritchie and Connelly had been fighting "and I was drunk enough to do anything, so I just did it", words which contradicted Dr Kennedy's finding 90 minutes later. Blaine also disputed the officers' statement that his penknife was open and denied using the words 'I wouldn't do anything to you boys'. In his concluding statement, Levy asked for a verdict of manslaughter, arguing that the prosecution had not called any evidence to show that Blaine had entered into any agreement with Connelly to kill Ritchie.

Humphreys, the consummate establishment man, was not sympathetic. If Blaine was present aiding and abetting the man who struck the fatal blow, he was guilty of murder, the judge said. "It is quite immaterial whether he intended that the man should be killed or whether – to use his own picturesque expression in one of his statements afterwards – in his belief it was merely a 'grievous bodily harm job'." Moreover, the judge said, the defence had not cross-examined Dimsey or Pearce about the meaning of the words they attributed to Blaine. These, if accepted to be correct, showed that he had participated in the robbery in which Ritchie was killed which was murder.

The jury took only 18 minutes to find Blaine guilty. Passing sentence, Humphreys said it was the only possible verdict. As he awaited his fate in HMP Wandsworth, Blaine's mood swung, like that of so many condemned men down the years, between cheerful and sullen. He often refused the hour's exercise he was allowed or to be shaved (condemned men were not allowed to do this themselves, lest they attempt suicide), though he generally ate and slept well. It was during this time he wrote down his life story as part of an appeal to the Home Secretary.

"I know I robbed a man when he was knocked out and deserve to be punished for it, but I do not think I am guilty of murder. The man guilty of this crime is free and the police know it," it concluded. "All I can say is I am sorry and I have found out my mistakes in this life. I hope my mother, father, brothers and sister are happy and never get to know about this." Perhaps they never did; they had been out of his life for many years by then.

At the Court of Criminal Appeal on 13 December, Levy referred to the case of Victor Betts and Herbert Ridley, who had murdered a bank messenger while robbing him in 1930. Although Betts was hanged, Ridley was reprieved because "he played a secondary part in the crime". Blaine, Levy argued, had firmly and consistently denied any knowledge of Connelly's intention to attack anyone; he had thought they were only going to smash a window and steal.

The court, however, said that the police evidence was that Blaine had admitted holding Ritchie while Connelly struck him and asked Levy why he had not challenged this claim when his client denied it. He feebly said that he could not dispute the police evidence and that he could not find any fault in the summing-up. The days when the veracity of the police might be attacked in court were some years away still. The appeal was dismissed in five minutes flat.

Blaine passed Christmas in a reasonably good frame of mind, which was not apparently much affected by being told on 27 December that a reprieve had been refused. Two days later, he was hanged by Albert Pierrepoint and Harry Kirk, getting a drop of 6'11".

It went off smoothly. The case went almost unnoticed in the hubbub about the man in the opposite condemned cell, [12] William Joyce. Five days later, Joyce was also executed. His body was buried in the middle of that night, on top of Blaine's in an unmarked grave as per normal practice, separated only by a layer of charcoal. Blaine is still there; Joyce was reburied in Ireland in 1976.

The Canadian Adjutant General informed Ritchie's sister Mary, who lived in Montreal, of all the proceedings, including the findings of a Court of Inquiry that he died "from injuries resulting from blows to the head inflicted by two men with robbery as a motive", while on authorised leave, and that no blame was attached to him. Mary later announced his death "Accidentally at London, England" in the *Montreal Gazette*. Ritchie was buried with full military honours at Brookwood Military Cemetery in Surrey in Grave 61, Row D, Plot 6. He is also commemorated among others of his parish who died in World War II in a stained-glass memorial window at Lakeshore Drive United Church in Morrisburg and was the subject of a speech by Joseph Hardman at the Orders and Medals Society of America Table Medal Seminar in 2016.

12. "In death as in life, I defy the Jews, who caused this last war": The execution of William Brooke Joyce for treason at HMP Wandsworth on 3 January 1946

There were some curious parallels between the cases of [8] John Amery and William Brooke Joyce, two renegades who decamped to Nazi Germany during World War II. They were the last two men to be executed for treason in Britain; [13] Theodore Schurch was hanged a day after Joyce for treachery. Although of very different backgrounds, both were deeply conflicted in their identity. Both were radio propagandists involved in attempts to recruit British prisoners of war to fight alongside Germany, albeit to different degrees. They were viciously anti-Semitic but believed themselves to be anti-Communist rather than pro-Nazi. They also portrayed themselves as fervent patriots and probably believed it, yet, when put on trial for treason, both sought to save their skins by claiming that they were not even British.

Joyce, the man of humble origins, is far better known now than Amery, the son of a cabinet minister. This is probably because he established an identity during the war and was at least competent at his sinister trade, whereas Amery made a complete hash of everything he ever did. Along with a handful of others among the 215 people hanged since the end of the war, Joyce has generated a cottage industry of publications, starting with

Rebecca West's *The Meaning of Treason* and continuing to this day.

Joyce was in some ways the epitome of how national identity became blurred in the first age of mass emigration. His parents were Michael Francis Joyce, a distant relative of the author James Joyce and a well-off Catholic landlord and businessman in County Mayo, and Gertrude Emily Brooke, born in Lancashire-born into an Anglican, Anglo-Irish family of doctors, who met on board a liner on the way to the US in 1905. Their forst son, William, was born in Brooklyn on 24 April 1906 and Michael obtained a birth certificate stating that in 1917. William himself told many people he had been born in Galway and other documents relating to him give different dates, years and locations. This issue came to matter at the end of his life. His parents had held Irish and British citizenship respectively but renounced these to become naturalised Americans. The family returned to Ireland in 1909 and settled in Salthill, County Galway, where Michael ran the horse-tramway system.

Both parents were strong Unionists, a dangerous thing to be as Irish nationalist tensions arose and exploded in the Easter Rising of 1916. William followed their views and became known for his schoolyard lectures on the dangers of Bolshevism and scorn for Irish nationalism at St Ignatius Collage, a Jesuit school he attended from 1915 to 1921. A school report said of him: "That boy will either do something very great in the world, or he will hang by the end of a rope". He might easily have perished in the Irish War of Independence, when British Army intelligence recruited him as a courier in the battle against the IRA. It has been stated that he hung around with the infamous Black and Tans at Lenaboy Castle, though others dispute this on the grounds of his youth at the time.

All this activity, Joyce later claimed, led to the local IRA plotting to assassinate him on the way home from school in 1921, despite their usual ban on killing minors. He escaped only because their intelligence was out of date and his family had moved to a new house, which enraged neighbours later burned down. He was then mustered into a different regiment for his safety, only to be discharged a few months later when they found out he was under military age. Two days after the Irish Free State was declared, Joyce sailed to Liverpool and then moved on to London. The rest of the family followed later, ultimately setting in Dulwich where Michael became a grocer. It was a big fall from the prosperity the family, now enlarged by the birth of another son, Edwin Quentin in 1918 and a daughter, had enjoyed in the US.

Joyce continued his education at King's College School, Wimbledon, on a foreign exchange and finished his High School Certificate at Battersea Polytechnic. In 1922, he applied to join London University's Officer Training Corps (OTC), claiming extensive experience in the conflicts in Ireland. He then took a first-class honours degree in

English Language and Literature with History at Birkbeck College in 1927. This alone makes him the best educated of all the people hanged in Britain since 1945; he also later took post-graduate courses in philology and psychology at King's College, London. During his time at Birkbeck, he entered the college's OTC, supported by a letter from his father stating that the family were "all British, not American, citizens".

Joyce's early years in London saw the emergence of the first European fascist parties, notably in Mussolini's Italy. He developed an interest, working with – but not initially joining – Rotha Lintorn-Orman's British Fascists. Ironically, it was while stewarding a meeting in support of the Conservative Party's Jewish candidate for Lambeth North, in the general election in 1924, that he was razor slashed. It left a permanent scar from his earlobe to the corner of his mouth. He blamed "Jewish Communists" but his first wife, Hazel Kathleen Barr, who he married in 1927 and gave him two daughters, Diana and Heather, later said that he "was knifed by an Irish woman". That same year, the Civil Service rejected him – "A little oily, don't you think?" said a comment on his application form – and he became a tutor in a 'crammer' school.

In 1930, Joyce joined Oswald Moseley's New Party, which later became the British Union of Fascists (BUF). He rose swiftly through the ranks, thanks to his powerful oratory, and became Director of Propaganda. By nature, he was apparently likeable and energetic, someone who might have found a higher vocation had he not fallen for a squalid cause. The journalist and novelist Cecil Roberts wrote of him: "Thin, pale, intense, he had not been speaking many minutes before we were electrified by this man ... so terrifying in its dynamic force, so vituperative, so vitriolic". He also became known for his willingness to get involved in street brawls, despite his diminutive stature, and was a powerful leader of his men

In July 1933, Joyce applied for the British passport that would ultimately be his downfall. To obtain this, he claimed to have been born in Galway; had he declared the truth, he would not have been eligible. Together with Moseley and two others, he was tried for taking part in a riotous assembly at Worthing in 1934 but acquitted. It was also this year that Michael Joyce burned all the documentation relating to his and William's nationality, perhaps fearing that William or the whole family might be deported if he got into legal trouble. After becoming Deputy Leader, Joyce was instrumental in shifting the party's focus from the corporatist-driven economic revivalism espoused in Italy towards anti-Semitism, as well as changing its name to British Union of Fascists & National Socialists in 1936.

During these peak years in his influence in national politics, the family homes in Chelsea and Norwood were centres of fascist activity. Visitors included Julius Streicher, editor of the Nazi newspaper *Der Sturmer*, who was to be executed for war crimes after the Nuremburg Tribunal. Another, Heather later said, was Maxwell Knight, the prototype for 'M' in Ian Fleming's James Bond stories. Joyce also worked with Dudley and Norah Elam as area administrative officer for the BUF's West Sussex division in the 1930s and stood unsuccessfully for London County Council. Divorcing Hazel in 1936 after she had an affair with another BUF member, he married former cabaret artiste Margaret Cairns White at Kensington Register Office on 13 February 1937.

After poor results at the 1937 election, the BUF was short of funds and Mussolini withdrew financial support. Moseley reduced the paid staff drastically and Joyce lost his job. The two were never close: Joyce regarded the aristocratic Mosley as a weak leader, while Mosley called him "little more than a conceited popinjay" and other well-born fascists saw him as a common oik, useful only as a stepping-stone to power. Financially troubled, Joyce returned to tutoring and formed the breakaway National Socialist League, with Margaret as assistant treasurer.

Here, during the slow drift to war, the emphasis was more on opposing war with Germany. Joyce was again tried for assault at West London Police Court in 1938 and under the Public Order Act at Westminster Police Court in 1939 but was acquitted each time. The League was dissolved shortly before war broke out, in August 1939. Special Branch detectives went to their Earl's Court residence to arrest Joyce and Margaret on 1 September, which was just two days before war was declared and eight after Joyce had renewed his passport again, but they had already fled to Germany. By some accounts, Maxwell Knight himself tipped them off.

Shortly after arriving in Berlin, he bumped into a former BUF colleague, Dorothy Eckersley, who had been married to the chief engineer of the BBC. She secured him an audition at Germany's state broadcaster, the *Reich-Rundfunks-Gesellschaft*. Before long, he was recruited to make radio announcements and write scripts for its English language service. Starting on 18 September 1939, he made the radio broadcasts for which he was to become infamous and earn him the nickname 'Lord Haw-Haw' – originally 'Lord Haw-Haw of Zeesen,' after the location of the broadcasting station.

In fact, the name, which was coined for the man heard by the *Daily Express* correspondent 'Jonah Barrington', originally referred either to Norman Baillie-Stewart, another renegade Englishman, or to Wolf Mittler, a German with flawless English, who Joyce soon replaced. "He speaks English of the haw-haw, dammit-get-out-of-my-way variety, and his strong suit is gentlemanly indignation," Barrington wrote. Joyce's voice was actually rather nasal – the result, he himself claimed, of being punched by a school contemporary for his 'Orangeman' views. Indeed, it was rather indistinct because he had moved around so much. Different people heard traces of Ireland, Oxford, Manchester and even Chicago in him.

Whatever the case, the name stuck once Joyce became the main voice of the Nazi regime in Britain and he was satirised as 'Lord Haw-Haw, the Humbug of Hamburg" by Max Miller and Arthur Askey. He sometimes introduced himself using the name. His "jeering, sarcastic and menacing tone" fitted the name just as well as Baillie-Stewart's genuinely plummy voice. The programmes, always beginning "Germany calling, Germany calling", garnered some six million regular and 18 million occasional listeners in the UK by 1940, in part to hear something other than heavily censored official news, in part because Joyce seemed exceptionally well informed about events, right down to the names of captured POWs and which locations would be bombed next. Josef Göbbels, the Nazi Minister for Propaganda, described his success as "really astonishing".

Others just found Joyce funny, albeit less so as the war dragged on and the toll exacted on Britain grew ever worse. (One piece of fan mail said, "You're much funnier than Handley", referring to Tommy Handley's clunky satire of him in *It's That Man Again*.) Joyce's broadcasts went out over a network of German-controlled radio stations in many occupied countries. Bombing raids led to the broadcasting base being moved from Berlin to Luxembourg and finally to Apen, near Hamburg. He also broadcast and wrote scripts for the Concordia

Bureau, which ran several 'black propaganda' stations, plus propaganda attempting to recruit British prisoners of war into the British Free Corps, the successor to Amery's Legion of St George, and published *Twilight Over England*, comparing supposedly Jewish-run Britain unfavourably with Nazi Germany. Allying with the USSR against Germany was a hideous mistake, he argued. "From my earliest days, I was taught to love England and her Empire. Patriotism was the highest virtue I knew," he wrote.

Like Amery, Joyce lived the high life in wartime Berlin, drank and smoked heavily and had a highly volatile relationship with his wife. She was frequently unfaithful, while he was often violent. They divorced in 1941, only to remarry six months later after her German lover was sent to the Eastern front. Hitler awarded him the War Merit Cross (First and Second Class) but they never actually met. As Germany's defeat drew near, Joyce's broadcasts grew ever more risible. The last took place on 30 April 1945, just before the fall of Berlin, and he was audibly drunk as he berated Britain for pursuing the war to unconditional surrender. "You may not hear from me again for a few months," he slurred at the end. He probably did not know at this pint that both of his parents had died during the war.

Next day, the SS drove him and Margaret to Flensburg on the Danish border, capital of Admiral Dönitz's short-lived government. Many senior Nazis were there, hoping to escape to neutral

Sweden. It was in woods near here that he was found on 28 May, gaunt and malnourished, as he gathered firewood. Captain Alexander Lickorish and Geoffrey Perry, a German Jew who had been born Horst Pinschewer, heard him speak and asked if he was William Joyce. Joyce gave his false German name and reached into his pocket, probably for his fake identity papers. Perry feared that he was going for a gun and shot him four times in the buttocks. Other papers found on Joyce soon proved his identity. Another of the officers later commented that if he had known the fuss that would ensue from taking him alive, he would have shot Joyce dead on the spot. Margaret was captured shortly after.

While he recovered at Lüneberg Military Hospital, Joyce gave a long statement to Captain Scarden of MI5. This claimed, "I was actuated not by a desire for personal gain, but solely from political conviction" and that he had hoped for an Anglo-German understanding until the very end. It concluded: "I know I have been denounced a traitor and I resent the accusation. I conceive myself to have been guilty of no underhand or deceitful act against Britain, although I am also able to understand the resentment that my broadcasts have in many quarters aroused. Finally, I would like to stress the fact that in coming to Germany and in working for the German radio system my wife was powerfully influenced by me. She protests to the contrary, but I am sure that if I had not taken this step, she would not have taken it either."

The couple were first taken to Brussels. Margaret was flown to Croydon on 3 June. The level of reporting was obsessive and vindictive. 'No Biscuits for Lady Haw Haw', gloated the *Daily Herald*, recounting an incident at the airport where officers had tea, biscuits and bully beef in a tent as they waited, took the food away as she came and then, after consultation among themselves, let her have a cup of tea. Once she was in custody, the speculation returned to when Joyce himself would be brought over.

Behind the scenes, the authorities were arguing about what to charge him with. Interim Attorney-General Sir Donald Somervell felt he could only be prosecuted under wartime defence regulations, which carried a maximum sentence of 14 years, and pronounced himself "incredulous" that the Director of Public Prosecutions, Sir Theobald Mathew, wanted to pursue a charge of treason. Mathew, no doubt spurred by public opinion, won the day. In addition, a new Treason Act was rushed through in the two weeks between his arrest and his extradition, requiring only one, rather than the previous two, witnesses would be needed to recognise his voice on the broadcasts. The reason for this was to become clear later.

On 14 June, it was reported that Joyce would appear at Bow Street Police Court the following Monday, 18 June, and questions were asked in the Commons about what action was proposed. The new Attorney-General, Sir David Maxwell Fyfe, replied that barring any unforeseen changes, the prosecution would begin before the end of the month. And so it did. Joyce was finally returned to the UK on 16 June to be charged. As his plane flew above the World War I graveyards of Flanders, he was heard to mutter: "England and Germany at war with each other ... madness, I tell you." It was reported that his cell at Bow Street Police Station was floodlit throughout that night as a security measure and that the doors to the yard, usually opened, were kept closed. As an added tidbit, it was claimed that he occupied the same cell as Dr Crippen had after he had been brought back from the US in 1910.

Joyce faced magistrates at Bow Street for the first time on 18 June amid intense media interest. "He was wearing a black suit and brown shoes but had no collar. His hair was closely cropped. His face looked grey and drawn. He stood to attention, squared his shoulders, and faced Sir Bertrand Wilson, chief Metropolitan magistrate, who heard the opening of the case," one report ran. Formal evidence of arrest was given and Joyce was remanded for a week to HMP Brixton. His later transfer to Wormwood Scrubs caused a near riot among prisoners and he was again transferred, for his own safety to HMP Wandsworth.

At his next hearing on 25 June, Lawrence Byrne, senior Treasury counsel, read Joyce's post-arrest statement and produced his birth certificate and passport declaration, noting that the details in them were not the same. His solicitor, C.B.V. Head, reiterated the claim that Joyce was not a British subject, and that the Crown had not proved that he was. When the trial was due to start at the Old Bailey on 18 July, Mr Justice Charles consented to an application by Joyce's junior counsel, Derek Curtis-Bennett KC, to hold it over to the next sessions so that someone could go to see original documents relating to his birth certificate in the US.

Nationality was vital to the defence case, Curtis-Bennett said – both Joyce's and his father's – and "it will be our submission that if Joyce was born in the United States, he cannot owe allegiance to the King ... I take upon myself the responsibility that it would be impossible to conduct this man's defence without the document." Byrne agreed and Charles therefore acceded. Urgent inquiries in the US, overseen by J. Edgar Hoover himself, established that Joyce was indeed born there and had obtained his British passports fraudulently. His American citizenship would have automatically ended when he took German nationality, meaning that he could not have been extradited for trial there either. Nonetheless, the authorities were determined that he would not escape.

On 17 September, Joyce appeared before Mr Justice Tucker at Court Number One of the Old Bailey, which had sustained bomb damage and still had its windows blacked out with tar. The new Attorney-General, Sir Hartley Shawcross, led for the prosecution. Joyce, in a letter to Margaret, dubbed the austere Shawcross 'Hot Cross Buns'. There were three charges of treason: that Joyce assisted the King's enemies by broadcasting propaganda to his subjects on many occasions between 18 September 1939 and 29 May 1945; by being naturalised as a German citizen before 26 September 1940; and that he "did aid and assist the enemies of the King by broadcasting to the King's subjects' propaganda on behalf of the King's enemies" between 18 September 1939 and 2 July 1940.

The sole witness on the matter of the broadcasts was Detective Inspector Albert Hunt, who had heard Joyce speak while policing a BUF rally and claimed to have recognised his voice during a broadcast in the first month of the war. This was very thin gruel. Hunt only recalled the broadcast saying that Dover and Folkestone had been destroyed. It was completely untrue as no bombing at all had taken place then and Joyce's counsel, Gerald Slade KC, remarked that it would have been an odd way for Joyce to begin his broadcasting career. While Hunt's memories of later broadcasts were better, these did not matter because Joyce definitely owed no allegiance to Britain after July 1940. Captain Lickorish and Joyce's interrogator, William Skardon, also testified for the prosecution.

Slade, who received death threats for defending Joyce, kept him out of the witness box. He probably calculated that his client's unrepentant Nazi views would do him no favours. Better, surely, to simply claim that the prosecution had not proven its case. The defence called, among others, Joyce's brother

Quentin, now a civil servant, who was of slighter build but bore a facial resemblance and shared his views. Quentin testified to the family background and his parents' deaths. None of the papers and documents saved when the family home was bombed had any information on his father's nationality, he said, but he remembered seeing his father burn some old papers about 11 years ago, one with an embossed American eagle. When a frayed marriage certificate was held up, he identified it as that of his parents.

Many more witnesses were brought forward to show that Joyce was indeed American by birth. As Slade put it, "if I am a Chinese, by screaming from the house tops 50,000 times that I am a British subject, I do not become one." Most of the real debate was on matters of law and the law of treason had evolved at a time before the mass use of passports. At the end of the second day, the first two charges were dismissed with the agreement of the prosecution because Joyce, as an American citizen, could not owe any allegiance to Britain once his passport had expired.

That left only the third count, that he made broadcasts while still in possession of a British passport. Slade argued cogently that any allegiance Joyce owed was only while he was resident in Britain and lapsed when he left. However, when he returned from deliberating Tucker, as Rebecca West put it, "with this usual eccentric excess of military smartness and his sustained tight-lipped derisiveness", ruled that he agreed with Shawcross and that it was a matter of pure law rather than for the jury to decide. He directed them that, on 24 August 1939, "in the passport applied for, the prisoner beyond a shadow of doubt owed allegiance to the Crown of this country, and that on the evidence given, if the jury accepted it, nothing happened at material times thereafter to put an end the allegiance he owed".

Slade could still argue that the prosecution had failed to prove beyond doubt that there had been any broadcasts in the material times and the first one the BBC definitely attributed to him was in August 1940. Shawcross, wisely, kept his last words very brief and, in the words of legal author Thomas Grant, "in the broadest of brushes", while Tucker's summing-up seemed more about defending his conduct of the trial than the evidence. It was enough for the jury, who took only 23 minutes on 19 September to convict Joyce. Some were surprised that Lord Haw-Haw, who had spoken such volumes in defence of his foul creed, had nothing to say before he was duly sentenced to death. He bowed stiffly to Tucker, waved to Quentin and his friends and ran down to the cells.

The defence announced an appeal on 27 September. Many people were troubled because Joyce was not actually entitled to a British passport and had only obtained one by lying. The *Yorkshire Post* commented: "Whatever detestation may be felt for the offences of which the jury found the prisoner guilty yesterday, it will be the wish of the country that his appeal should be heard with the utmost fairness, as it will be. More is at stake here than the fate of William Joyce; the traditions of British justice, upon which so much depends, have to be faithfully upheld. If they were lost sight of, through determination to bring swift punishment upon the head of one who has been widely reviled as a traitor, grievous harm would be done to an essential part of the British heritage."

More succinctly, historian A.J.P. Taylor remarked: "Technically, Joyce was hanged for making a false statement when applying for a passport, the usual penalty for which is a small fine". Many lawyers also thought the appeal should have been allowed. N. Long-Brown KC wrote to the *Daily Telegraph* after Joyce's execution describing it as "a blot on British justice". Had Joyce remembered to post his unwanted passport back, Long-Brown said, he could not have been convicted.

The appeal, before Lord Chief Justice Goddard, Mr Justice Humphreys and Mr Justice Lynskey, was on four grounds: that no English court could try an alien for alleged crimes committed abroad; that Tucker erred in law by accepting the prosecution's legal arguments about allegiance; that Joyce had never asked for protection; and that the question of allegiance should have been for the jury to decide. With characteristic sarcasm, Goddard asked Slade if he really meant to say that "an alien can go backwards and forwards across the Channel, owing allegiance when he arrives at Dover and no longer owing it when he lands in Calais".

The appeal was dismissed, but, as the case raised major issues in law, Shawcross allowed it to be heard in the House of Lords, the highest court in the land. The same points were argued again when the five law lords headed by the Lord Chancellor presided over the case over the course of 10-13 December. Here, in the Palace of Westminster, the rhetoric soared above that of the trial. Rebecca West wrote that it was "as good an entertainment as first-class tennis" and Joyce showed a "dignity and refinement" that he had lacked before. By four to one, the lords upheld the verdict; Lord Porter dissented, arguing that Tucker had misdirected the jury and allegiance was a question of fact for them to decide.

That was the last roll of the dice. On 22 December, it was announced that Joyce would be executed on 3 January 1946. He conducted himself with conspicuous courage and dignity in his last weeks in Wandsworth, during which time his only visitors were his wife, herself a military prisoner at HMP Holloway, and his siblings. He was politically unrepentant, writing in a letter to Edwin: "In death as in life, I defy the Jews, who caused this last war, and I defy the power of darkness which they represent. I warn the British people against the crushing imperialism of the Soviet Union. May Britain be great once again and in the hour of the greatest danger in the West may the standard be raised from the dust, crowned with the words 'You have conquered nevertheless'. I am proud to die for my ideals and I am sorry for the sons of Britain who have died without knowing why."

He discussed religion and philosophy with the chaplain, writing to Margaret of the consolation they had given him. Before death, he professed a belief in God as "the supreme reality" and accepted a blessing from Father Marshall-Keene, a previous acquaintance, and took communion on the morning of 3 January. At 9.00 a.m., he walked unflinchingly the few yards to the death chamber to be hanged by Albert Pierrepoint. The scar on his face reportedly split wide open because of the pressure on his head as he fell. Outside was a crowd estimated at 250-300, considerably more than Amery had attracted. That might have pleased Joyce, had he known. Extra police were there in case of any demonstration by sympathisers, but it all passed quietly enough; a few fascists gave furtive salutes and slunk away.

Later that day, Joyce's body was buried on top of [11] Robert Blaine's, separated by a layer of charcoal. Mass was offered for his soul at his old school in Galway. In 1976, his remains were exhumed and returned for burial in the Protestant section of the New Cemetery at Bohermore in County Galway, after campaigning by his younger daughter, now Heather Iandolo. A Tridentine Mass was celebrated at his reburial.

Alone among the 32 British citizens and supposed British citizens caught in Germany at the end of the war, Margaret Joyce was never charged with treason, even though she also made hundreds of broadcasts, was unquestionably British and never renounced her citizenship. In an official document, an MI5 agent said that this decision was made on compassionate grounds – her husband's execution. It has also been claimed that Joyce cut a deal with prosecutors not to reveal his own links with MI5 in return for sparing her, although in truth there was little consistency in how the authorities dealt with renegade broadcasters. Of the 14 captured, only Amery and Joyce were ever charged with treason.

Margaret was quietly taken back to Germany two days after his execution and interned there until her release on 2 January 1948. She died in London in 1972, still a fervent Nazi. Heather, who became a schoolteacher and renounced her father's anti-Semitic views but retained fond memories of him, continued to air the notion that he was working for MI5. His older daughter Diana died in 2009. In 2011, now a widow of 82, Heather appealed to the Criminal Cases Review Commission to have the verdict overturned on the grounds of his alleged deal with MI5 and the familiar one of his citizenship. This did not go anywhere and it is hard to imagine a real double agent acting as Joyce did.

Joyce has received extensive coverage in the annals of true crime, but has also inspired fictional works, notably Ethel Mannin's *Every Man a Stranger*, whose protagonist, Lance Kannon, bears some resemblance to him. The man himself expected, deserved and received no sympathy from the British people. Only a few highly educated people familiar with legal niceties were uneasy about his execution and there is a strong case for concluding that the Establishment wanted him dead out of repugnance at his actions, or perhaps in part because his swipes at toffs and capitalists had a ring of truth to them.

It was certainly unusual that Shawcross led the prosecution in person, not least after his constitutional expert said there was no case in law. It has also been noted that Mr Justice Tucker had called Joyce a traitor in 1939 and should arguably have been ineligible to preside at his trial. Others have regretted that his execution enabled Joyce to put on a good show. All the same, there was a strong case for saying that he had sought some of the benefits of citizenship in the country he claimed to love and as such had some sort of duty of allegiance to it. Other British fascists thought the same, if only because they had been unable or unwilling to get out in time. He was also intelligent enough to know that a patriot cannot simply substitute his vision of the country for the one shared by the vast majority of his countrymen and for there to be no consequences if he does.

13. "A poor, uneducated fool who was caught young": The execution of Private Theodore William John Schurch for treachery at HMP Pentonville on 4 January 1946

The last of the three men who faced the gallows for crimes other than murder within a month the turn of 1945-6 was much more obscure than the posh wastrel sociopath [8] John Amery and the ranting ideologue [12] William Joyce. Theodore Schurch's crime was subtly different: where Amery and Joyce, as civilians, were tried for treason in criminal courts, he was a soldier in arms, which brought his crimes under the Treachery Act of 1940, and he was tried in a military court. The final outcome, however, was the same. He was also the only British soldier to be executed for acts of treachery committed during World War II, and one of only two to die for that offence, alongside Duncan Scott-Ford, a merchant seaman who paid the penalty in 1942 for giving information to a German agent in Lisbon.

Schurch was born to a Swiss father, Theodore Sherman Schurch, and an English mother, Eunice Henrietta (née Chapman), at Marylebone on 5 May 1918, was baptised at the Swiss church and was registered as a Swiss citizen in his father's village, Reubach in the canton of Berne. He had one sister, Pauline Eunice, born in 1923. The family lived successively in Stoke Newington, Stamford Hill and North Wembley, while his father worked as the head night porter at the Savoy Hotel.

Curiously, a death notice was published in the *Harrow Observer* on 14 July 1996 that Theodore Schurch, of 81 Harrowdene Road, North Wembley, had died aged 72 on 25 June. This man, it recorded, had worked at the Savoy and lived in North Wembley for 32 years; he had come to Britain in 1915 and "developed a great fondness for it" but remained a Swiss subject. Clearly something is wrong here for he could not have come to Britain in 1915 and been in 72 in 1996.

The coincidence of names and occupation is improbable, however, so the likeliest explanation is that there was a typographical mistake and the man who died in 1996 was indeed Schurch's father and was much older than 72. At the time of his son's arrest, a Special Branch report described both parents as "highly respectable, constitutionally minded persons who are not in sympathy with any other nation". Schurch himself said they never knew of his political activities, objecting mainly that whatever he was doing kept him out late at night.

The younger Schurch left school without qualifications in 1934 aged 15 but managed to secure himself work as a costing accountant for several local firms in his home area. At the last but one, Lancegaye Safety Glass in the Wembley Exhibition Grounds, it was his misfortune to meet Irene Page, the daughter of the owners, who worked there as a telephone operator. She belonged to a circle of suburban fascists at a time when admiration for Mussolini and Hitler was not uncommon and she came into work on Saturdays in a black shirt. Some think it was her "large, well-formed bust" rather than her views that attracted Schurch at first, but he was an easy mark in that respect.

By his own account, he had been bullied at school. "Ever since I can remember, I have been looked at askance on account of my foreign name," he later said. It was probably true. Britain between the wars was no less xenophobic and probably more insular than most European countries. Either way, he happily tagged along to British Union of Fascists (BUF) meetings at a house in Willesden. As well as being attracted to their ideology, for the first time in his life that he felt like he belonged somewhere.

An unprepossessing young man, despite standing over six feet tall, with "a shrunken face and crooked, protruding teeth", Schurch looked older than his years. He was also talkative, friendly and able to make a good impression on some of his colleagues. A report after his capture said that he was "gifted with an innate shrewdness and natural intelligence which compensates for his obvious lack of education". Indeed, by 1945, he was fluent in five languages.

At BUF gatherings, Schurch met the party leader Oswald Moseley and possibly also Joyce, then its deputy leader. A more important encounter still was with the Italian owner of a Cardiff trading firm called Bianchi, a committed fascist who told him that he would be useful to the party despite his youth. At Bianchi's bidding, he applied to and was accepted into the Royal Army Service Corps (RASC) in May 1936. It was also Bianchi who, during Schurch's training, took him out to lunch, told him to volunteer as a driver and gave him the £5 he needed to buy a regimental dress uniform. Through gifts like this, more than he would readily see in his humdrum job, Schurch became inveigled ever further into their web and he certainly developed a taste for what money could buy.

In 1937, again at the behest of the BUF, he volunteered for service in the British mandate of Palestine, sailing out there that November. His local handler, he claimed – it was never verified - was a wealthy, well-connected Palestinian Christian called Homsi, who ran the regional General Motors franchise from a garage on the Jaffa Road in Jerusalem and gave Schurch all of his instructions, including transferring from driver to technical mechanical transport clerk, plus money whenever he needed it.

As part of the RASC command where the forces fuelled their cars to travel around the Mandate, Schurch was in the loop about the movements of senior officers, including General Wavell. He said that he passed this information and other gossip about military deployments onto Homsi, who could in turn pass it anti-British intelligence operatives and their German allies. Schurch's treachery thus long predated the war. It took an even more sinister turn when war came.

In 1941, his unit was sent to Egypt. Schurch asked to take some long-accumulated leave but was refused. When he received his pay, he secured a pass on which he forged the name of Captain John Richards and went AWOL, dodging the military police all the way back to Tel Aviv where he contacted Homsi and told him of his new location. Then he returned, served a field punishment and volunteered for front line service in the expectation of helping the Italians.

During the winter of 1941-2, Schurch spent two months in the military hospital at Tel El Kebir with "temporary mental derangement" after an attempted suicide. He was later to claim that this was the result of belatedly realising what an invidious position he had put himself in. In view of his three further years of serving Axis intelligence, this strains credulity. It is just possible, however, that his capture by the Germans at Tobruk in 1942, along with hundreds of others, was genuine, since the port city in Italian Libya fell only two days after his arrival.

Sent to an Italian-run POW camp at Benghazi, Schurch asked to see a military intelligence officer. Colonel Mario Revetria believed that he might well be useful and had him returned to Benghazi, where thousands of POWs from the Tobruk and Benghazi raids were being held captive. First, he was sent back to Tobruk to find out more on the operations of HMS Sikh and HMS Zulu, which had just been sunk. On his return, he was dressed as an officer, resumed the identity of Captain John Richards from the Inter-Services Liaison Department and tasked to seek information from British officers.

In October 1942, Schurch was sent across the lines at El Alamein with his real identity documents to pose as an escaped POW and get whatever information he could. He was sent to a transit camp near Alexandria, where he stayed for a few days before going back to the Italians, something he did at least two more times. His task was to find information about the activities of the newly formed Long Range Desert Group, later called the Special Air Service (SAS), as it roamed the desert near Tripoli attacking convoys. Exactly how much damage Schurch really did is hard to judge, but one modern author, Ben Macintyre, blames him in part for Squadron B losing 12 men and three of its six officers before the end of December. The Germans certainly seemed to know where to find them a lot of the time. Indeed, Schurch himself attributed the capture of two patrols in part to his work.

There was some dark comedy in Schurch's spying career too. On one occasion in December 1942, he was sent, dressed as a British army captain, to speak with a Private John Elliot Bowman, another ex-RASC man. Bowman immediately recognised him as Driver 'Issi' Schurch, who he had known in 1937, while Schurch did not recognise the unwashed, heavily bearded Bowman and tried to pump him for information on SAS activities until finally Bowman sourly asked him: "How are you going on, Issi?" Schurch and the Italian sentry then went through a pantomime in which the latter addressed him as 'Captain Schurch', said that he had been recognised as a British secret service agent and would have to be flown to Italy that night. As he left, Schurch breezily told Bowman: "If we meet in Italy, I'll get you a job as my batman."

Others who met him in different situations became suspicious of him for different reasons: the immaculate Italian boots he was wearing after claiming to have trekked across the desert; the way he breezed past sentries and back out again that little bit too easily; the extra order of wine he was given at meals; the little implausible details in his back stories. Schurch struggled to look the part in a world where officers had middle class accents and was simply not cunning or worldly enough for the role of a spy.

In early 1943, with the campaign in North Africa basically over, Schurch was shipped over to Italy and tasked with locating a British wireless station in Vatican City. This mission was not successful. His next, in February, was to go to Camp 50, a special interrogation centre at the Cavalry Barracks in Rome, to speak to the captured head of the SAS, Colonel David Stirling. Stirling later recalled seeing 'Captain Richards' there several times. However, he said, an RAF officer had warned him to be careful of saying anything to Richards and passed him only untrue information and such true details as he believed Richards to know already.

"Captain Richards told me he had a Swiss mother and a London-born father. He was an obvious Cockney. I could identify him," Stirling concluded. This reversed the nationalities of Schurch's parents, presumably to substantiate his very English assumed name, but it was not a very good cover. All Schurch really got out of Stirling was the name of his successor, Captain 'Paddy' Mayne.

He returned to the same camp shortly after to seek information from officers including Lieutenant Archibald Hart about the work of the Special Boat Service and others. Hart, who had been captured in Sicily, briefly shared a room with 'Captain Richards', who he recalled telling him that his father was the manager of a large London hotel, another slight twist on reality. He and his other roommates had also been warned, by an Army batman, to be wary of Richards. Richards was taken away shortly afterwards, ostensibly to go to hospital, when another British officer recognised him.

On 25 April, again posing as Richards, Schurch was sent back by German intelligence sent back to gain information about two British submarines, HMS Sahib and HMS Splendid, which had just been sunk off Italy. From Lieutenant John Henry Bromage of the Sahib, and Lieutenant Hardy, navigation officer of Splendid, he managed to find out which base 'S' squadron submarines were operating from and who the commander was. Bromage later recalled meeting 'Richards' and discussing prison life with him.

Richards said, as he had to others, that he had been captured at Benghazi in February 1943.

Bromage also met and talked with Hardy, which 'Richards' might have overheard, but his memories were vague on that point. His account was very revealing as it shows that Schurch had seen the way the wind was blowing and hoped to get out of the web into which he had spun himself. After their first conversation, Schurch asked to meet him alone on or about 3 May. There, he told Bromage his real name and background, with a few unimportant embellishments. He said he had been captured at Benghazi and sent to a transit camp as an ordinary prisoner, "but had later been sent for by the Italians who had learned of his German parentage and had threatened that unless he co-operated with the Italians, they would 'frame' his parents in London". He had agreed to do so and passed them a mix of true and inaccurate information to deceive them.

Several other British officers already knew this, Schurch said, and he asked what he should do when he was recaptured. Bromage advised him to apply for a court martial. Two or three days later, Schurch saw Bromage again privately and produced a typed document in English with about ten questions relating to the armament of modern submarines. Bromage gave incorrect answers to some and said he did not know the answers to the rest. It also emerged that shortly after Bromage arrived at the camp, 'Richards' warned several members of the Sahib's company "to be very wary of 'stooges' in the camp, saying jocularly that he may be one himself", a pathetic attempt at double bluff. Bromage made a verbal report about all this to a British commander when he left the camp to be taken to Camp 39 at Padua on 17 May. Schurch, he said, "was in a highly nervous condition and very seedy during the whole period at the Camp in Rome".

In September, when Italy was negotiating its surrender to the Allies, Schurch was sent to Perugia to seek information about people supposed to be working for British intelligence, but was arrested by the Germans, who believed him to be an escaped POW, and put on a train heading to Germany. Ever resourceful in adversity, he managed to escape before it left, though not without damage to his ankle. He made his way back to Rome, where he recuperated and called on Colonel Helfrich, head of the German intelligence service, the ABW. Helfrich was impressed by his credentials and continued to use him for the next two years. He also took the precaution of obtaining a Swiss passport from the Consulate-General in Como in October 1944.

The details about his activities in this period are rather sketchy and did not form part of the charges he ultimately faced. Exactly when the British intelligence services wised up to him is unclear. According to a secondary source, they were first told of what he was doing in 1943 and his name appeared in a 1944 list of British subjects who were believed to be aiding the enemy. Those whose testimony was used against him all claim to have been suspicious of him and not to have said anything that might have helped him, but it is clear that he did garner some useful information.

On 26 May 1945, an American officer arrested Schurch at La Spezia as he waited for a train to Rome, on initial suspicion of being a deserter. He was questioned by none other than James Jesus Angleton, then commander of the Secret Counter-Intelligence Unit Z and later for 20 years head of counter-intelligence for the CIA. Schurch gave full details of his involvement in Axis intelligence and was handed over to Captain R.A. Archer of the Special Investigation Branch. Aware of how much trouble he was in, he spilled the beans in style. Angleton noted how composed he was throughout the interview and the massive, mostly accurate detail he gave of the incidents, personalities and places he had encountered during nearly ten years of service. He also coughed up the names of 62 enemy agents operating in Italy and the Tyrol.

As to Schurch's claim that he had been motivated by an ardent and now lost love for fascism, however, Angleton was unmoved. Schurch's "first acts of treachery enabled him to enjoy the taste of expensive pleasures which he could no longer psychologically do without", he noted, and right up until his arrest Schurch was doing everything in his power to accomplish the missions given to him. Archer concurred.

Next day, Captain Lascaris was brought to an identity parade where he unhesitatingly picked Schurch as the man he had seen in the uniform of a British Officer at the aerodrome in Derna. This was enough for Archer to arrest Schurch and hand him over to military custody. Schurch claimed that he had lost his faith in fascism when he had seen senior figures in the German and Italian high commands totally failing to live up to the ideals of the movement. "I quite realise from what I have done in the past years the consequences and I am quite willing to face them, but if in any way I can help the British authorities in whatsoever manner they want me to I am quite willing to do so. As I am still a British soldier I wish to be treated as such and be dealt with by the British Government," he wrote.

That happened soon enough. Schurch's court martial began on 12 September at the Duke of York's HQ on the Kings Road in Chelsea, which was built in 1801 and had served many military purposes ever since. (It had also hosted the trial during the war of Josef Jakobs, who became the last man to be executed – by firing squad – at the Tower of London. Sold off by the Ministry of Defence in 2003, it now hosts the Saatchi Gallery, housing and upmarket shops.) Schurch was charged with one count of desertion in North Africa in October 1942 and nine of treachery contrary to Section 1 of the Treachery Act 1940. Five of these related to obtaining information from POWs and members of forces and communicating it to the enemy between 13 September and November 1942. The final three related to seeking information from POWs about military and naval operations in the Mediterranean in April and May 1943.

The Judge Advocate was Major Aubrey Melford Stevenson KC, a future High Court judge. Colonel R.B.R. Colvin DSO, commander of the Grenadier Guards, presided, with five other members. Captain C. Lawson of the Judge Advocate General's Office prosecuted, aided by Major R.A.L. Hilliard, while Lieutenant Alexander Brands KC appeared for the defence. Hilliard and Brands had previously squared off at the trial of the German POWs [7] Armin Kühne and Emil Schmittendorf. Before the trial began, Schurch was allowed to object to any of the proposed jurors. He asked them to state their religion and promptly objected to Major F.A. Holland, who was Jewish. This was allowed and the 'member waiting', Major Harbinson, who was Church of England, took Holland's place. All the rest were either Presbyterian or Church of England.

The hearing was then adjourned for five days at Brands' request, as he had only been instructed the day before. Lawson agreed that he also needed to ask for extra time and added that "it was desirable that the accused should have further time to prepare his defence in view of the fact that the only penalty the law permitted in the case of the first nine charges was that of death".

On 17 September, after an adjournment for both sides to complete their preparations, the prosecution called five witnesses who had made written statements about Schurch and identified him as the person they had met as 'Richards'. Lascaris' evidence relating to Schurch's activity in North Africa was pretty insubstantial. Much more revealing testimony came from Stirling, Hart and Bromage, leaving no doubt about what he had been up to.

Brands went over how Schurch joined the British Army in 1936 and went overseas, both at the instruction of the BUF. He was then contacted by a certain person and given information, which he believed to be non-treasonable and told that, unless he carried on doing what he was doing he would be 'framed'. This affected his peace of mind so badly he once attempted suicide – he suffered from a persecution complex as it was. At first, he did help the enemy, but "when his peace of mind returned, he realised what a serious step he had taken" and the reports he gave to the Italians were either false or about things they knew already.

Hilliard countered by showing how, in seven cases, Schurch intentionally mingled with British POWs and obtained information which he handed to the enemy. When serving in Egypt in 1942, Hilliard said, "to enable him to make contact with the enemy intelligence service, he agitated for posting to the frontline unit". He was thus in Tobruk to be captured by the Germans, made contact with the Italian Intelligence Service and then "turned into a position which can only be described as an agent of that intelligence service".

Similarly, he had mixed with British POWs around Rome, obtained information and passed it on, as his own statement showed. His act of returning from the transit camp in Alexandria with information that the enemy wanted and crossing back to their lines clearly constituted desertion. Investigations, Hilliard added, were still being carried out relating to certain parts of the statement and he asked for these to be read *in camera*. The court agreed.

Schurch called no witnesses in his defence but gave evidence under oath and was examined by both counsels. There may have been some truth in his claims of being trapped, but he would surely have known it was not a defence in law. His previous offences were stating a falsehood to an NCO, absence from duty and twice being AWOL. In evidence, Schurch admitted becoming a fascist as a boy, in reaction to being bullied at school because of his foreign origin and name. Brands tried to elaborate on the persecution complex until Melford Stevenson stopped him by saying that "this is a court martial and not a court of psychiatrists".

As to why he got involved with the enemy, Schurch answered: "Because I found that as a regular soldier the persecution against me was much worse in the Army than it was in civilian life. I attempted suicide. I volunteered to go up to the front line to get away from it all. My persecution complex was so bad then that I decided to join the enemy." Only when his calm returned did he realise "what a serious step I had taken". It was too late to back out and he was threatened that "all the plans had been laid to cast suspicion on my people in England". For this reason, he made the best he could of it and gave the Italians useless information.

Hilliard pounced on this. "Do you say that for two and three-quarter years you hoodwinked this intelligence service? Were you not working for the Ministry there, with access to their records and received by General Hezler, chief of the intelligence service in Italy? Were your services such that you were brought into contact with the heads of the services?" Not all, replied Schurch, but he admitted that he was taken to a man he took to be Hezler as a trusted agent.

Melford Stevenson told the court that Schurch had made a statement "upon which each of the charges treachery in this case is founded" and the defence had never challenged its admissibility. The details in this were backed up by the evidence of witnesses. The defendant had denied any treasonable intent in court and it was the jury's task to examine the evidence and decide whether "anyone could possibly have indulged in the activities in which this soldier did indulge without intending to give assistance to this country's enemies"; he had also claimed that he never gave accurate information to the enemy but his statement showed that he had repeatedly given exactly the information he had been told to by Italian military intelligence.

Schurch himself had the right to address the court but he left this to Brands, who did not ask for a not guilty verdict but a recommendation to mercy. "I think you will agree with me when I say he is of a low mentality and poor education," Brands began. Schurch gave the impression of being "an exhibitionist", who had absorbed the BUF's ideas at a time when "many people more illustrious than himself held the same views". He was suckered ever deeper into his activities until finally, in 1941, he realised that he was to all intents and purposes a spy, hence the attempted suicide. He also began to realise how dismally the leaders of the Axis states failed to live up to the ideals they espoused. Now, once it was too late, he decided to mend his ways. Since his capture, he had given every possible assistance to the authorities.

"I wish you to regard him as a poor uneducated fool, who was got at by those who knew better, and jockeyed into position from which he could not retract," Brands said. "He had to the dirty work for the other people who stayed in the background, who today are going free. Now he will pay for his work with his liberty, if not his life." The proceedings took only 145 minutes. When the court resumed after a 20-minute adjournment, Schurch was told that its findings would be promulgated to him later. He would have known straight away that he had been found guilty on at least some of the charges. In fact, he was found guilty on all ten and the mandatory sentence was passed.

From the military detention facility, he was sent to in Woolwich, Schurch made two more statements appealing for clemency. In the first, he once again went over how he had been seduced by the "high sounding doctrines" of the BUF when still young and had initially believed that the information he was supplying was "for an innocent purpose" until he finally realised his situation and tried to extricate himself from it by attempting suicide. He was then forced to continue, he claimed, by the threat of reprisals against his parents, so instead he offered only false information to the Axis. When captured, he made the full, voluntary statements that largely convicted him and much more that he could have withheld on other German and Italian agents.

The second statement gave fuller details about Homsi and his initial activities in Palestine, plus some more details about some Italians he had been involved with in London before his departure to Palestine and believed to be spies. "If there is any way I can help the British authorities in any capacity, I am willing to do so as I could take you to a lot of places and round up a lot of people who are 100% fascists and national socialists but who have now and always have had a good cover under alibis," he concluded.

Perhaps he could have but the authorities were not interested. On 4 January 1946, Schurch was hanged by Albert Pierrepoint and Alexander Riley at HMP Pentonville. As a small matter of bureaucracy, the Home Office had to write to the War Office confirming that it was ready to assist, as it had been in the case of [5] the five recently executed German

POWs, provided it was "clearly understood that the executioner and any prison staff are employed as agents of the military authorities and not in their capacities as civilian employees of the prison department".

There was an odd postscript to his story as late as 2017, when the BBC reported that Schurch's name is commemorated on the Commonwealth War Graves Commission's Brookwood Memorial as a casualty of war. His name is on Panel 17, Column 3. This provoked angry reactions in later years from some whose ancestors were real war victims. The memorial, unveiled in 1958, commemorates war casualties whose graves were unmarked. Schurch had been a serving officer at the time of his execution and was indeed buried in an unmarked grave. Thus, ironically, the Imperial War Graves Commission had no discretion to exclude him. According to one author, at least 18 executed murderers are commemorated there, mostly men who later murdered their wives or girlfriends. [3] Howard Grossley and [26] Walter Clayton, who was hanged for strangling his girlfriend on Morecambe Beach in August 1946, are certainly among them.

14. "I am nobody": The murder of Samuel Hammond Gray by William Batty at 45 Prince Street, Dudley Hill, Bradford, on 14 August 1945 and his execution at HMP Armley on 8 January 1946

As the case of [4] Thomas Richardson and others that came later showed, the dislocation of wartime created many new relationships and probably destroyed an equivalent number of old ones. Some married in haste, fearing that their lives would be cut short, as many indeed were. GI brides were whisked off their feet but it did not always end happily ever after 'over the pond'. Sometimes servicemen came home to Britain that the girlfriend they hoped to marry and settle down with – or even the woman they had already married – had found someone else.

As always during wartime, soldiers and other men took their chances where they could get them, sometimes by force. A few paid dearly for it. Richardson's own case was not so much a love triangle as a love quadrilateral; he was one of two, if not more, men consorting with a married woman in Leeds and shot dead a rival out of jealousy while the woman's husband was away serving with the forces. In the far less documented but probably more representative case of William Batty, just down the road in Bradford, the victim was a love rival too, though at least he appears to have been the only one.

Batty was a 27-year-old labourer who lived at his family home at 65 Ireton Street, about 1.5 miles away from the home of his eventual victim. Little is known of his childhood other than that he was afflicted with tuberculosis and had to be treated in sanatoria. This cleared up after a final bout at the age of 17. As a result of it, though, his schooling was disrupted and he only attained Standard 5.

From his teenage years onwards, Batty was a habitual criminal, whose misdeeds had escalated in seriousness ever since he was first fined five shillings for riding a bicycle without a red rear light in September 1934. If he kept on the straight and narrow for a couple of years after that, his career exploded in some style thereafter. In February 1937, he stole a wristwatch, for which he was fined £18 and bound over in the sum of £5 for two years. Two months later, he was listed as a deserter from the Army. That October, he was accused of stealing a car worth £319 and in November of taking a car without the owner's consent and driving it while under the influence of alcohol, for all of which he was fined £1 plus costs and bound over in the sum of £5 for three years.

On New Year's Eve 1937, an application was made to vary the conditions, presumably because he was struggling to, or even not attempting to, pay his fines, and he was ordered to live at a Church of England Temperance Society Lad's Home for three months. It took him only three weeks to violate these conditions and earn himself a fine of 7s.6d, which was discharged two days later. Batty had not learned much, though. That April, he was convicted of breaking into a warehouse and stealing linen, with another offence being taken into consideration. It seems that he had tested the magistrates' patience too far this time because they gave three years in Borstal.

Batty was out by January 1940 when he was accused of shopbreaking but was discharged when no evidence was offered. The same occurred a month later, when he was accused of breaking into a garage and stealing a car and a licence. All this had taken place in Bradford. In May, he was in York where he was again up for taking a car without the owner's consent, with three other offences, one in Bradford, being taken into consideration. It earned him one month's imprisonment. Back in Bradford next February, he was in trouble for breaking into a store and committing larceny, with four offences being taken into consideration; he was sentenced to ten months.

Finally in April 1943, he was up for housebreaking and stealing goods to the value of £1,239.3d on one count, and the same with goods worth £426. These were very substantial sums of money and it seems probable that the goods were mostly jewels that he tried unsuccessfully to fence. This time, 13 other cases were taken into consideration. Batty was sentenced to three years of penal servitude and was ordered to pay costs of £33.8s.6d. Evidently, he was released early because he was at liberty by mid-1945 at the latest. In all, he had been in court 16 times by the end of the war. For reasons unknown, he had never been called up to serve in the armed forces. It is scarcely an exaggeration to call Batty a one-man crimewave. He was also a disastrously unsuccessful criminal, with no moral boundaries and no self-control.

Another Bradford man, one who kept out of the courts and the papers, was Samuel Hammond Gray. The son of a man of the same name and his wife Sarah Anne, Gray was 33 at the time of his return to the city in 1945. He lived at 45 Prince Street in the Dudley Hill area, near the main arterial route out to the south-east of the city with his wife Nellie, by whom he had two sons, Peter and Alan. The house was part of a row of 'back-to-backs' and was approached down an alleyway off the main street. Gray had gone to serve in Burma in 1941, as a driver in the Royal Corps of Signals.

At some point in 1942, Nellie met Batty in a pub and began an affair with him. Her choice of lover was not a good one and she must have worked that out before very long. According to Nellie – who, to be fair, may not have been telling the whole truth on this matter – she told Batty from the start not to take their affair seriously and that he would have to disappear from the scene when her husband returned because she still loved Samuel. "You mean I'm just here to give you a bit of fun," he allegedly asked on one occasion. She replied, "You've got it in one", and repeatedly reminded him as much.

The source of all this is unclear and Nellie herself would deny in court that there had been an affair.

Batty, she soon realised, was a jealous man with a violent streak and possibly suicidal tendencies, not one likely to slink back into the shadows when his mistress's husband showed up. In July 1945, he pulled out a Luger and spun the chamber around, then left it in a raincoat pocket at the house. He told her he had bought this, together with 50 rounds of ammunition, in Leeds and said various other things that made her uneasy about his intentions. She also claimed that she had tried to end the relationship but that he had refused to accept it. Indeed, by her account, he continued to say that he would shoot Gray when he came back on multiple occasions "because he wanted me to go with him". The last time was just before Gray returned.

Matters came to a head on 9 August, the same day that the second atomic bomb was dropped on Nagasaki. Out of the blue, Gray sent a telegram to Nellie, saying that he would be coming home on leave the next day. At this point, he had been away continuously for three years and there was no chance that he would ever be required to go back on active service. He may well have rejoiced inwardly that he had survived the war. In fact, he did not; he was shot dead on his own doorstep the day before it officially ended. On hearing the news of his rival's return, Batty at first said he would talk over the situation with Gray, but ominously added: "If he won't let you go, I'll shoot him".

Two days later, on 11 August, Gray arrived home. That evening, he was sitting in the living room with a cup of tea when he heard a man's voice asking her neighbour from number 47, Margaret Ripley: "Where is the next-door neighbour, Margaret?" Then there was a knock at the door. Nellie opened it. The man standing there was, of course, Batty. He gestured to her to come out and talk to him, but she ignored him and closed the door in his face. Shortly after, at 11.10 p.m., Alice Spilsbury, who lived at number 20, saw Batty sitting on her wall as she walked home. He asked her if she would go through the passageway opposite and tell Mrs Gray that someone wanted to see her. She refused and told him to get off the wall for good measure. Saying nothing more, he complied.

When Mrs Spilsbury looked out again a few minutes later, he was not there, but when she left her home to visit her friend Mrs Hallworth higher up the street at number 15, she saw that he had only moved to the opposite side about two houses beyond the passage to number 45. She quickened her step to avoid him. Almost at once, she said, he put his hand into a coat pocket and took something out. There was a flash and a loud noise. Initially she did not realise it was a gun but an ex-serviceman like Gray would have known exactly it was. Nellie was to testify that they both heard it but said nothing about it and, astonishingly, added that "we attached little importance to the shot". Even then, Batty did not leave the vicinity. When Mrs Spilsbury left her friend's home at 1.20 a.m. on 12 August, he was lying in a doorway opposite number 15.

On 14 August, Nellie received a letter from Batty. She had no choice now but to confess the truth to her husband. Gray, who would probably have suspected something and may have availed himself of the services of local girls in Burma like most soldiers did, said that he forgave her and would make a new start with her. Meanwhile, Batty spent the evening in the Cross Keys Hotel, drinking and playing dominoes. Milkman Albert Edward Leeming saw him leave at about 10.00 p.m. when the beer ran out and the taproom closed. He seemed quite sober, Leeming said. Batty then made his way to Prince Street, where Reuben Fearnley, a lorry driver who lived at number 87 and had seen him once before, spotted him lurking in the passageway by number 45 at about 10.20.

The Grays were sitting in their living room with Margaret Ripley, who had come to collect a newspaper. Nellie, who knew that Batty was hanging around in the vicinity, watched out anxiously for him. At one point, Batty even asked a passing girl to knock on the door for him before finally plucking up the courage to do it himself. The door opened inward to the left, straight into the living room. When Gray answered it, he asked to talk to Nellie. "May I ask who the hell you are?" replied Gray, or in other versions "Who are you? What do you want?" "I am nobody," said Batty, presumably dramatising the humiliation of rejection. Without further ado, he drew out his revolver and fired a single shot into Gray from close range.

Nellie said later that this took place at about 10.35 p.m., and that she recognised Batty's voice, heard a shot and saw Gray collapse backwards onto the floor inside the doorway. The bullet entered his body in the upper part of the abdomen, midway between the navel and the breastbone. It passed through the stomach, aorta and the body of the 11th dorsal vertebrae, damaging the spinal cord before exiting his back, then travelled into the house, smashing a vase on a dresser at the back of the living room. Gray's abdomen rapidly filled with blood and he had no chance of survival.

Batty ran out through the passageway into the street as Nellie Gray tried to tend to her husband and Margaret Ripley ran for help. There were a lot of people out and about on that warm summer evening where it had just turned to dusk. Some were drawn out by the commotion; others were just taking the chance of some air; others were on the way home from the pubs or the cinemas. Ripley – who, like Nellie, had not seen the assailant because Gray and the door blocked her view, recognised his voice, having seen him at the house many times – called the police.

Others, some of whom knew Batty by sight and some who did not, got a good look at him. James Arthur Sefton and his wife Elsie May, who lived at number 37, later testified that they heard the shot as they turned into Prince Street from Tong Street on their way back from the Dudley Hill Picture House. They saw Batty, who Elsie had known by sight for a few weeks, running along the roadway. He passed close by them, his right hand thrust deep into his jacket pocket, his left hand on his chest holding either the lapel of his coat or his chest. Agnes Feather of number 57, another wife of an absent soldier, was also on the way back from the pictures when she saw Batty leaning against a wall on the left-hand corner where Tong Street met Prince Street. She had known him for 12 years, though they did not speak to each other now.

Continuing along, Mrs Feather met Fred Mitchell, a miner from number 63 who did not know Batty, and walked down the street with him. When someone spoke to her about the incident, she went back to the top of Prince Street but did not see Batty again, so instead they went they went to 45 to find Gray lying on the floor, groaning. After running away, it appears that Batty hung around uncertain of what to do. Harry Kay, John Lavery and Jack Gallagher all saw him at close quarters as they stood talking near the junction with Tong Street. None of them knew him before and he did not join the conversation, but none of them had heard a shot or knew that anything was amiss at that point.

The police were apparently alerted at 10.59 p.m. and Sergeant William Ryall arrived from Cutler Heights Police Station at 11.07 to find a crowd of people in Prince Street. They directed him to number 45, where Agnes Feather was applying a cold compress to the stricken man's forehead. Gray was already unconscious and beyond help, though Ryall gave him first aid. Dr George Reginald Granton arrived, carried out a cursory examination and pronounced him dead. As the body was lifted up, Granton found the bullet under Gray's left shoulder and handed it to Detective Sergeant Gordon Dewhurst. It had presumably ricocheted off the back wall, because only one had been fired by all accounts.

"The murder created a sensation in the neighbourhood of the dead man's home. By midnight, a fairly large crowd had gathered," the local press reported. A nine-year-old schoolboy found the cartridge shortly afterwards in a passage about five yards away from the house, as the body was being moved out. He handed it Mitchell, who handed it to Ryall. Detective Inspector Cecil Walton found the cartridge case. All three items were passed on to Detective Superintendent Thomas Rushworth, who in turn passed them to Dr Lewis Charles Nickolls, director of the North-Eastern Science Forensic Laboratory in Wakefield – 'Elsie', to his colleagues because of his initials - for forensic analysis.

Batty himself made his way back to Ireton Street and knocked first on the door of number 33. This was the home of his mother's friend Florence Heavysides, with whom she often spent the evening. There was nothing unusual about his demeanour, Heavysides said later. Told that his mother had gone home at 9.45 p.m., he went on to number 65 and knocked. It was now 12.15 a.m. on 15 August, which was to be VJ Day. Mrs Batty said: "The police are looking for you. They've been here and searched all over." He replied, "If they come again, say you haven't seen me", and turned to go but was immediately arrested by Detective Constable Stanley Metcalfe, who had been waiting close by with PC Croydon since calling earlier and finding him to be out.

They took him back into the house and cautioned him. His first words were: "I can tell you where I've been tonight. I know nothing about it". They took him to the Town Hall and cautioned him again. Asked by Metcalfe if he cared to say now where he had been the previous evening, he said "No", and when charged with murder at 1.15, he said: "I have nothing to say". Bradford's chief police surgeon Dr Ralph Rimmer, who had just Samuel Gray's body, now checked his killer on arrival at the station and found that he had consumed some alcohol but was not drunk at that point and showed no evidence of organic disease or mental health problems.

Later that morning, Rimmer carried out a post mortem that established the full extent of the damage the bullet had done and found from powder marks around the wound that it had been fired from no more than an inch and a half away. Cause of death was shock and haemorrhage, he inevitably concluded. Meanwhile, Mitchell and Kaye both picked out Batty from an identity parade as the man they had seen at the top of Prince Street after the murder. He made his first appearance in front of magistrates at Bradford City Court later that day.

Describing him as a "pale-faced man with a small moustache [and] wearing working clothes", the newspapers said that he "appeared to be calm, though his face was flushed". Only formal evidence of arrest was given. DS Rushworth applied for a remand to give time for the necessary papers to be forwarded to the Director of Public Prosecution.

Batty was duly remanded until 23 August and given legal aid. While he awaited the next hearing, police searched for the revolver, asking for anyone who found it or who could supply information as to its whereabouts to get in touch. Successive remands followed as the case was built up. The medical officer at HMP Armley, Dr Francis H. Brisby, kept him under observation and reported, two weeks after his incarceration, that despite his limited education, Batty was of quite good intelligence, there was no recent recurrence of his illness and his mind was "clear and alert"; there was nothing suggestive of mental illness and he was fit to stand trial. Indeed, since Batty was claiming it was all an accident, there would be no real effort to ascertain the true state of his mental health.

Batty finally came to trial at the West Riding Assizes in Leeds on 29-30 November before Mr Justice Lynskey. Geoffrey Hugh Benbow Streatfield KC, who was less than two years from being elevated to the bench where he acquired a particularly grim reputation, led for the prosecution; Charles B. Fenwick KC led for the defence. The killing was ascribed to simple jealousy. The police called no fewer than 22 witnesses: Rushworth, Walton, Dewhurst, Ryall, Dr Granton, Dr Rimmer, two other professional witnesses and 14 others who collectively established the sequence of events of both 11-12 and 14-15 August.

Nellie Gray testified to the course of her relationship with Batty and her attempts to break it off, while Margaret Ripley said categorically that she recognised Batty by his voice, as she had seen and spoken to him many times. Nickolls, who had examined all the firearms exhibits on 25 August, testified that the cartridge case he had been given to examine came from same gun as the one handed to him for testing. In addition, the powder burns around Gray's wounds showed that he had been shot at extremely close range.

The defence did not dispute the basic facts but instead alleged that the aggressor was Gray. Under questioning from his counsel, Batty simply denied threatening to shoot or kill Gray, said that he had never owned a revolver, pistol or gun, and claimed that he and Nellie "were devoted to each other". He claimed that it was Gray who had pulled the gun and pointed it at him, shouting: "I know who you are and what you want". Gray then pointed something at his chest, he said "No, don't" and twisted Gray's wrist to his body. Then there was a loud bang. "Gray staggered back and I had the gun in my hand. I gripped the pistol when Gray pressed it to me and I twisted his hand. I ran with the pistol, I was frightened. I did not know that Gray was seriously injured," he claimed. He only realised he was holding the gun as Gray fell. Frightened, he put it under his coat and later threw it over a railway embankment as he went home.

Fenwick tried putting this to Nellie Gray, saying: "I suggest that your husband had a pistol and that there was a sharp struggle between them, involving Batty seizing your husband's wrist, and that immediately after there was a shot". She said that neither was the case and also denied in the teeth of all the evidence to the contrary that Batty had ever been her lover. She had to admit that he had stayed overnight at the house many times over the past three years, because Margaret Ripley, herself the wife of a serving solider, had said as much. Ripley added that there were only two bedrooms and the master bedroom had a double bed, leaving the insinuation as clear as day.

No doubt many held the cheating wife largely responsible for what happened. That, however, was for the court of public opinion. In the court of law, the jury needed only 25 minutes to decide they did not believe Batty's story. He was clearly sane, his crime was witnessed and premeditated, and the sentence was inevitable. Asked if he had anything to say, he enigmatically replied: "I protected my life just to forfeit my life". This was presumably a continuing claim of self-defence. Batty's solicitor said on 4 December that there would be an appeal, on grounds yet to be decided, but it was dismissed on 20 December. No reasons for this have ever entered the public domain and it is doubtful that there could have been any substance to it.

On 8 January 1946, Batty was hanged at HMP Armley by Thomas Pierrepoint and Harry Allen, who recorded it simply as "Very good job". "No more than half a dozen people were in the vicinity when he was hanged," a newspaper report stated and, indeed, it is hard to imagine that there was the slightest shred of sympathy for him locally. Gray was buried in Tong Cemetery in Bradford, in Section A, Grave 130. Prince Street has been almost completely redeveloped since the murder, with only a few older houses left.

15. "Now you can meet the boyfriend": The murder of Charles Alfred Elphick by Michał Nieścior at 69 Abinger Road, Portslade, on 21 October 1945 and his execution at HMP Wandsworth on 31 January 1946

Many stories of wartime romance and betrayal were playing out up and down the country in 1945 as many returning servicemen found that their wives and girlfriends had not just stayed at home knitting and waiting for their safe return. For a few unlucky men in these love triangles, these stories were to end with them lying dead and sometimes their rivals following suit a few months later at the hands of the state. In each of these cases, the cheating wife lived on after the man who killed on her account was hanged. Not one of the husbands who killed the woman he returned to went to the gallows as a result.

Among the cases in the year after VE Day that did end that way, those of [4] Thomas Richardson, [14] William Batty and [15] Michał Nieścior were all different but had something in common in that the (male) victim was the rival of the perpetrator and the rivalry evolved in circumstances that would almost certainly not have occurred but for the coming of war. Less than a week after Batty faced the hangman at HMP Armley for murdering the husband of the woman who had been dallying with him in wartime, Polish-born Nieścior paid the price for a very similar crime, which also took place on the doorstep of the victim's house, at Portslade-by-Sea, Sussex.

Charles Alfred Elphick had married his wife, Jessie Eileen, who signed herself 'Jean', in 1934. They lived with their daughter, Joan, at 69 Abinger Road, part of a row of Edwardian terraced houses just south of the A270 which demarcates the old Portslade village to the north from Portslade-by-Sea, originally known as Copperas Gap, to the south. Portslade-by-Sea took its name in late Victorian times, when the whole coastal strip between Brighton and Worthing was developed. There was no seaside glamour here, however: it was essentially the industrial centre of Brighton and Hove, and it was far from being a wealthy town.

According to Jessie, the marriage was happy until 1939, when war broke out and Charles was called up. By then, he was 36 and towards the upper end of the age range for active service. He spent three years of the war still in Britain. From June 1942 to August 1945, he served as a signalman with the Royal Corps of Signals. This was the same corps as [14] Samuel Gray served in and in the same theatre of war, Burma, so it is not impossible that they knew each other.

Like many other deserted wives, Jessie's eyes strayed and she began attending dance venues in Brighton. It was at one of these, called Sherry's that she encountered Nieścior in May or June 1944. He had been invalided out of the Polish Navy with a duodenal ulcer, came to Britain and worked as a chef at the Polish Rest Home for Sailors on the seafront at 98 Marine Parade. It was definitely Jessie who made the running. At some point afterwards, she rang him at the Royal Crescent Hotel, asked if he remembered her and if he had a girlfriend. He said "No" and she told him they should meet again. Next time they did, he stayed the night at her house. After the first month, they were meeting every night.

By Jessie's account, Nieścior looked on her as his wife and addressed her as such. "We both got very fond of each other and he was very passionate towards me and I to him," she later admitted. By November, the relationship was serious enough that Jessie wrote to her husband telling him she had a new partner. He responded by stopping the allowance he had been paying her. From February 1945, she ceased to write to him so Elphick did not know that her new man had moved in with her in April 1945. In August, as the war in the Far East came to a close, Charles was given 96 days' leave ahead of being demobbed, which in practice meant that he was almost certainly going to be home for good. Now 42, he looked considerably older, with his portly frame, his grey temples and his mostly bald head.

When he got home on 10 August, the day after the second atomic bomb was dropped on Nagasaki and brought Japan to its knees, the girlfriend of another Pole opened the door and Elphick was confronted by the sight of a stranger sitting up in his bed; Jessie was in the bath in the kitchen. Her first words to her husband, she later admitted, were: "What are you doing here? I've finished with you a long time ago. Now you can meet the boyfriend." Words, not surprisingly, were exchanged. Elphick ordered Nieścior out and Jessie said: "That goes for me too". Her husband, she later said, was angry, though she had seen him angrier. The three spent a tense night together under one roof. Next day, she and Nieścior moved out to lodgings at 53 Gardener Street, close by.

Game, set and match to the interloper, it seemed. Except that it was not that simple. Jessie was pulled each way by love, guilt, the excitement of a passionate affair and no doubt reproaches and disapproval from people around her. From the start, she returned every morning to make breakfast for Elphick and Joan. This led to rows with the jealous, controlling Nieścior. Only nine days later, she moved back into the marital home. "I had gone so far with Nieścior that I did not know to break it to him. He dreaded it. I did not find that week all that I thought of him was right. I realised what I had left with my husband and daughter," she later stated. "You can't go back, you can't go back," he told her. "I must," she replied. "You can't," he said again. But she did.

After staying with Elphick that night, she saw Nieścior next evening but, she claimed, did not dare to tell him that she intended to move back in permanently because Nieścior had already threatened to kill her if she did. "He said if he saw me walking with [Elphick], he would put a knife in me and no one would know the difference," she said. She feared he really might, because "I knew his temper". Jessie's account was, of course, entirely self-serving although she did at least have the grace not to deny the affair. Nieścior for his part claimed that she told him at one point that her moving back in would make no difference because she would still see him any time he liked. This she denied.

The following day, however, she met him at the Crescent Hotel – and despite the fact that Elphick saw them together, she spent the night with Nieścior at his lodgings at 96 Old Shoreham Road. She returned next morning to find Elphick out and went back to Nieścior's. Next time she went home, she found the door locked and bolted, and back she went again. This time, she spent three nights there but after that, she claimed, she told Nieścior she was finished with him. Quite what had been going on in her head is hard to say. On Saturday 1 September, she returned to her husband and somehow convinced him that she really had decided to stay with him for good.

To make a new start and, no doubt, to get away from Nieścior for a while, the family then went for a short break at Jessie's mother's home in Hastings. When they returned on 9 September, she found that a window had been smashed the electric switch had been pulled from the wall and the dial on the wireless had been smashed. In the kitchen, they found a coat that had been cut to pieces and a skirt that had been ripped up. More scarily still, there was a knife mark in the mattress of the bed where they slept. Clearly someone had broken in and done his utmost to scare them. There was only one realistic suspect. She remonstrated, but Nieścior denied everything.

What Jessie left out of her statement about this time, however, was very pertinent. She clearly remained torn between the two men and had written three letters to Nieścior while she was still on holiday with her husband. Badly written though there were, they leave no doubt about her feelings for him, or the kick it was probably giving her to dangle a moonstruck lover on a string.

"Hello darling," one began. "Just a few lines to let you know I am still at Hastings with my mother and Joan. Well, Mickel [sic], hope you haven't missed me too much, darling!! I don't know quite what I am going to do or how long I shall stay here and it's all through your own fault, you know why, for you certainly did not prove your love for me the last night I was at [illegible] and anyway, darling, if you don't see me for one or two weeks and you still love and make up your mind what you are going to do, then I will come and see you at the Crescent. But if you don't want me then we must say goodbye, maybe you will find another girlfriend while I am away. So Mickel darling, try and be a good boy and I'll be seeing you soon. Don't worry about anything for you know you can trust me now, I wonder? ... So this is all for now. I want to come and see you now but maybe you will still be bad-tempered with me again ... Darling, keep smiling. Ever yours, Jean."

Another read: "How are you feeling these days? I miss you more than you'll ever know. Well darling, it seems years since I last saw you, hub." This was presumably short for 'husband'. "I am here with my mother and Joan, thinking about you all the time. Darling, do you still love me? I wish you were here tonight. I wonder what you have been doing with yourself and anyway, don't be surprised to see me at the Crescent any time."

The third, probably from after the holiday, came from another location where Jessie was staying with her sister. "I bet you think I have a boyfriend here. Well Mickel, you are wrong for I have not," it began. After some characteristically English words about the weather, she asked: "Darling, have you any other girlfriends, I wonder!! I like to know, cross my heart, and anyway, I still love you darling (honestly cross my heart) and I still miss you, it seems years since I last saw you dear. Anyway, perhaps you are not missing me after all. Anyway, I will be seeing you soon and take care of my cycle because I might need it again." This referred to a bicycle she had lent him a few weeks before the night it was all to explode in her face. "I wish I was never going to see Portslade again ever!! Then I'd be happy. I hear that Mr Elphick is at Hastings again. I don't know when I shall go back there, so now I shall say cheerio. Darling, all my love and kisses. Your Jean".

Between her return to Portslade and 21 October, by Jessie's account, she saw Nieścior three times although she continued to sleep at home. She was later to claim that she saw him out of fear that he would kill her husband. On 19 October, she received a letter from him, dated the day before and referring obliquely to a quarrel when they met two nights before. Addressed to "my darling wife" and in impenetrable English, this ran: "Just a few lines to remind me at Brighton. I'm wondering because you don't wont see me any more.

"I see you change your mind and you forget your promise and forget that time when I was been in hospital and you are come every night to see me and you are allways been cry of me when I was very ill and that I never forget and I don't forget your love all the time we was been together. Now I don't know what is happen with you and what is wrong with you. Please let me know what you think is going to do now but I like to what do you really think about me and or life together. My darling wife, please don't be angry what I am going to tell you but it seems to me you don't believe me or are you afraid of something some think like that. I have give you my word and promise, you know that I am yours and I won't change my mind, you start to worry to me and make my bad tempered."

"Dearest Jean, I am very don't sorry about last night when you tell me about coupons and you and I try to give you single coupons," he continued, presumably referring to clothing coupons. "You must know I was been only joking with you but now I am no now. You are is very take offence. Please Jean, forgive me, I am very sorry for you for all I was being alone, please forgive me that. I do not that never, darling Jean." Nieścior continued that he had got a place for them to live, just two minutes' walk from the Crescent and now did not know what to do with it. "Please let me know what to do with home because it costs lots of money on one month ... I only will tell I still love you I didn't change me feeling to you, just the same as befor and I will wait for you when you came and tell me what I must start to do. Please write. All my love for you and to Joan. Your forever loving, Michal."

It seems clear that there had been an argument over something he did not understand to be serious or that perhaps she had engineered to finish things. The reference to the house must tie in with the testimony of Charles Walter Mason, caretaker at the Polish Rest Home for Sailors, that Nieścior asked his help to find some lodgings for his wife and daughter, though when Mason did so he apologised and said he would not need them after all. Presumably there was no answer from Jessie.

Rebuffed and humiliated, Nieścior brooded. On the evening of 21 October, he cleaned the kitchen at the rest home thoroughly, locked the door and gave the key to another former seaman who worked there, Paul Danilo, at 6.45 p.m. He had clearly armed himself with a knife. He then spent a little time with Mason at the Cannon Arms pub, saying as he left at 7.35 that he was going on to the Dome in Brighton. Witold Siedlar, another seaman who worked there as a cook, saw Nieścior standing at the entrance at about 8.00 p.m. but did not see him come in again that night.

What he was doing in the following three hours is unknown and probably unimportant but at 11.20 p.m., he arrived outside 69 Abinger Road on Jessie's bicycle. Nieścior was to claim later that Jessie told him Elphick had made threats against him and that he kept a knife under his pillow. All of this she also denied. Given that the weapon Elphick chose was not a knife, it seems probable that this much was true. Her claim that she never mentioned him to her husband is harder to believe.

The couple were in bed in the front bedroom at the time when they heard the letterbox rattling. They heard someone trying the windows, then jumping from the windowsill to the garden. Jessie immediately "had a feeling" it was Nieścior but did not say so at first. All was quiet for a few minutes, then they heard the back door being tried. To get there, it was necessary to go 50 yards down the street and climb a high wall, so this showed that the would-be intruder was in earnest.

At this point, Elphick got up, put his trousers on, turned on the hall light and went downstairs. It went quiet again but just as Elphick came back upstairs, they heard Nieścior shouting "Open this door" and banging hard on it. "You know who that is," Jessie said. A look through the clear glass panel on the door confirmed that it was his rival, fully tooled up. "He's got a darn big knife," Elphick said. "You get out of the way, I'll open the door," she told him, with more courage than sense. Elphick said "I'll get something to hit him with first", went to the kitchen tool cupboard and picked up a scaffolding hammer. Again, she said, "You get out of the way, I'll open the door", and Elphick stayed behind her.

Jessie later claimed to be afraid that Nieścior would kill her first. As she opened it, she saw Nieścior with the knife in his hand. "Listen, let me talk to you, let me talk to you," she begged, but Nieścior shouted over her shoulder at Elphick either "This is for you" or "I'll finish you", she was not sure which, and slashed at him. A brawl ensued, with Jessie trapped between husband and lover as they went for each other with deadly weapons. Nieścior got no further in than the doormat and the fracas continued outside, over the gatepost.

Finally, all three fell over a low garden wall onto the pavement, Jessie landing on top of Nieścior. She felt the knife underneath her and tried to grab it but he got there first, cutting her left hand. According to Nieścior, he managed to grab Elphick's hammer and hit him with it, a claim borne out by the blood found on it later. Frederick Haville of number 75 and Albert Edward Strange of number 92 were both woken by screams at different times. Haville looked out and saw the two men fighting in the porch. Nieścior broke away and ran into the centre of the street, followed by Elphick, who was dressed in a singlet and trousers, but wore no shoes.

Jessie, Haville and Strange both confirmed, picked up the bicycle and told Elphick to go back into the house, and he did so. She then made to get onto the bicycle and go to the police, but found the chain was off and she started to push it down the road towards Shelldale Road. Nieścior grabbed her by the coat and pulled her from it to prevent her from leaving, then said "All right, we go for the police". Fearing she had no alternative, she said, she walked away from the scene with him. Strange stated later that as he half-dragged her past his house, Jessie cried out "You've killed my husband" and Nieścior replied: "I'll kill you too". Strange recognised the voice of the man he had seen at the house many times before.

According to Haville, Elphick came back out three or four minutes later. He ran after them as far as Bampfield Street and was only about two yards behind Nieścior according to Strange, but then turned back. When Haville found him, he was staggering about, bleeding from the left arm, and had face injuries. Together with Strange, Haville helped Elphick towards his house. Elphick called out to his daughter, who opened the door from the inside. The two men laid him down in the scullery, where Haville laid his coat under him and tried to bind his wounds, while Strange called for a doctor and the police.

Holding her left sleeve and ignoring her screams, Nieścior marched Jessie to the corner of Bampfield Street, right into Trafalgar Road and on towards the Catholic Church at the bottom of Vale Road. Here, she said, he took the knife out of his left pocket and tried to drag her up Vale Road. Trying to pull herself free, she protested that they had to go to the police but Nieścior pulled at her coat, tearing the sleeve, then took the knife out again and said: "This goes through you, then through me. I finish everything tonight." She said that she did not understand what was happening. "You don't want me. You can't have him," he shouted.

At length, she persuaded him to go back towards the house with her. Once they got to the corner of Bampfield Street and Abinger Road again, they saw a light and people milling around. "I believe the police are there," the Pole said. "Now look out," said Jessie and ran. When she got back into the house, it was to find her husband on the floor of the kitchen and four men attending to him, one of whom was a local GP, Dr George Mitchison. PC William Caldicott, then Inspector William Hunt and Detective Constable Nice arrived at the scene. They found bloodstains on both gate pillars, on the pathways, on both walls inside the front door, on the passageway to the scullery and in the scullery itself. The hammer was lying on the table with "a good deal of blood" on it.

Elphick was rushed to Southlands Hospital in Shoreham-by-Sea, arriving still conscious at 12.30 a.m. on 22 October. Dr Kenneth William Oldham, the assistant medical officer, tended to him. Meanwhile, Nieścior made good on his promise. At 1.30 a.m., Sergeant Walter Broadbridge was on duty at Brighton when the Pole walked in, his clothes soaking from the heavy rain. He held his right hand up to show a small cut about an inch long between the knuckle and the wrist and said in broken English, "I have been fighting. Man fought me, I fought him. I came to the police for this", indicating his hand.

Asked why he had been fighting, Nieścior said: "I knocked at the door. Man came to the door. I live with his wife for three years while he was away." He told Broadbridge the other man's name, adding that he had walked all the way from Portslade. Broadbridge had another officer dress the wound, which he did not think needed hospital treatment, though in fact it took two weeks to heal. Nieścior gave his name and showed his identity card, saying he had come from the Royal Crescent Hotel. Evidently believing the story, Broadbridge said that if wanted to take any action, he should go to a JP in the morning and take out a summons.

Nieścior left and went back to his workplace, where he washed and replaced the knife, then went to bed in one of the vacant rooms. In the interim, the police were getting a truer picture. Siedlar opened the door to Hunt at 3.30 a.m. and showed them where to find

Nieścior. At first, Siedlar said, Nieścior refused to hand over the keys to the kitchen, saying that only the Lieutenant Commander could have them, but was eventually persuaded otherwise. They got in to find the knife lying across two sinks, still very wet. He was taken to Brighton Police Station, cautioned and told he would be taken back to Portslade Police Station to be charged with unlawful wounding. He declined the services of an interpreter, saying he understood English, but Marceli Reimus, a Chief Petty Officer in the Polish Navy, was fetched anyway.

Nieścior was charged at 6.45 a.m. and he made a statement that reads nothing like the English he actually spoke. He had gone to return the bicycle, he claimed. When he knocked on the door, Elphick came downstairs, switched on the light and looked through the window. "When he saw it was me, he quickly ran upstairs and returned with a small axe. Mrs Elphick came down just after him. She opened the door. Mr Elphick tried to hit me with the axe, which he had raised ready to strike. Mrs Elphick came near me. I raised my right arm to defend myself, and I received a cut on my wrist. With my left hand, I caught his hand and, losing balance, we all fell down in the small yard in front of the house. I was underneath but got myself free. I hit Mr Elphick with his own axe, which I got hold of whilst lying on the ground. Then I left quickly," he continued. "Mr Elphick ran after me and I ran away to the police to report the matter."

This clearly omitted a lot of detail, to say the least, as it made no mention of the knife he brought or the wounds he inflicted. Things soon got much worse for the Pole, because the charge was upgraded to murder. After an initial improvement, Elphick's condition had suddenly began to deteriorate at 9.25 and he died 15 minutes later. Jessie was at his side and one can scarcely imagine what was going through her mind. When told of this at about 11.35 a.m., according to Hunt, Nieścior responded: "Let them take me from here and shoot me right away".

Dr Leonard James performed a post mortem at the Royal Sussex Hospital and found five head injuries, including one of four and a half inches running all the way down from the right eye across the cheek. There were two serious wounds to the chest. One, three inches below the left collarbone, had perforated between the second and third ribs, bruising the heart; the other went two and a half inches into the neck. The right lung had collapsed and there was a large amount of blood and fluid from severed vessels, plus 15 superficial cuts and scratches on the upper torso. Cause of death was shock, following numerous stab wounds.

Nieścior appeared at Hove Magistrates Court on 23 October, 5 November and lastly 20 November 1945. In prison, he was emotional at times but gave no trouble. The medical officer found it hard to speak conclusively about his mental health because of his limited English but was certain that he was fit to plead. At the last hearing, Jessie gave evidence, describing how she "dared not tell Nieścior she was going to return to her husband, because he told her that if she did, he would kill her". She burst into tears part of the way through her testimony.

The trial took place at the Sussex Assizes in Lewes on 10-11 December before Mr Justice Wrottesley, with Tristram Beresford KC leading for the prosecution and Eric Neve KC for the defence. It would be the last capital murder case over which Sir Frederick John Wrottesley (1880-1948) would preside before being appointed to the Court of Appeal the following year. Appointed a judge in the King's Bench Division in 1937, he had been better known for his work in civil cases, but he studied criminology when he was elevated and became known for his profound knowledge of criminal law and common-sense approach.

Wrottesley had passed sentence of death over Johannes Dronkers and other spies during World War II; wife murderer Harry Dobkin in 1942; and George Silverosa and Sam Dashwood, two young thugs who murdered a pawnbroker in London that same year. He was also on the court that rejected the appeals of Karl Gustav Hulten, the US Army deserter and his girlfriend Elizabeth Jones, whose six-day crime spree, culminating in the murder of a taxi driver in 1945 was one of the most avidly followed of its day and indirectly spawned George Orwell's celebrated essay, *Decline of the English Murder,* which was published in *Tribune* magazine in 1946.

The facts of the current case were not in much dispute. Paul Danilo identified the knife shown in court as one of those from the kitchen at the Polish Rest Home for Sailors. He also testified that Nieścior had often talked of Jessie Elphick but had never mentioned any quarrel he had with Charles Elphick. The main prosecution witness was Jessie herself. Inevitably, the defence tried to portray her evidence as unreliable because of her past behaviour. Wrottesley, however, told the jury that her admitted adultery did not necessarily make her a perjurer.

Everything hung on Nieścior's claim that he was acting in self-defence. This was at least a tenable claim. Perhaps uniquely among all the defendants facing capital murder charges in post-war Britain, he had been in a fight with a man who was prepared to use a lethal weapon against him – there are many types of scaffolding hammer, but all are heavy and made of metal – and who may have been trying to kill him. Had Nieścior been the one killed, Elphick would surely have used the same line of defence, though with far more justification.

Nieścior stood by his statement: he had come back to return the bicycle and carried his knife because Jessie had told him that Charles kept a knife with him in bed; he only took it out after Elphick attacked him; he first hit Elphick with his own axe and he lashed out blindly, not intending to kill. He had no answer as to why he wanted to return the bicycle so late at night. And, as the prosecution pointed out, he had called round, armed and dangerous, and aggressively demanded to be let in. He had threatened Jessie with the knife as well as stabbing Elphick with it. He had the weapon, a motive and a readiness to kill. That was enough.

On 11 December, the jury of 11 men and one woman took only 45 minutes to find Nieścior guilty of murder. Jessie broke down in tears again as sentence of death was passed. His appeal for a verdict of manslaughter to be substituted was dismissed by Justices Humphreys, Lewis and Collins at the Court of Criminal Appeal on 14 January 1946; Humphreys observed that he had brought a knife to the house of a man he was at odds with and can have had no intention in his mind other than of using it.

Nieścior also petitioned the Home Secretary, similarly pointing the finger of blame at Jessie. "Time and time again, she was telling me her husband intended to kill me – that she did not confess in front of the court. I was in a constant state of fear that it may be fulfilled," he wrote. "Then he came up to me with an axe and did wound me in my arm. I defended myself with a kitchen knife." This cut no ice with the authorities either. The date of execution was fixed on 18 January and he was duly hanged at HMP Wandsworth by Albert Pierrepoint and Steve Wade on 31 January. Charles Elphick was buried in a war grave at Portslade Cemetery, his tomb slab recording only a few personal details and the date of his death.

The end of the rope – The hanged of post-war Britain

SOURCES

[1] George Smith

European Theater Operations Board of Review Opinions, Volume 22:

http://www.loc.gov/rr/frd/Military_Law/pdf/ETO-BOR_Vol-21.pdf

The Spectator, 24 September 1937

Northern Whig, 25 September 1937

The Scotsman, 18 October 1937

Detroit Free Press, 9 December 1944

Manchester Evening News, 8 January 1945

Williamsport Sun-Gazette, 9 January 1945

Belfast Newsletter, 9 January 1945

Gloucestershire Echo, 8 & 9 January 1945

Derby Daily Telegraph, 12 January 1945

Dundee Courier, 12 January 1945

Pittsburgh Press, 13 January & 11 May 1945

Democrat & Chronicle (Rochester, NY), 13 January 1945

The Advertiser (Adelaide), 16 January 1945

Chris Bishop, Eastern Daily Press, 8 September 2006

Times Free Press (Chattanooga), 16 November 2014

David Venditta, The Morning Call, 11 July 2015

Capital Punishment UK:

http://www.capitalpunishmentuk.org/sheptonm.html

Edward Burman website:

http://edwardburman.com/news/2016/7/8/the-strange-life-of-sir-eric-teichman

Wikipedia - Oise-Aisne American Cemetery Plot E:

https://en.wikipedia.org/wiki/Oise-Aisne_American_Cemetery_Plot_E

Ancientfaces:

https://www.ancientfaces.com/person/leonard-s-wojtacha/54168579

Honingham Village:

http://honinghampc.norfolkparishes.gov.uk/category/village-history/history-honingham-hall/

Norfolk Heritage Explorer:

http://www.heritage.norfolk.gov.uk/record-details?TNF278-Parish-Summary-Honingham-(Parish-Summary)

Wymondham College ... Remembered:

http://www.wcremembered.co.uk/usaf.html

Martin Bowman, We're Here to Win the War for You (Amberley, 1988)

Bill Cotton, They Would Have Come Looking for Me, Wouldn't They? (Badgerwood, 2005)

J. Robert Lilly & J. Michael Thompson, Executing US Soldiers in England, World War II: Command Influence & Sexual Racism, in Peter Hodgkinson (ed.), The International Library of Essays on Capital Punishment, Volume 3: Policy & Governance (Routledge, 2016)

True Detective, November 2020

[2] Aniceto Martinez

European Theater Operations Board of Review Opinions, Volume 22:

http://www.loc.gov/rr/frd/Military_Law/pdf/ETO-BOR_Vol-22.pdf

Lichfield Mercury, 23 February 1945

Charlotte Observer, 8 February 1993

Express & Star, 1 July 2017

Shepton Mallet Nub News, 15 February 2021

Capital Punishment UK:

http://www.capitalpunishmentuk.org/sheptonm.html

Wiki Visually – HMP Shepton Mallet:

https://wikivisually.com/wiki/Shepton_Mallet_(HM_Prison)

Wikipedia - Oise-Aisne American Cemetery Plot E:

https://en.wikipedia.org/wiki/Oise-Aisne_American_Cemetery_Plot_E

Wikipedia - List of Individuals Executed by the United States Military:

https://en.wikipedia.org/wiki/List_of_individuals_executed_by_the_United_States_military

Airfield Research Group:

https://www.airfieldresearchgroup.org.uk/forum/staffordshire-other-sites/11640-flaxley-green-pow-camp-rugeley?jjj=1530473167505

J. Robert Lilly & J. Michael Thompson, Executing US Soldiers in England, World War II: Command Influence & Sexual Racism, in Peter Hodgkinson (ed.), The International Library of Essays on Capital Punishment, Volume 3: Policy & Governance (Routledge, 2016)

J. Robert Lilly, US Military Justice in the European Theater of Operations, World War II

[3] Howard Grossley

National Archives: PCOM 9/1073

Extra, 2 September 1945

The end of the rope – The hanged of post-war Britain

Abby Bolter, Wales Online, 15 November 2017

Island Farm POW Camp Wales:

www.islandfarm.wales

Welsh Icons News:

http://welshicons.org/cymrupedia/buildings-structures/cardiff-hm-prison/

Documentaries: 'The Great Escape' & 'Lily':

http://www.seanchaifilms.net/

John Eddleston, Blind Justice: Miscarriages of Justice in Twentieth Century Britain? (ABC-Clio, 2000)

Charles Whiting, The Great German Escape (Pen & Sword, 2010)

Steve J. Plummer, The Greatest Escape (Cloth Wrap, 2015)

Tony Couzens, The Cwmaman Files (Self-published, 2015)

Paul Johnson, The Brookwood Killers: Military Murderers of WWII (Pen & Sword, 2022)

True Crime, August 2017

[4] Thomas Richardson

National Archives: HO 144/2228, HO 144/22229

Shields Daily News, 30 April 1945

Manchester Evening News, 22 May 1945

Manchester Evening News, 8 June 1945

Liverpool Echo, 8 June 1945

Hull Daily Mail, 9 June 1945

Daily Mirror, 9 June 1945

The end of the rope – The hanged of post-war Britain

Yorkshire Post & Evening Intelligencer, 9 June & 18 July 1945

Nottingham Evening Post, 16 July 1945

Liverpool Echo, 17 July 1945

Aberdeen Evening Express, 17 July 1945

Dundee Evening Telegraph, 18 July 1945

Bellshill Speaker, 20 July 1945

Motherwell Times, 20 July 1945

The Guardian, 17, 18 & 23 July 1945

Duncan Campbell, The Guardian 15 September 2013

Crimeandexecution.com on Facebook:

https://www.facebook.com/CrimeandExecution/photos/a.141806745979037.30452.141796299313415/219789931514051/

Ancestry:

https://www.ancestry.co.uk/genealogy/records/lily-motson-24-2zv9cj

John Eddleston, Murderous Leeds (DB Publishing, 2015)

[5] Erich König & four others

Newcastle Evening Mail, 2 July 1945

Liverpool Evening Express, 2 July 1945

Liverpool Echo, 3 July 1945

Birmingham Mail, 4 & 5 July 1945

Hartlepool Northern Daily Mail, 4 & 6 July 1945

Northern Whig, 7 July 1945

The end of the rope – The hanged of post-war Britain

The Scotsman, 7 & 10 July 1945

Birmingham Daily Post, 7 & 13 July 1945

Nottingham Evening Post, 9 & 10 July 1945

Daily Herald, 11 July 1945

Derby Daily Telegraph, 11 July 1945

Coventry Evening Telegraph, 12 July 1945

Belfast News-Letter, 13 July 1945

Yorkshire Evening Post, 27 August 1945

Western Morning News, 29 August 1945

David McKie, The Guardian, 23 December 2004

Lewis Cohen, Gazette & Herald (Devizes), 10 July 2008:

Manchester Evening News, 18 April 2010

Kriminalia.de:

http://www.kriminalia.de/wp-content/uploads/2016/10/The_Executioner_At_War.pdf

Axis History Forum:

https://forum.axishistory.com/viewtopic.php?t=153782

Island Farm Wales:

http://www.islandfarm.wales/German_And_Italian_Escape_Attempts_From_Other_Camps_In_Great_Britain.htm

Steve Fielding, Pierrepoint – A Family of Executioners:

https://fullenglishbooks.com/english-books/full-book-pierrepoint-read-online-chapter-22

The end of the rope – The hanged of post-war Britain

Capital Punishment UK – Pentonville Prison:

http://www.capitalpunishmentuk.org/penton.html

Stephen Stratford, British Military & Criminal History, 1900-99:

http://www.stephen-stratford.com/pow_trial.htm

Wartime Memories Project:

http://www.wartimememoriesproject.com/ww2/pow/powcamp.php?pid=2962

Volksbund Deutsche Kriegsgräberfürsorge:

http://www.volksbund.de/home.html

Wikipedia – London Cage:

https://en.wikipedia.org/wiki/London_Cage

Comrie local website:

http://www.comrie.org.uk/business-directory/9180/steinmeier-legacy-fund-news/

Visit Scotland:

https://www.visitscotland.com/info/see-do/cultybraggan-camp-21-p1189351

Secret History: Execution at Camp 21:

https://www.youtube.com/watch?v=H1jA4dmgpJo

Alexander Scotland, London Cage (Evans Brothers, 1957)

Roderick de Norman, For Fuehrer & Fatherland (History Press, 2009)

David Leslie, Banged Up: Doing Time in Britain's Toughest Jails (Black & White, 2013)

Charles Whiting, The Great German Escape (Pen & Sword, 2010)

Kenneth Roy, The Invisible Spirit: A Life of Post-War Scotland 1945-75 (Birlinn, 2014)

Helen Fry, The London Cage (Yale, 2017)

Master Detective, February 2021

[6] Ronald Mauri

National Archives: MEPO 3/2299

Bedfordshire Times & Independent, 8 May 1936

Biggleswade Chronicle, 22 October 1937

Time, 20 November 1939

Marylebone Mercury, 22 June & 13 July 1940

Coventry Evening Telegraph, 6 March 1941

Western Morning News, 6 March 1941

Daily Record, 6 March 1941

Derby Evening Telegraph, 21 June 1941

Daily Herald, 24 June 1941

Liverpool Daily Post, 25 June 1941

Western Daily Press, 26 June 1941

Western Times, 27 June 1941

Gloucestershire Echo, 12 & 18 July 1945

Nottingham Evening Post, 4 June, 13 July & 7 August 1945

The Guardian, 13, 16 & 17 July 1945

Nottingham Journal, 13 & 16 July 1945

Daily Telegraph, 16 July 1945

Aberdeen Press and Journal, 17 July 1945

The Argus (Melbourne), 17 July 1945, p16

The Courier-Mail (Brisbane), 20 July 1945

Birmingham Mail, 7 August 1945

Liverpool Evening Express, 7 August 1945

Manchester Evening News, 7 August 1945

Belfast Telegraph, 20 September 1946

Nathan's Genealogy:

http://nathansgenealogy.wikia.com/wiki/Rinaldo_(Ronald)_Bertram_Mauri

True Detective, September 2012

[7] Emil Schmittendorf & Armin Kühne

The Guardian, 6, 8, 9 & 14 August, 6 & 16 November 1945

Newcastle Journal, 8 August 1945

Liverpool Evening Express, 8 August 1945

Yorkshire Post & Leeds Mercury, 8 & 10 August 1945

Nottingham Evening Post, 9 August 1945

Lancashire Daily Post, 16 November 1945

Evening Despatch, 16 November 1945

Rachael Clegg, The Star, 27 April 2010

The end of the rope – The hanged of post-war Britain

Axis History Forum:

https://forum.axishistory.com/viewtopic.php?t=153782

The Chris Hobbs Site:

http://www.chrishobbs.com/sheffield5/lodgemoor1945death.htm

Kriminalia.de:

http://www.kriminalia.de/wp-content/uploads/2016/10/The_Executioner_At_War.pdf

Island Farm Wales:

http://www.islandfarm.wales/German_And_Italian_Escape_Attempts_From_Other_Camps_In_Great_Britain.htm

Capital Punishment UK on Facebook:

https://www.facebook.com/permalink.php?story_fbid=986908854680461&id=315934825111204

Erick Koch Wordpress:

https://erickoch.wordpress.com/2016/11/30/murder-in-medicine-hat-a-nearly-forgotten-episode-in-ww2/

Wikipedia - List of Individuals Executed by the United States Military:

https://en.wikipedia.org/wiki/List_of_individuals_executed_by_the_United_States_military#

Charles Whiting, The Great German Escape (Pen & Sword, 2010)

David Bentley, The Sheffield Murders, 1865-1965 (ALD Design & Print, 2013)

[8] John Amery

National Archives: PCOM 9/1117, HO 45/25773, HO 144/22823

Birmingham Mail, 30 April, 30 May, 30 July, 12 September 1945

The end of the rope – The hanged of post-war Britain

Birmingham Daily Gazette, 2 May 1945

Sunday Mirror, 13 May 1945

The Sphere, 19 May 1945

Daily Herald, 31 May 1945

The People, 10 June 1945

Sunday Post, 8 July 1945

Liverpool Evening Express, 28 June 1945

Gloucestershire Echo, 9 July 1945

Liverpool Echo, 9 & 30 July, 12 September 1945

Newcastle Evening Chronicle, 30 July 1945

Lincolnshire Echo, 17 October 1945

Manchester Evening News, 28 November 1945

Lancashire Evening Post, 5, 8 & 17 December 1945

Sydney Morning Herald, 20 December 1945

George Rosie, The Independent, 2 February 1995

Bernard McGinley, New Statesman, 2 July 2001

Vanessa Thorpe, The Guardian, 17 February 2008

Ronald Harwood, Daily Mail, 5 March 2008

Daily Telegraph, 14 February 2018

John Amery, *L'Angleterre et L'Europe*, (Paris, 1943)

Leo Amery, John Amery: An Explanation (1946)

David Faber, Speaking for England: Leo, Julian & John Amery, the Tragedy of a Political Family (Free Press, 2005)

Rebecca West, The Meaning of Treason, (Phoenix, new ed., 2000)

Alan Whicker, Whicker's War (HarperCollins, 2005)

Roy Maclaren, Empire & Ireland: The Transatlantic Career of the Canadian Imperialist Hamar Greenwood, 1870–1948 (MQUP, 2015)

Josh Ireland, The Traitors: A True Story of Blood, Betrayal & Deceit (Hachette, 2017)

Adrian Weale, Patriot Traitors (Viking, 2021)

William D. Rubenstein, History Today, 1 February 1999:

http://ifamericaknew.org/history/amery.html

N. Copsey, John Amery: The Antisemitism of the 'Perfect English Gentleman', Taylor & Francis:

http://www.tandfonline.com/doi/abs/10.1080/0031322202128811411

John Simkin, Spartacus Educational:

http://spartacus-educational.com/2WWameryJ.htm

[9] John Young

National Archives: MEPO 3/2296

The Courier-Mail (Brisbane), 9 June 1945

Daily Mirror, 7 July, 9 November & 10 December 1945

Daily Herald, 31 July & 11 November 1945

Lancashire Evening Post, 7 August 1945

Gloucestershire Echo, 7 August 1945

The Guardian, 8 August 1945

Essex Newsman, 9 & 20 November, 21 December 1945

The end of the rope – The hanged of post-war Britain

Capital Punishment UK on Facebook:

https://www.facebook.com/permalink.php?story_fbid=1002368416467838&id=315934825111204

True Crime Library:

https://www.truecrimelibrary.com/crimearticle/couple-battered-to-death/

Leigh-on-Sea Message board:

http://www.knowhere.co.uk/Leigh-on-Sea/Essex/South-East-England/messages?start=3

Professor Keith Simpson, Forty Years of Murder (Harrap, 1978)

Dee Gordon, Foul Deeds & Suspicious Deaths in Southend-on-Sea (Wharncliffe, 2007

Molly Lefebure, Murder on the Home Front: A True Story of Morgues, Murderers & Mysteries during the London Blitz (Hachette, 2011)

[10] James McNicol

Chelmsford Gazette, 18 August 1945

Thanet Advertiser, 24 August 1945

Chelmsford Chronicle, 24 August & 16 November 1945

Essex Newsman, 20 November & 21 December 1945

Motherwell Times, 21 & 28 December 1945 & 4 January 1946

The Scotsman, 22 December 1945

Sussex History Forum:

http://sussexhistoryforum.co.uk/index.php?topic=6045.0;wap2

Dee Gordon, Foul Deeds & Suspicious Deaths in Southend-on-Sea (Wharncliffe, 2007)

The end of the rope – The hanged of post-war Britain

True Crime, July 2022

Adam Ball - Southend Guy Paranormal:

https://www.youtube.com/watch?v=JD2tby6aup4&list=PLLZNGUi1qn_y2AlpC7YixePoaxtU-qyVv

https://www.youtube.com/watch?v=r5vVIU-pDho

[11] Robert Blaine

National Archives: MEPO 3/2309, PCOM 9/708, CRIM 1/1728

Ottawa Journal, 19 September 1945

Ottawa Citizen, 19 September 1945

Winnipeg Tribune, 19 September 1945

The Gazette (Montreal), 21 September 1945, 18 January 1949

Western Morning News, 17 November 1945

Evening Despatch, 13 December 1945

Coventry Evening Telegraph, 29 December 1945

Sussex History Forum:

http://sussexhistoryforum.co.uk/index.php?topic=6871.0;wap2

OMSA:

www.omsa.org/wp-content/uploads/2017/08/OMSA-Awards-Handbook-Vol-2-Honors-Registry-14-August-2017.pdf

Nickel in the Machine:

http://www.nickelinthemachine.com/tag/execution/

Carmen/Dufferin Municipal Heritage Advisory Committee:

http://carmandufferinheritage.ca/local%20heritage/war%20memorials/solders_at_roseisle.html

Veterans Affairs Canada:

http://www.veterans.gc.ca/eng/remembrance/memorials/canadian-virtual-war-memorial/detail/2928726

James Morton, Gangland Soho (Hachette, 2012), Chapter 12

Amy Bell, Murder Capital: Suspicious Deaths in London, 1933-53 (Manchester University Press, 2015)

Robert Baker, Beautiful Idiots & Brilliant Lunatics (Amberley, 2015)

Gary Powell, Death Diary: A Year of London Murder, Execution, Terrorism & Treason (Amberley, 2017)

Fitzrovia News, Volume 147, 2017:

https://towerarchive.files.wordpress.com/2017/12/fitzrovia-news-fn147-lowres.pdf

True Detective, Winter Special 2017

[12] William Joyce

Liverpool Echo, 29 May & 26 June 1945

Daily Herald, 4 June 1945

Coventry Evening Telegraph, 18 June 1945

Nottingham Evening Post, 28 June 1945

Shields Daily News, 18 July 1945

Yorkshire Post & Leeds Intelligencer, 20 September 1945

Hull Daily Mail, 3 January 1948

Byron Rogers, The Spectator, 9 July 2005

Ted Jeory, Daily Express, 22 May 2011

Obituary - Geoffrey Perry, The Independent, 17 October 2014

The end of the rope – The hanged of post-war Britain

Daily Telegraph, 3 January 2016

The Guardian, 4 January 2016

Stephen Stratford, British Military & Criminal History, 1900-1999: http://www.stephen-stratford.com/william_joyce.htm

Ricorso:

http://www.ricorso.net/rx/az-data/authors/j/Joyce_W/life.htm

W.H. Lawrence, Rex v Lord Haw, Hein Online:

http://heinonline.org/HOL/LandingPage?handle=hein.journals/hastlj2&div=13&id=&page=

J.W. Hall (ed.), The Trial of William Joyce (Notable British Trials series, William Hodge, 1946)

Rebecca West, The Meaning of Treason (Virago, 1982)

A.J.P. Taylor, English History 1914–1945 (OUP, 1965)

Francis Selwyn, Hitler's Englishman (Penguin, 1987)

J.A. Cole, Lord Haw-Haw: The Full Story of William Joyce (Faber, 1987)

David O'Donoghue, Hitler's Irish Voices: German Radio's Wartime Irish Service (Beyond the Pale, 1998)

Mary Kenny, Germany Calling: A Personal Biography of William Joyce, Lord Haw-Haw (New Island Press, 2003)

Nigel Farndale, Haw-Haw: The Tragedy of William and Margaret Joyce (Macmillan, 2005)

Colin Holmes, Searching for Lord Haw-Haw: The Political Lives of William Joyce (Routledge, 2016)

Thomas Grant, Court No. 1 – The Old Bailey (John Murray, 2019)

[13] Theodore Schurch

National Archives: KV2/76, KV 2/77, WO 71/1109, WO 204/13021

Gloucestershire Echo, 12 September 1946

Newcastle Evening Chronicle, 12 September 1946

Liverpool Daily Post, 13 September 1946

Yorkshire Evening Post, 17 September 1946

Dundee Evening Telegraph, 17 September 1946

Hull Daily Mail, 17 September 1946

Dundee Courier, 19 September 1946

Harrow Observer, 14 July 1996

David Sanderson, The Times, 22 September 2016

BBC Website, 11 November 2017:

http://www.bbc.co.uk/news/uk-england-surrey-41947492

Andy Brookman, Britain at War:

https://britainatwar.keypublishing.com/

Stephen Stratford, British Military & Criminal History, 1900-99

http://www.stephen-stratford.com/schurch.htm

Gallowglass Security blog:

http://gallowglasssecurity.com/gsp-and-gallowglass-security-at-the-saatchi-gallery/

Wikipedia, James Jesus Angleton:
https://en.wikipedia.org/wiki/James_Jesus_Angleton#World_War_II

Ben Macintyre, SAS: Rogue Heroes – The Authorised Wartime History (Penguin, 2016)

The end of the rope – The hanged of post-war Britain

Graeme Kent, On the Run: Deserters Through the Ages (Biteback, 2013)

Janet Dethick & Annie Corke, Twixt the Devil & the Deep Blue Sea (Lulu.com, 2013)

[14] William Batty

National Archives – ASSI 45/105/4

Yorkshire Post & Leeds Intelligencer, 17 & 18 August, 30 November, 1 & 4 December 1945

Yorkshire Evening Post, 15 August 1945 & 5 January 2016

Genes Reunited:

https://www.genesreunited.co.nz/boards/board/genealogy_chat/thread/803365

Stephen Wade, Yorkshire Murders & Misdemeanours (Amberley, 2009)

John Eddleston, Murderous Leeds (Breedon Books, 1997)

True Crime, January 2012

[15] Michał Nieścior

National Archives: ASSI 90/14, ASSI 36/79

Hartlepool Northern Daily Mail, 20 November 1945

Dundee Courier, 12 December 1945

Derby Daily Telegraph, 31 January 1946

Coventry Evening Telegraph, 31 January 1946

Findagrave:

https://www.findagrave.com/memorial/163476015/charles-elphick

Judy Middleton, Portslade in the Past:

http://portsladehistory.blogspot.co.uk/2016/12/portslade-and-second-world-war.html

Oxford DNB: Sir Frederick John Wrottesley

John Eddleston, Murderous Sussex (Breedon Books, 2011)

True Detective, November 2015

Printed in Great Britain
by Amazon